# THE
# UNCERTAINTY
# MINDSET

# THE
# UNCERTAINTY
# MINDSET

## INNOVATION INSIGHTS FROM
## THE FRONTIERS OF FOOD

## VAUGHN TAN

Columbia University Press   *New York*

Columbia University Press
*Publishers Since 1893*
New York    Chichester, West Sussex
cup.columbia.edu
Copyright © 2020 Vaughn Tan
All rights reserved

Library of Congress Cataloging-in-Publication Data

Names: Tan, Vaughn, author.
Title: The uncertainty mindset : innovation insights from the frontiers of
food / Vaughn Tan, School of Management, University College London.
Description: [New York City] : [Columbia University Press], 2019. |
Includes bibliographical references and index.
Identifiers: LCCN 2019057472 | ISBN 9780231196888 (hardback) | ISBN
9780231196895 (trade paperback) | ISBN 9780231551878 (ebook)
Subjects: LCSH: Restaurant management. | Restaurants–Technological
innovations.
Classification: LCC TX911.3.M27 T36 2019 | DDC 647.95068/4–dc23
LC record available at https://lccn.loc.gov/2019057472

Columbia University Press books are printed on permanent
and durable acid-free paper.

Printed in the United States of America

Cover design: Vaughn Tan

# CONTENTS

# Contents

# PREFACE

I N November 2010, I visited my first culinary research and development (R&D) team. Several months earlier I had met José Andrés, ThinkFoodGroup's head chef and cofounder, at a talk he had given at Harvard. I went to breakfast with Andrés the day after, during which he mentioned offhand that ThinkFood-Group's success was largely due to their investment in a dedicated R&D team based at their Washington, DC headquarters. Over ham and eggs, I somehow convinced Andrés to let me spend a few weeks with them.

As soon as I got out of the airport, I beelined downtown to the cluster of restaurants owned by ThinkFoodGroup, a rapidly growing international restaurant group with an innovation lab. It had begun to gust and rain heavily when I emerged from the Penn Quarter subway station. Fortunately, Oyamel, the restaurant I'd been instructed to go to, was only a few blocks away and the ranks of midrise office and apartment buildings kept some of the rain from street level. Russell Bermel, then Andrés's assistant, met me at the door and took me through the brightly daylit, blue and white, ground-floor dining room filled with lunchers happy under a ceiling mobile of gently moving butterflies—forests of *oyamel*, the sacred firs, are one of the principal wintering grounds for the monarch butterfly in highland Mexico. Then we descended into the basement kitchen, where the R&D chefs were working that day.

The large, but nonetheless cramped, low-ceilinged, windowless room was lit by bright fluorescent light. It was filled with the noise, heat, and movement of a kitchen in the middle of a lunch rush, and the floor had become slick with water and a thin film of grease. Skirting line cooks, busboys, and potwashers, we eventually came to the farthest corner of the kitchen where the walk-in refrigerator was located. There, we joined two chefs who stood looking annoyed at five bowls and three binders of recipes laid out on a battered stainless steel prep table that had been temporarily commandeered from the vegetable prep cook. As I was about to introduce myself, we heard a shouted, "Backs!" and Bermel pulled me up against the table with the others to get out of the way of a frenzied line cook who ran past us to the walk-in, wrenched open the door, snatched up a tray of prebraised pork, and ran with it back to his station before the door had swung fully shut. Bermel said, "Welcome to the ThinkFoodTank."

My first impression of the ThinkFoodTank when I saw it in Oyamel's basement was of a haphazard, ramshackle operation. As an organizational researcher, I did not expect to rapidly discover an innovation team both more creative and more effective than the product innovation teams I'd been a part of at Google—much less one organized in ways that violate many conventional innovation management principles. But once I saw past these superficials, I realized that it was a team of rare quality: fast-moving, adaptable, intensely curious, self-organizing, and highly effective. It just happened to be organized in ways that were not only unexpected but in fact ran *counter* to what I expected from having worked in a supposedly highly innovative technology firm and from being immersed in conventional innovation management theory.

The conventional approach to designing an innovation team is to assemble it with great care from handpicked employees, isolate it from the rest of the organization's distractions and politics, and give it plenty of resources. The ThinkFoodTank, by contrast, was scrappy, small, and lightly resourced. It worked wherever space could be found, drew experts from across and outside the group as needed, and was tightly integrated into the daily operations of ThinkFoodGroup's many restaurants and new openings. It had evolved this unconventional but effective way of organizing innovation work without advice from management experts.

The ThinkFoodTank violated so much conventional wisdom that I returned several times in 2010 and 2011 to try and make sense of how it worked at all—let alone as well as it did. I eventually spent over a month with ThinkFoodTank as it moved around the group's restaurants, seamlessly introducing process innovations and launching new restaurants with apparent ease despite the tremendous number of moving parts involved. Early on, Andrés had described his R&D team as "Delta Force." I quickly saw what he meant. ThinkFoodTank functioned at a high level even when unpredictable work was thrown at it—it was an innovation dream team.

ThinkFoodTank was so surprising that it made me want to see if other culinary innovation groups worked in similar ways. Between 2011 and 2016, I spent time observing the inner workings of some of the best cutting-edge culinary innovation teams in the world—acclaimed by consumers, critics, peers in the high-end culinary industry, and observers in science, technology, and innovation.[1] In the United States, other than ThinkFoodGroup,

I went to The Cooking Lab (publishers of *Modernist Cuisine: The Art and Science of Cooking, Modernist Cuisine at Home,* and *Modernist Bread*). Outside the United States, I went repeatedly to Amaja (a restaurant in southern Argentina that worked closely with a culinary R&D team called the Patagonia Food Lab; both are pseudonyms) and the Fat Duck's Experimental Kitchen in the United Kingdom, and worked with the MAD Foundation in Denmark (an organization spun off from the cutting-edge Danish restaurant Noma and which convenes the MAD Symposium, the pre-eminent international cutting-edge culinary conference).

As an organizational sociologist studying innovation teams, I was steeped in conventional management theory that emphasizes carefully designing R&D teams so they contain the correct people, providing them with the correct resources, and identifying the correct targets for innovation work. Conventionally well-managed organizations can be highly efficient, but only when conditions are predictable, stable, and controllable. But innovation is not about efficiency, and reality is seldom so accommodating.

These teams had in common an unconventional approach to choosing what to work on, how to work, how to find new members, and how to motivate them—because they explicitly recognized the impossibility of predicting the future. Without management experts to tell them otherwise, they simply acknowledged that there was no way to know in advance what would be correct in their industry—they had what I call *the uncertainty mindset.* This mindset suffused and influenced how they were organized. It led each team to build robust responsiveness and flexibility by injecting uncertainty into its structure and ways of working. Their homebrewed organizing principles, born out of this mindset, made these teams tremendously effective at adapting to the rapidly changing environment of cutting-edge, high-end cuisine, finding new problems to solve, and thus generating a constant stream of culinary innovation.

At the frontiers of food, I discovered a fundamentally different approach to innovation that I became increasingly convinced was relevant beyond cuisine. Cutting-edge cuisine is a model system for understanding the uncertainty mindset and its consequences for organizations in other industries. This book explores how the uncertainty mindset arose in cutting-edge cuisine, what it is, and the principles for organizing innovation that it produced.

## THE TERRITORY AHEAD

This book weaves together information from hundreds of interviews, thousands of hours of field observation, and archival research—unless otherwise indicated, all quotations and figures are from my own fieldwork and research. I did much of the field research under nondisclosure agreements, which some of the teams have been able to waive fully or partly. This book thus uses a combination of real names and pseudonyms for people and teams. I have also further disguised one of the teams at its request, while trying to retain the flavor and feeling of its original location and accurately conveying the team dynamics that are the focus of this book. My goal throughout is to present a portrait of the industry of cutting-edge, high-end cuisine, to introduce some of its most effective innovation teams and the unconventional ways in which they worked, and to explain what insights they hold for other organizations.

These teams had the uncertainty mindset because their environment was clearly and undeniably uncertain. Part I explains how high-end cuisine became highly unpredictable as it transformed into an industry undeniably obsessed with continual innovation, while part II describes the many different forms culinary innovation can take.

Teams with the uncertainty mindset assume that the future is truly uncertain instead of simply being risky. Part III explains how risk is fundamentally different from true uncertainty and outlines the ways in which an uncertainty mindset affects how a team is organized.

The uncertainty mindset changes how teams find new members, set team goals, and motivate themselves—the next three parts of the book explore how it influenced these important aspects of team organization. Part IV explains how it led these teams to a counterintuitive way of thinking about job roles and finding new members. Part V explains how it allowed them to create environments in which their members could learn how to pursue the open-ended goals required by innovation work. Part VI explains how it led these teams to take on projects that induced desperation among their members to motivate them to do intellectually and emotionally uncomfortable innovation work.

Finally, part VII offers a brief outline of what each team featured in this book has done in the intervening years. I conclude by explaining how the uncertainty mindset can update conventional thinking about how businesses should define employee roles, hire new employees, set and pursue goals, manage learning, motivate employees, and choose projects—these unconventional, counterintuitive changes have the potential to make organizations more innovative and adaptable even beyond the frontiers of food.

# ACKNOWLEDGEMENTS

I owe a great debt to the R&D teams whose members let me stand around getting in the way. At ThinkFoodGroup and ThinkFoodTank: José Andrés, Greg Basalla, Russell Bermel, Rick Billings, Sam Chapple-Sokol, Terri Cutrino, Charisse Dickens, Michael Doneff, Rubén García, Rodolfo Guzman, Jorge Hernandez, Aitor Lozano, Ann McCarthy, Justin Olsen, Joe Raffa, Hollis Silverman, Robyn Stern, Michael Turner, Rob Wilder, and Josh Whigham. At the Fat Duck and Fat Duck Experimental Kitchen: Heston Blumenthal and many others whom I can't name due to a nondisclosure agreement. At the Cooking Lab: Jonathan Biderman, Maxime Bilet, Sam Fahey-Burke, Wayt Gibbs, Scott Heimendinger, Nathan Myhrvold, Caren Palevitz, Kim Schaub, Anjana Shanker, Aaron Versoza, and Johnny Zhu. At MAD: Caroline Eybye, Mark Emil Hermansen, Arielle Johnson, Peter Kreiner, Aurora Lea, Matt Orlando, René Redzepi, Melina Shannon-DiPietro, Mikkel Westergaard, and Lars Williams. At Amaja and the Patagonia Food Lab (both pseudonyms)—many people whom I can't name due to a nondisclosure agreement. My fieldwork with these teams was largely funded by research support from Harvard Business School, University College London, and Pelle Øby Andersen at the Food Organization of Denmark.

Amy Edmondson, Jeff Polzer, and Chris Winship were—and are—the best advisors I could have asked for.

Special thanks to the team at Columbia University Press for believing in a strange and uncategorizable book: Noah Arlow, Lowell Frye, Ben Kolstad, Shashi Kumar, Julia Kushnirsky, Marielle Poss, and especially my editor Eric Schwartz. Margy Avery and Michèle Lamont offered invaluable advice on changing publishers midstream, while Bradley Abruzzi, Michael Russem, Shannon Sewards, and Simon Smith helped me avoid late-breaking legal and design pitfalls.

Many readers improved this book through their comments (the errors remaining are mine): Joshua Abrams, Sandra Berrios-Torres, John de Cuevas, Josh Evans, Aaron Greenspan, Heng Min Zhi, Paul Henninger, Sujin Jang, Arielle Johnson, Markus Karner, Joshua Kauffman, Diana Kudayarova, Lam Yishan, Katharina Lange, Eleanor Lee, Christina Leung, Tse Wei Lim, Chris Muller, Sriven Naidu, Jerry Neumann, Ann Owens, Jake Parrott, Gus Rancatore, Venkatesh Rao, Dan Schrage, Luciana Silvestri, Santiago Suarez, Chatham Sullivan, Omid Tavallai, Matt Wells, Darryl Wee, Merry White, Alex Wiltschko, Ben Wurgaft, Brad Zlotnick, and Tiona Žužul.

I'm thankful too for those who provided me homes away from home during and after fieldwork: Kate Hamblin and Hugo Thurston in Oxford, Diana Kudayarova and Tse Wei Lim in Cambridge and New York, Merry White and Gus Rancatore in Cambridge, Ann Owens and Dan Schrage in Los Angeles, Trinie Thai-Parker and Luke Wohlers in Seattle, and the Winemakers Club in London—John Baum, Guillaume Gerbet, Colin Grandfield, Ben Hearn, Alberto Segade, Dany Teixeira, and Tamas Tengelics.

Last—but most of all—love and thanks to my parents, Jane Teo and Alan Tan, for continuing to put up with my bullshit.

# PART I

A Partial History of New Ideas in Food

# 1

## FROM THE MARGINS TO THE CENTER

I T is a midsummer day in 2011 at Amaja, then and now one of the most influential proponents of cutting-edge, high-end cuisine in the world. The dining room occupies a third of the ground floor of an eighteenth-century seaside warehouse in a city on the Argentine coast of Patagonia, at the southern extreme of South America. It features almost none of the usual trappings of fine-dining restaurants. The low-ceilinged room is framed by splintered, limewashed pillars and beams, each a single massive timber. The uncarpeted floors are wide boards of dark pine. The restaurant seats about thirty-five people at fifteen smoked oak tables, each with a wide, white candle burning in a wax-encrusted saucer and a small vase containing an arrangement of unassuming flowers and leafy branches—there are no tablecloths. At each place setting is a stoneware plate, a rough linen napkin rolled around a knife and fork, and a water glass. The chairs are austere: polished dark oak with no upholstery save a seat pad, softened a little with furs draped over their hard backs.

Though close to downtown, the neighborhood is still largely industrial. The area is gentrifying but the road leading in from the city begins as patchy asphalt, then turns into potholed gravel. Two oil lamps sputter on iron rods driven into the cracked concrete in front of the entrance. Through the restaurant's wide dining room windows, down-at-heel houseboats moored nearby and a field of weeds are visible; from the smaller windows in the bar, a few of the many surrounding warehouses can be seen.

The austere room and gritty neighborhood are unusual for a high-end restaurant, but what's really unusual here is harder to see. For a start, one of the houseboats tied up nearby—a double-level, two-bedroom craft with an open-plan enclosed top deck—is part of the restaurant. It's the dedicated test kitchen, staffed by a small team of chefs who rarely cook for paying guests. Their time-consuming and failure-prone brief is to develop new dishes and ingredients. The existence of this dedicated research and development (R&D) unit is both a reason for and the result of the restaurant's identity and philosophy.

Soon after it opened in 2003, Amaja committed itself to cooking only with ingredients local to and seasonal in Patagonia, to produce what its chef-owner, Tomás Irigoyen, described to me as "an unmistakable representation on the plate of this particular time and place." Dishes are retired and new ones introduced as ingredients come into or go out of season. At this far-southern latitude, these changes happen so frequently that many of the twenty or more dishes that make up the full tasting menu might turn over entirely every six months. Today, a few tables of special guests, all friends of the restaurant or visiting chefs, will be the first to taste a dish that features charred leek stems and an ingredient that the restaurant's chefs believe has never before been used successfully in high-end cooking: massive hand-dived mahogany clams nearly two centuries old. Having discovered these clams through a trusted supplier, the R&D chefs have spent the last four months trying to figure out how to cook them so they don't have, as the head chef said, "the texture of a piece of rubber."

The restaurant's R&D work goes beyond making new dishes out of existing ingredients and into the realm of basic or fundamental culinary research. On this particular day in the test kitchen, a small selection of the research projects underway include: incubating woody overwintered carrots to try and make their native enzymes break down the cellulose and turn them tender, sweet, and edible again; building a culturing box to attempt to adapt a Japanese fungus to South American grains and legumes for a project to create a Patagonian miso; a dessert course combining beets, strawberries, and "green flavors" of lovage and dill; trial fermentations using different salt levels and preparation processes for making garum from South Atlantic bycatch fish; modifying the protein chemistry of milk to create a more reliable dairy equivalent of a soymilk protein skin product called yuba; a comparative tasting of foraged flowers to find the best flavor pairing with raw, unfiltered rapeseed oil; trial lacto-fermentations of unripe wild top-setting garlic; an experiment to identify the best way to clarify a fishbone fumet.[1] These basic and applied research projects only sometimes bear fruit that the restaurant guest can detect in the form of new dishes. Maintaining so extensive a program of basic research while producing a steady stream of highly refined new dishes requires a dedicated R&D team. This investment in R&D has allowed Amaja to build a global reputation around culinary innovation.

Continual innovation has been critical to both Amaja's identity and its success. Innovation is the reason it has become esteemed by professional food critics in traditional media and guides such as Michelin and Gault-Millau. Far more important, innovation has also allowed it to win the affections of a much larger group of global food tastemakers who exercise their influence online, in the informal world of food discussion boards, social media, and blogs. Lovers of high-end innovation in food, these culinary neophiles travel the world in search of culinary novelty. When they find it, they report on it in greater detail and more swiftly than traditional critics or guides. This group of neophile tastemakers emerged just as the culinary cutting edge began to form, and they have played a crucial role in creating it by driving other neophiles to the restaurants they love most: restaurants like Amaja that invest in R&D that allows them to constantly transform their menus in surprising and unexpected ways. At least three of them will eat in the restaurant today, having flown in from Asia and Europe after being drawn here by blogposts and forum postings enriched with course-by-course photography of various instantiations of Amaja's menu. Largely due to these tastemakers and their influence networks, on any given day Amaja might have over a thousand people on a waitlist for a meal that would cost nearly three hundred dollars before drinks, tax, and service.

And yet, this is just a normal midsummer day at Amaja. In the context of conventional high-end dining in 2011, it might still have seemed unusual to have a dedicated R&D team working on basic and applied culinary innovation and so tightly imbricated in a network of nontraditional critics and tastemakers. But the transformations that brought innovation from the margins of high-end cuisine to the center were already well underway.

## A TYPE OF INNOVATION MOVEMENT TAKES SHAPE

The 1960s were a time when the upheavals in the art world were particularly profound and rapid.[2]

Artists like Bridget Riley, Joseph Beuys, Andy Warhol, Donald Judd, and Dan Flavin (to name just a few) explored new art materials, new methods of manipulating those materials, and ways of working outside of the conventions of art. The result was a wave of new ways of thinking about what art could be: process-based art (like Fluxus), pop art, minimalism, conceptual art. Similar upheavals happened in high-end cuisine in the opening decades of the 2000s: new methods of cooking were developed, new ingredients and flavor combinations discovered, experiments conducted with new ways to tell the story of a meal, new audiences identified. Now, at the end of the second decade of the 2000s, new ideas in high-end cuisine proliferate faster than even the most committed Michelin star-hunter or chef-groupie can keep track of. High-end cuisine has become an innovation-oriented industry—culinary R&D is now a deliberate activity around which restaurants are organized.

Nearly everything we eat today—ingredient, cooking method, flavor combination, dish—had to be invented, whether that inventor was credited or not. However, until as recently as two decades ago, innovation was rarely seen as a good reason for a restaurant's existence. Most high-end chefs came up with new dishes between cooking for paying guests, and their restaurants distinguished themselves primarily through the quality of their ingredients and the sophistication of their technique.[3] The novelty of their food was icing on the cake instead of the cake itself. Menus changed, often seasonally, but guests did not routinely expect to encounter entirely new dishes on a restaurant's menu, let alone an entirely new menu. Innovation happened, but only the rare restaurant anchored its efforts on making continual innovation the core of its identity, and only a handful of restaurants invested in dedicated R&D chefs and labs—some examples include El Bulli in Spain, the Fat Duck in the UK, and Les Prés d'Eugénie in France.

This was because constant innovation disrupts traditional restaurant organization. From the guest's perspective, a restaurant is a place where food is cooked and served, and where someone else has to make sure that everyone is having a good time. This is accurate, but it is also incomplete. From the restaurant's point of view, it has to be a factory that reliably produces exactly what its customers want to buy and, given the high overheads in high-end cuisine, it has to be efficient while being consistent.

## CONSISTENT, EFFICIENT COOKING MACHINES

It's hard to be either consistent or efficient, and it is even harder to be both at the same time. If you have ever tried to cook an omelet exactly the same way more than once, you know that it is hard to exactly replicate even so simple a dish. If you are not a professional cook or serious amateur and have nonetheless decided to take on the challenge of making *boeuf bourguignon* for the first time, you soon realize that using time and ingredients efficiently requires both practice and a surprising depth of knowledge—even if you're only cooking a peasant French dish of beef braised in red wine.

In a high-end restaurant, the difficulty is compounded because the food is not simple and the overheads are high. Each dish is an assembly of many components, each made from what is often a complex recipe requiring multiple ingredients and cooking techniques. Yet guests who return and order the same thing still expect to get a dish they recognize. For high-end restaurants to become efficient and consistent at producing complex dishes, they have traditionally depended, like factories all do, on extensive documentation, intense specialization, and clear hierarchies.

Recipes are the best-known form of restaurant documentation: lists of ingredients and quantities accompanied by instructions about how to use them. If the ingredients and instructions in a good recipe are followed precisely, the dish should turn out as expected: it should taste, look, and smell the same each time.

Writing a good recipe requires understanding what processes and ingredients are essential to the final result and the ways in which they are essential. This is not as simple as it appears, because cooking is a complex physical and chemical process that to date has largely been understood and taught in the guise of a complex of interlinked processes that have been known to work together—i.e., empirically—instead of as formal mechanisms.

This empiricist approach to cooking arises because a cook often has only a fuzzy idea of the connections between what he or she did and the dish that resulted. Many actions that are essential to the result are not likely to be recognized as such, while inconsequential actions often are mistakenly thought to be important. For instance, the first version of a *macaron* recipe probably didn't include the now standard instruction to tap each tray of piped, unbaked shells hard on a counter to dislodge large air bubbles in the liquid batter and produce a more evenly shaped finished product.[4] Such a process detail might have developed only after a pâtissier making many batches of macaron shells noticed that some trays baked up more evenly than others and, through experimentation, figured out that the difference came down to accidentally rough treatment of the more successful trays of shells. The converse—inconsequential actions without the effects they are believed to have—are legion. For instance, searing meat on all sides, long thought to "seal it" and keep it juicy through the cooking process, does nothing of the sort, and adding salt to dry beans during cooking does not toughen them.[5]

Ingredients matter too. Ramen noodle dough is made from only flour and water, with a tiny quantity of alkaline salts kneaded in. The alkalis give the dough its distinctive flavor, aroma, and texture by altering the structure of the gluten that develops, making the dough springy and yellow, with an aroma recalling that of orange flower water. But the taste, smell, and feel of the finished dough depends to a large extent on what salts are already in the water used (the chemical composition of tap water in most cities changes slightly from day to day), the gluten and protein composition of the flour (which differs across producers, and often varies from batch to batch even from the same producer), and the precise chemistry of the alkali salts used.

Ingredients vary and they react with each other unpredictably. Even trivial-seeming particularities of each ingredient can therefore dramatically affect a recipe's results. To make recipes consistent, chefs must be able to distinguish between details of the ingredients which are crucial and those which are not. These become evident when a recipe produces inconsistent results even if followed precisely. When this happens to a chef, she might investigate whether the ingredients in the recipe need to be more precisely specified: only type T45 flour milled by Minoteries Viron, only the alkali salts made by Koon Chun, only deionized water. She might refine the recipe by choosing specific ingredients and then adjusting their proportions until the results are desirable and consistently replicable. The more complex the recipe—the more ingredients and steps it contains—the more repetition is required to test and refine it so it accurately and unambiguously documents the methods and materials needed to reproduce a particular dish consistently.

Rigidly structured division of labor is the other pillar of restaurant organization. In a large high-end Western restaurant, the service kitchen staff are divided into specialized stations. A station can be responsible for complete dishes, components of dishes, some dishes and some components, or coordinating the work of the different stations (a crucial role that manages the workload of the kitchen by telling the other stations when to start cooking a dish and assembling components prepared by other stations into finished dishes).

How any particular kitchen divides work among stations depends on many things, including the restaurant's size, how many people it employs in the kitchen, the kinds of equipment needed, and what dishes are on the menu. Most restaurants serve meats that are either quickly cooked before serving or precooked and finished just before service—so most restaurants have a station dedicated to cooking meat, often outfitted with a large grill and high-heat cooking range. The nature of the menu and the design and organization of the kitchen mutually determine each other. For instance, a pasta restaurant will usually have a station (that doesn't exist in other types of restaurants) equipped with a specialized kettle that can quickly heat a lot of water and cook multiple orders of pasta simultaneously. A restaurant with a large dessert menu will likely have a sizeable pastry station run by a dedicated pastry chef, while a restaurant with a small and simple dessert menu might not have a pastry station at all.

The contrast between the rigidly organized restaurant kitchen with many cooks and a home kitchen run by a lone cook is stark. Where a home cook would carry out every step of every recipe for every dish for a meal, the division of a restaurant kitchen into stations means that each station is responsible for a fraction of the steps or a fraction of the recipes that make up the restaurant's menu. Consequently, cooks working at each station cook the same things and use the same equipment every day, over and over again, and become efficient at doing those things quickly and correctly.

Efficiency with time and material is crucial in high-end cuisine. Even under ideal circumstances, high-end restaurants don't make much money despite how much they charge. A finished dish that isn't as it should be is often destined for staff meal or the trashcan. No money will be made on it—worse, it must be remade at the expense of both materials and time. Higher rents and labor costs, wear on expensive equipment and breakage of delicate glass and servingware, wastage in costly supplies, theft by customers and staff, and unpredictability in the number of guests who want to eat mean that overheads are higher and margins are thinner in high-end restaurants than many other industries and in lower-end restaurants. Consistency is essential for a restaurant to win repeat custom; efficiency is essential for it to survive.

## INNOVATION IS THE ENEMY

Innovation foils attempts to be consistent and efficient. Every new dish introduced means the kitchen has to relearn how to be consistent and efficient—at best.

In 2010, Amaja's R&D team developed a new snack, a dish of deep-frozen raw cod liver shaved over crisps made of milk protein. Raw cod liver is practically liquid at room temperature, solidifying only when frozen to below -18°C (-0.5°F). The shavings melt in the mouth and release an intense wash of oceanic flavor. But making the dish nearly broke Amaja's service kitchen. Even the heat from gloved hands causes frozen cod livers to begin to liquefy, and the deep-frozen liver shavings begin to melt the moment they are created. This meant that the dish could not be preassembled or even premade. The snack station had to take raw cod livers from the super-cold blast freezers used in the pastry kitchen and shave them over the milk crisps (a dish component that itself had a 60 percent failure rate) using a mandoline shaver that had been precooled with liquid nitrogen, with someone standing by to rush each dish to the guest's table as it was completed. Even so, many plated dishes of the frozen cod liver melted before they could get to the guests and had to be remade. When it first went on the menu, the frozen cod liver dish was the essence of inconsistency and inefficiency, a wrench flung into the carefully calibrated gears of the kitchen machine—and also an intensely delicious burst of cold and umami, provoking thought and surprise by the contrast between the powerful flavor and the speed with which it vanished on the tongue.[6]

Beyond disrupting consistent and efficient production, innovating is difficult when the result is to be held to an extraordinarily high consumer standard—the new thing must be both new and good before it can be allowed to reach the customer. Apple cannot release a new iPhone until it has been refined to the point that customers used to the distinctive style and build quality of previous Apple products will be satisfied. The same is true for a high-end restaurant whose guests and critics expect even new dishes to be conceptually consistent with previous dishes and as flawlessly executed. The creation and refinement of a new dish is best handled by people who are focused on creating new things and the inevitable failure that entails, instead of on replicating existing things and becoming successful at that through repetition. These two different sets of tasks draw on fundamentally different skills and inclinations.

Just as innovation-focused companies in consumer hardware and pharmaceuticals build specialized and highly trained teams to manage and conduct R&D and then transfer it to production, a restaurant anchored on innovation benefits from an R&D team dedicated to developing and testing new recipes, redesigning the service kitchen to accommodate new recipes, and teaching the service chefs how to cook new dishes. As high-end restaurants began to focus on pushing more innovation onto their menus more frequently, they found that they could only do this by redesigning the traditional organizational structure. They created internal R&D teams to do two things simultaneously: break routines that create efficiency and consistency by introducing new dishes and processes, while building new routines that allow those new dishes and processes to be done efficiently and consistently. As culinary innovation became more important in high-end cuisine, it became normal for a high-end restaurant to have an experimental kitchen or lab space, to have a dedicated culinary R&D team, and to spend a lot of money on research that the guest doesn't directly experience. Innovation soon became central in high-end cuisine—and a cadre of standalone culinary R&D labs and restaurants with dedicated R&D teams began to emerge by the end of the 2000s.

This industry disruption spread surprisingly quickly considering how important efficiency and consistency have always been to restaurant operations. In turn, this is because in the last decade, coming up with new ideas in food has become critically and commercially important enough for many restaurants to make innovation central to their identities. But even the rapidly growing importance of culinary innovation for a restaurant's commercial success would not have driven the innovation in high-end cuisine that we've seen had it not been for other developments that simultaneously made the work of culinary R&D easier to do and more important for a restaurant's professional reputation.

# 2

# THE UNDERCURRENTS OF THE NEW

**H**IGH-END cuisine is both the food itself and the social and cultural context in which it is embedded: the preferences and preconceptions of critics and diners, the professional norms of the high-end culinary industry, and scientific and technical developments in adjacent industries.[1]

Three trends and two long-standing dynamics produced today's flood of culinary innovation, transforming high-end cuisine into an industry where the state of the art changes frequently and unpredictably. These trends began in the late 1980s and 1990s but came to a head around the same time during the last decade: the group of tastemakers and influencers in high-end cuisine suddenly expanded, communication between chefs and scientists intensified and accelerated, and easily useable knowledge and organizational platforms for culinary innovation became available.

## MORE AND DIFFERENT
## TASTEMAKERS AND ARBITERS

In the last two decades, the group of restaurant taste arbiters expanded dramatically from a small number of professional critics working primarily for newspapers and magazines to a much larger number of mostly amateur critics that included bloggers and social media personalities. The seeds of this expansion were planted shortly after the eating public began to post course-by-course commentary accompanied by photographs and video about what they were eating at restaurants. This happened first on online bulletin boards like Chowhound and eGullet in the late 1990s, then on food blogs in the early 2000s, and in the last six to eight years on social media platforms like Twitter, Instagram, and Periscope.

Chowhound, founded by Jim Leff and Bob Okumura in 1997, was one of the first food-only online forums. eGullet, founded in 2001 by Steven Shaw and Jason Perlow, was another. These two multithread bulletin boards were the precursors of serious food blogs as we know them today. For people disproportionately interested in food, the online forums of the late 1990s and early 2000s rapidly became places where a community of shared interest could form even when its members were spread around the country or the world.

Food and restaurant lovers of all types—from interested know-nothings, to singlemindedly obsessed *otaku* amateurs, to professional critics and chefs—discovered Chowhound and eGullet and realized that they were anonymous, freely accessible places to ask a question or express an opinion. They piled in quickly and the dividing and recombining threads of conversations about specific topics put people with similar interests into contact with each other. People passionate about tacos, or cheap eats in Queens, or Laotian salads could find one another and communicate almost in real time. Their communication, in the form of individual posts and threads of sequential posts, was stored permanently and made publicly visible.[2]

Culinary neophiles rapidly recognized this as a tremendous enabler. A business traveler from Ohio heading to New York City for a work trip could search the boards for places to eat. The same traveler could also start a thread asking for restaurant recommendations and, within hours, have thirty replies linking to other relevant posts or threads from people she knew only online, if at all. As the communities of culinary neophiles grew, they began to realize that the posts and threads they'd written on these early forums were becoming the most reliable and up-to-date repositories of information about where to find the most cutting-edge restaurants and chefs and what to think about them. Eaters who cared about cutting-edge food no longer seriously looked at reviews in major newspapers—they looked instead to the boards for guidance from a group brain more attuned to what they were looking for.

As these communities of high-end culinary neophiles and repositories of information and opinion about innovative food and restaurants coalesced around each other, the group of people whose opinions mattered for restaurants began to expand beyond the circle of professional critics. The new online crowd of amateur restaurant reviewers increasingly found and posted about cutting-edge restaurants before professional critics wrote about them. Among culinary neophiles, these posters became influential critics in their own right.[3] Their crowdsourced reviews were more frequent and numerous than professional critical coverage of restaurants in newspapers, and they were able to cover a larger number of restaurants. These crowdsourced reviews swiftly highlighted the restaurants whose menus changed often and whose dishes were new and unusual, since these were the restaurants that merited the most new postings.

Around 2008, a few years after Chowhound and eGullet became widely influential, food blogs by prolific diners emerged as the next wave of influencers in high-end cuisine. Some food blogs were about particular cuisines, cities, or price ranges—but most of the successful ones were narrowly focused and thus appealed deeply to their specific audiences. Food blogs focusing on innovative food and restaurants soon emerged.

Personal food blogs such as *Food Snob* (written by a young banker who later joined the organizing team for MAD, one of cutting-edge cuisine's key conferences), *Gastroville* (intellectual property lawyer turned Michelin-starred chef), *Docsconz* (doctor, later organizer of culinary tours), *Chuck Eats* (still a mystery), *A Life Worth Eating* (software engineer, later a publisher of food and coffee journals), and *The Ulterior Epicure* (attorney, later food writer) documented their authors' high-end dining activities by posting extraordinarily detailed reviews of meals, featuring course-by-course photography and often detailed analyses of the chefs' motivations in cooking what they did.[4] These bloggers had more freedom than newspaper critics—they weren't bound by constraints of anonymity or impartiality, didn't have to appeal to mass audiences, and didn't have to visit the same restaurant repeatedly before writing a review.

Instead of visiting and reviewing a small number of established high-end restaurants, these bloggers went where the boards led them—and the boards led them to restaurants, often not yet reviewed in more conventional outlets, where chefs were pushing the boundaries of what was technically possible in cooking and service. Casual neophile diners came to rely increasingly on these online blog reviews and posts when searching for new restaurants and choosing which ones to visit. By sending diners like these to restaurants that frequently changed their menus, the food boards and blogs systematically and disproportionately rewarded restaurants that invested in culinary innovation.

Meanwhile, almost exactly when power dynamics in restaurant reviewing and criticism were changing, an opportunistic business strategy by a restaurant award program called The World's 50 Best Restaurants—known in the industry as the

50 Best—pushed the system firmly in the direction it was already headed. Launched in 2002, the 50 Best list rapidly claimed a large share of the global market for high-end restaurant endorsement that the Michelin Guide had dominated for decades. The Michelin Guide was originally a travel guide for French roadtrippers published by Michelin (the automobile tire manufacturer) to encourage more driving and thus increase tire sales. It continues to provide its users with brief but carefully calibrated ratings and reviews for restaurants spanning a wide range of price points. These days, it also covers many countries and is best known for its influential listing of Michelin-starred, high-end restaurants deemed worthy of special trips. Because of its nature as a guide dependent on carefully calibrated standards, Michelin relies on a small team of full-time, anonymous, trained, professional reviewers in each country. Especially when awarding stars, Michelin reviewers visit restaurants several times before assigning a rating.

In contrast, the 50 Best began as a marketing strategy by the UK-based industry magazine *Restaurant*. Initially aimed at professionals and restauranteurs instead of the general public, the 50 Best's jury structure is the conceptual inversion of the Michelin Guide's small team of professional reviewers. Where Michelin might have ten or so professional reviewers per country (it does not disclose exact numbers[5]), the 50 Best's jury is unpaid and consists of about a thousand chefs, journalists, and influencers around the world, each of whom nominates and votes on the restaurants in the list.

This allowed the 50 Best to cast a wide net—and the jury's naturally diverse criteria for restaurant quality meant that it frequently rewarded high-end restaurants that the Michelin Guide passed over. Most significantly, where the Michelin Guide implicitly emphasized the importance of execution and reliability over innovation, the 50 Best seemed to do the opposite. The 50 Best soon gained a reputation for being in touch with current trends and especially for highlighting innovation-driven restaurants.[6]

Both the Michelin star list and the 50 Best list are tremendously influential in the way ostensibly trustworthy restaurant lists are: they act as consumer-friendly filters about where to go and what to eat. Getting onto (and staying on) any of these prestige lists is more than just professional validation. It requires major initial and ongoing investment from the restaurant and can mean the difference between a successful year and bankruptcy. When Noma, a restaurant in Copenhagen, entered the 50 Best list at thirty-third place in 2006, bookings were up 15 percent the week after the announcement. Bookings kept increasing when it went to fifteenth place in 2007, tenth place in 2008, third place in 2009, and then an unexpected first place in 2010. The 2010 list was announced on April 26, 2010. Within a few days, the wait-list for Saturday nights for the next three months had swollen to over a thousand people (Noma seats around thirty-five to forty people at dinner). Restaurants like Noma that could constantly create new dishes were the ones that social media and internet influencers visited the most. These restaurants rose to the top of the 50 Best list, which also made them commercially viable and sometimes even commercially successful.

## CHEF NETWORKS FORM
## AROUND INNOVATION

While the power dynamics of restaurant criticism were changing to favor culinary innovation, changes with a similar effect were taking place in the high-end restaurant industry. Within the last decade, information about innovation in cuisine began to spread more quickly among chefs through chef conferences and social media. This diffusion began slowly in the 1990s as a simple exchange of information between a small group of chefs and scientists, grew in the early 2000s, and then finally became focused in the last decade.

In 1992, Nicholas Kurti and Hervé This began gathering chefs interested in the physics and chemistry of cooking at a small conference called Molecular and Physical Gastronomy held in Erice, Italy, which was convened six times between 1992 and 2004.[7] At Erice, chefs and scientists could meet and share information from two domains of knowledge that had previously not had much contact.

Madrid Fusión, an initially Spain-centered high-end culinary conference, was established in 2003. Bringing together chefs from across the world (but primarily Europe and America), Madrid Fusión became a place where chefs could demonstrate new recipes and techniques to colleagues and the media—somewhat like the Consumer Electronics Show of high-end cuisine. The StarChefs International Culinary Congress, launched in the United States in 2006, served much the same purpose. Madrid Fusión and StarChefs were both meetings of chefs primarily focused on demonstrations of technique. These conferences highlighted the results of the culinary R&D that chefs around the world were doing—but they didn't create a cutting-edge culinary community. Cutting-edge cuisine still lacked a venue where chefs working on the frontiers of food could share the methods, motivations, and ideology of culinary innovation and form networks of mutual support.

This venue was provided by René Redzepi, Noma's chef-owner, when he started the MAD Symposium in Copenhagen in

2011. MAD was designed as the missing alternative to the traditional cooking demonstration-driven chef conference. Redzepi's motivation was to "create a place where chefs and those interested in the restaurant industry and food system could engage in serious discussion about what cooking could and should be."[8] The 250 or so attendees that first year included emerging and established chefs, social media influencers, scientists, and policymakers—and the symposium was structured not primarily as a series of demonstrations by chefs but instead more like a TED Conference, with ideas worth hearing presented in carefully produced segments.

Though the ideas about food system integrity and sustainability that were presented at MAD1 were important, the symposium had a more influential but less visible role to play in catalyzing the move to innovation in high-end cuisine. Because it was the first year for an unknown symposium in what was then a marginal culinary city, Redzepi had invited his closest professional peers and people he admired. The remaining attendees in that first year were food writers and young chefs interested in innovation who had been following Noma's work. Consequently, MAD1 brought innovation-driven chefs together with many of cutting-edge cuisine's most committed advocates and ardent enthusiasts. During pre-MAD meetups, in the coffee breaks between talks, over lunch or dinner, during the official and informal after-parties, those who came to MAD1 talked about their restaurants and careers. MAD1's theme was "Planting Thoughts," an attempt to question preconceptions about food and the restaurant industry—but many of the off-schedule discussions went deep, unprompted, into the motivations, problems, joys, and benefits of treating innovation and R&D in cuisine as a channel for a chef's creative expression.

With each successive symposium (there have been six in total as of 2019), MAD became more established as a place where progressive chefs, influential restaurant critics, and important people in the food industry could meet and get to know each other—and they talked about innovation in food during these meetings. MAD brought together hundreds of the restaurant industry's emerging cutting-edge community in a relatively intimate setting, gave them a context for creating a shared and convincing narrative for innovation in cuisine, and allowed informal but strong professional networks of cutting-edge senior and junior chefs to form.[9]

Chef conferences, MAD in particular, dramatically accelerated the tendency of the cutting-edge culinary community to use social media not just to broadcast their work but also to communicate with each other. A few years before MAD was founded, chefs had begun to use social media—Twitter at first, Facebook and Instagram later—to document new dishes and new techniques they had developed or encountered. Every chef conference made these social media networks in cutting-edge, high-end cuisine more densely interconnected. Even now, the best way to reach a well-known chef quickly may be to Tweet at him or her, or to send a Twitter or Instagram direct message. Through these social networks, information about culinary innovation spread more quickly and widely in the professional community than ever before. Because of their immediacy, high-end chefs became acutely aware of how frequently their peers were creating new dishes or new cooking techniques, how often the influencers they followed commented favorably on new dishes, and therefore how culinary innovation through R&D could enhance a high-end restaurant's ability to draw critical attention and bookings.

## EMERGING PLATFORMS FOR
## CULINARY INNOVATION

While chefs were becoming more aware of the importance of being on the culinary cutting edge and more eager to engage in R&D, most of them lacked the considerable technical knowledge needed to run systematic culinary research programs. However, within the last decade, professional chefs have gained easy and well-structured access to scientific and organizational information about culinary R&D.

### *Culinary Technical Knowledge Platforms*

Foundational information about the physics and chemistry of cooking had already been available since the publication of Harold McGee's *On Food and Cooking* in 1984. McGee's book allowed dedicated chefs to understand many of the physical and chemical mechanisms underlying their cooking, but it was not written as a cookbook or instruction manual and did not give chefs a structured body of practical applications that they could transform in their own fashion. Nonetheless, McGee's book played an important role in popularizing the idea of science-driven innovation in food, especially after being significantly updated and expanded in 2004. It led more professional and amateur chefs to experiment with science as a way to cook better and to create new dishes.[10]

As with food criticism and reviews, an online community of culinary experimenters formed around posts on food bulletin boards and personal blogs. One of the first technical topics in cooking to arouse interest online was a cooking method popularly referred to as sous vide. In sous vide cooking, food is sealed into an evacuated package, then immersed in temperature-controlled water until it reaches the same temperature as the surrounding water—this allows more precise control of the final temperature to which the food is cooked than other cooking methods allow. The eGullet thread on sous vide cooking began with a question from user Fay Jai on February 23, 2004 about whether home cooks could use the method.[11] This question rapidly collected a small crowd of about thirty frequent posters interested in temperature-controlled cooking, experimenting with it at home, and sharing their discoveries. Over the next six years, the thread of their posts and conversations eventually became the best repository of information about using sous vide cooking in a nonindustrial setting. That general pattern—virtual communities forming around highly specialized threads on specific technical topics relating to food—recurred on the eGullet and Chowhound food boards and was one of the first major steps toward making the knowledge McGee had assembled directly usable for chefs.

In the second half of the 2000s, amateur and professional chefs began to also use blogs to record their experiments in food science and show off the new dishes they were able to create through experimentation. These blogs were the crucial next major step in making information that enabled culinary innovation more accessible to interested chefs. Progressive chefs followed updates on techniques and new dishes on blogs written by people like Aki Kamozawa and Alex Talbot (*Ideas in Food*), Shola Olunloyo (*Studiokitchen*), Michael Laiskonis (*mlaiskonis*), Mikael Jonsson (*Gastroville*), Dave Arnold and Nils Noren (*Cooking Issues*), and Martin Lersch (*Khymos*).[12] These bloggers posted in detail about combining scientific understanding and experimentation to develop innovative solutions to specific problems they faced in food and cooking.

However, these sources of information about culinary science were still unsystematic and poorly-structured. The boards contained plenty of disorganized, difficult to navigate, and often haphazardly field-tested or documented information that was unsuited for immediate use by a chef working in a professional kitchen. The blogs went into great detail about specific problems and their solutions, but infrequently gave general principles and recipes that less technically inclined chefs could easily adapt to their own needs.

This utility gap was finally filled in 2011, when The Cooking Lab published *Modernist Cuisine: The Art and Science of Cooking*, a five-volume book surveying the science relevant to cooking and focusing on its practical applications to high-end cuisine.[13] This book was the result of five years of work by The Cooking Lab, an R&D team working out of an extensively equipped laboratory and test kitchen based in the offices of ex-Microsoft CTO Nathan Myhrvold's company, Intellectual Ventures, based near Seattle in the city of Bellevue. With a list price of $650, it was the most expensive cookbook ever published at the time.

*Modernist Cuisine* began, in fact, in the sous vide thread on eGullet. Myhrvold had been active on the thread almost from the first post. He noted simultaneously the volume of practical information on sous vide collected in the thread and available nowhere else and also the many gaps in understanding that still remained. *Modernist Cuisine* began as an attempt to produce a more complete sous vide cookbook. It gradually ballooned into a book that brought together existing knowledge and the results of new research The Cooking Lab carried out on the science of cooking, one designed to provide well-structured, practical information that chefs could use directly.[14]

*Modernist Cuisine* went beyond explaining the physical and chemical mechanisms underlying cooking by giving usable tested recipes that illustrated those mechanisms in practice. And the notes on these practical applications of theory were presented as a kitchen manual containing extensively tested applied methods and actual recipes based on the science surveyed in the book. These recipes showed how understanding those mechanisms let chefs cook in ways that were previously thought to be difficult or impossible, or in ways that were unprecedentedly efficient or consistent. Until the publication of *Modernist Cuisine*, most chefs developed their techniques empirically. Through repetition, they figured out how to achieve a particular result but seldom fully understood the mechanisms by which that result was achieved. When they were nonetheless able to successfully replicate the result consistently, their methods were often handed down both intentionally (through training programs such as cooking schools and apprenticeships) or unintentionally (through incidental observation).

For instance, a traditional method for making a hollandaise sauce is to whisk egg yolks with butter and optional flavorings while cooking the mixture gently over simmering water in a bain-marie (or water bath)—this method was first recorded in the mid-seventeenth century and has not changed significantly since.[15] Correctly made, hollandaise is a thick but airy and velvety emulsion of butterfat emulsified with water through the action of slightly heated egg yolk. Using yolk as an emulsifier requires the cook to have enough experience and judgment to heat the mixture to the narrow temperature window where the egg yolk's proteins will emulsify and thicken the sauce without coagulating and causing the emulsion to break. For this reason, hollandaise has traditionally been thought of as one of the more fragile and temperamental of the classic French sauces, prone to apparently unsystematic, inexplicable failure in the hands of inexperienced cooks who have been trained to follow hollandaise recipes and techniques in an almost ritualistic way. About hollandaise, Thomas Keller, owner of the French Laundry, Per Se, and other restaurants, and often considered one of the best and most technically sophisticated American chefs said, "you were taught how to make a hollandaise sauce, and you were never really taught why it works. You were just taught how to make it, and you were taught how to fix it if it broke, and that was it."[16] This approach made many recipes seem like temperamental formulae that could not be tampered with without chancing failure, and thus made it difficult to think of them as systems that could be taken apart and reconfigured.

McGee's *On Food and Cooking* popularized the idea that scientific knowledge—a closer understanding of the mechanisms behind cooking processes—could help people cook better. Returning to hollandaise, a scientific approach to developing a less temperamental recipe might begin with an intention to make a stable butterfat and water emulsion with a different, less temperature-sensitive emulsifier than egg yolk, or to keep the yolk but experiment with a different way of controlling temperature to reduce the chances that the sauce will overheat and split. However, applying known scientific mechanisms (such as different emulsifiers or heating methods) to recipe or technique development requires not only the knowledge of the mechanisms but also an understanding of how to apply the scientific method—the idea of developing testable hypotheses and using them to advance systematically, changing one recipe parameter at a time, toward a finished product. This approach to recipe development was (and remains) largely alien to traditional empiricist culinary training.

While *Modernist Cuisine* introduced some new science to professional chefs, its main contribution was to make existing science comprehensible and immediately accessible in the form of usable recipes. One such recipe was for a modernist hollandaise—still featuring egg yolk but stored in a pressurized cream whipper, then cooked and pasteurized in a temperature-controlled water bath held at 65°C (149°F) for thirty minutes instead of cooked over simmering water.[17] The modernist hollandaise can be made well in advance of use (compared to traditional hollandaise which is usually made just ahead of service) and entirely without risk of overcooking the sauce. If kept thereafter at this temperature or lower, the yolks in the sauce are safe to consume but will not coagulate—and when dispensed from the pressurized cream whipper, it aerates to an even lighter texture than the traditional version. This recipe was based on a technique developed by Daniel Humm for his restaurant Eleven Madison Park at least two years before, but the knowledge spread slowly through chef conferences until *Modernist Cuisine* published an extensively tested version that both explained how the method worked and gave an easily understood recipe featuring it.

*Modernist Cuisine* was a boon principally to high-end chefs—the same ones who were most likely to have the resources to invest in a program of culinary innovation. Not only was the book extremely expensive, the recipes and methods were also labor-intensive and more suited to use in high-end restaurants because they were developed by researchers working with a team of trained, high-end chefs. For the vast majority of high-end chefs who had little or no formal scientific training, the scientific information McGee had compiled had been tantalizing but hard to use. *Modernist Cuisine* presented these chefs with a compendious manual of basic and applied knowledge organized into books on fundamentals, techniques and equipment, animal and plant ingredients, ingredients and preparations, and plated recipes—over 2,400 pages in total, lavishly illustrated for visual appeal. This professionally accessible scientific information was important to the rise of high-end culinary innovation as the norm, analogous to a software platform that enables the growth of an ecosystem of applications built on top of it.[18]

## Legitimating the Culinary Innovation Team

Just as vital to the emergence of the culinary cutting edge was the growing social and professional legitimacy of the idea of organizing a restaurant around a culinary R&D team.[19] This had been slowly growing since the 1990s as restaurants such as the Fat Duck and El Bulli, and restaurant groups like ThinkFood-Group, set up their pioneering R&D operations and worked to legitimize innovation as a measure of quality in high-end cuisine.[20] But between 2008 and 2013, culinary R&D as a restaurant organizational form finally entered the professional mainstream consciousness. Mugaritz, El Bulli, and the Fat Duck—some of the most prominent of the cutting-edge restaurants—published books documenting their creative processes and emphasizing how dedicated culinary R&D teams made continual innovation possible.[21]

Other books supplemented this growing belief in the importance of culinary R&D. Lisa Abend's *The Sorcerer's Apprentices* (2011) documented a six-month service season in El Bulli, highlighting the crucial role of a dedicated R&D team in making an innovative restaurant possible.[22] Colman Andrews's 2010 biography of Ferran Adrià (founder of El Bulli) similarly emphasized the importance of the R&D work done at El Bulli and attributed the restaurant's influence to that investment in R&D.[23] Widely read and discussed among high-end chefs, these books, together with related articles in innovation-focused new food magazines like *Fool* and *Lucky Peach* and television series like *The Mind of a Chef* and *Chef's Table*, transformed the idea of building high-end restaurants around innovation and R&D into one that might almost be considered normal.

Relatively few high-end restaurants are owned entirely by their chefs—the costs of opening and operating one are now so high that chefs often work with partners who supply the operating capital and financial expertise. Some chefs also go into business with a front of house partner who handles the guest-facing service aspects of the restaurant. For both money people and front of house people, investing in culinary innovation or an R&D team was often perceived as a chef's indulgence.

The apparent success of a growing number of restaurants that had invested in dedicated R&D teams (most prominently, Momofuku, Noma, the Fat Duck, and El Bulli) made the idea more familiar and acceptable for people who ran the restaurant business operations. These successful innovation-led restaurants emphasized how they were able to routinely create new dishes and attract diners, or pitch and produce TV shows and books, because of their dedicated R&D teams. By 2012, chefs operating or setting up ambitious restaurants could point to numerous stories of this way of organizing a restaurant when trying to convince their investors and operating partners of the value of investing in dedicated R&D teams. This explanation allowed nonchefs running restaurants to understand culinary R&D as a potentially valuable part of an ambitious business strategy instead of simply a chef's expensive whim.[24]

## TWO AMPLIFYING DYNAMICS IN HIGH-END CUISINE

Two long-standing dynamics in high-end cuisine amplified the effects of these three trends, creating the enormous volume of culinary innovation we see today. First is the inherent inclination of chefs to learn new techniques and use them in ways that further their creative visions and reputations. The end results of high-end culinary R&D—inventions such as new dishes or new flavor combinations—are protected by widespread disclosure and long-term association with the inventor instead of patents or secrecy. Chefs or restaurants become famous for creating particular dishes, flavor combinations, and each chef vigorously promotes her inventions and her right to be recognized as their creator.[25]

Though copying another chef's invention is frowned upon, the culture of high-end cuisine actively pushes chefs to share techniques and methods and encourages them to constantly learn new techniques. For instance, a pastry chef might intern at master pâtissier Pierre Hermé's factory in Alsace to learn how to make macarons, then start his own macaron business. He might win acclaim for developing new flavor combinations for macarons made using Hermé's techniques—but would be poorly regarded by his peers if he decided to make a rosewater, raspberry, and lychee macaron and claim it as his own creation. Any pastry chef familiar with the landscape of modern pastry would immediately recognize it as an imitation of Hermé's classic Ispahan flavor combination, which he introduced while working at Ladurée.[26] Combined with this culture of knowledge-sharing, the strong norm against outright imitation fed on the increased availability of information about culinary R&D to strengthen high-end cuisine's emphasis on innovation.[27]

Second is the naturally competitive nature of chefs working in high-end cuisine. Innovation has became increasingly important for a restaurant's critical and commercial success and for a chef's professional reputation among chef peers. Social media channels, online bulletin boards, and chef conferences make chefs immediately aware of culinary innovations from their peers. The real-time updating of social media like Twitter and Instagram creates an image of the world of high-end cuisine that emphasizes continual innovation. Information about a new dish or cooking technique might once have taken months or years to percolate through the industry—but a photograph of a new dish in a restaurant in Brazil can be Instagrammed and seen by chefs around the world within minutes or hours. For ambitious high-end chefs and restaurants, adopting social media as a way to communicate with one another has had the side effect of making it clear that the frontiers of food are advancing in unpredictable directions and at high speed. While the velocity and scope of culinary innovation is inspirational and exposes chefs to new techniques and possibilities, it has also created constant social pressure for chefs to innovate to keep up with their peers.

## EVERYTHING SUDDENLY COMES TOGETHER

Figure 2.1 shows how the various currents in support of high-end culinary innovation gradually gained strength over several decades, eventually coming together within the last decade. Suddenly, the previously small group of culinary tastemakers and influencers expanded dramatically, communication between chefs and others outside the industry intensified and sped up, and easily useable knowledge and organizational platforms for R&D were made available. Knowledge was repeatedly infused into high-end cuisine from bench science, art, and industrial food chemistry, as those worlds became increasingly connected by chefs and other individuals who moved among them often and easily.[28] In high-end cuisine, these three trends created the flood of new ideas in food that we see today. In the last decade or so, culinary innovation has become practically irresistible. As more of the most ambitious young chefs set their sights on innovation, they made it increasingly difficult for other ambitious chefs to do anything else. As a result of this innovation arms race, high-end cuisine became an industry marked by rapid and unpredictable change.[29]

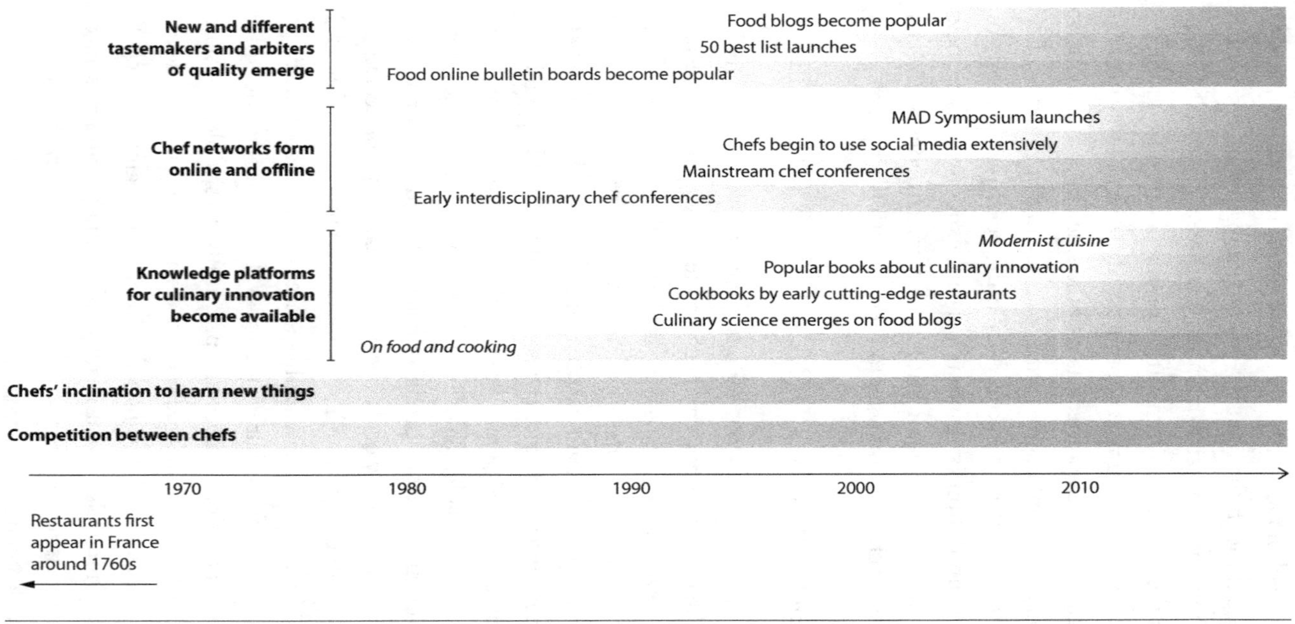

FIGURE 2.1 Trends and dynamics combining to support the emergence of a cutting-edge culinary community and movement.

At the high end, what began as a small, scattered movement in the 1980s and 1990s for organizing restaurants around continuous innovation became a coherent, influential trend by the late 2000s. In turn, this fundamentally changed how some of the most ambitious high-end restaurants organized themselves, transforming them from businesses striving for consistency and efficiency to businesses striving to balance consistency with constant innovation.

# PART II

What Is Innovation in Food?

# 3

## WELL-KNOWN, BARELY UNDERSTOOD

**M**Y second day at Amaja's test kitchen was one of those beautiful days that seem only possible close to the poles of the world. The sky was clear but for a few cloud traces, the sun was already warm at 7 a.m., and a cold salt-scented breeze came off the South Atlantic. I arrived at the restaurant at 10 a.m., when work had been underway for several hours. The large rented houseboat containing Amaja's test kitchen and the Patagonia Food Lab was tied up less than a hundred meters from Amaja's entrance, at a mooring shared with three smaller houseboats and a sixty-foot, three-masted sailboat being prepared for an art expedition to Antarctica. A large roll of freshly cut turf, soil backing beginning to dry out and crumble off, lay stacked in the shade by the houseboat's main door. Thrown haphazardly in front of the door and blocking it was further evidence of early morning industry: a big pile of densely woven, damp cotton bags stuffed to overflowing, ramson heads poking out. The door opened to reveal César Pareto holding a stack of empty three-gallon lidded tubs.

"Help me get this stuff off to the side. They just dump them here when they come in, like this is a loading dock. You want to watch out for those," he said, nodding at the bags of ramsons.

"They're full of ticks. We had to get the stagiaires tick kits last season. Want to drive out with me for some dead yeast?"

Absolutely.

A grubby compact car was parked on the concrete by the houseboat's mooring. It was used by the Amaja kitchen team for expeditions to foraging sites not easily reached on foot or bicycle. Warmed by the sun, it was scented with fresh green garlic, meadowsweet, and damp socks; dried vegetation and soil had been thoroughly rubbed into much of the upholstery. After unloading the foraged herbs—a sack each of ramsons and yarrow that had been left behind in the trunk—and moving a slippery stack of heavy-duty trashbags and muddy rubber boots off the passenger seat, we got in. Joggling over the potholed street leading away from Amaja, we headed for a small brewery thirty minutes north.

Pareto was thirty-five at the time and on his second career. After studying English and fine arts at Wesleyan (a tattoo of the first stanza of *Paradise Lost* spirals up and around his left forearm), he became an art director for commercial and music videos. The music industry soon lost its appeal. Winning a personal injury lawsuit from a traffic accident let him quit to go to cooking school at the French Culinary Institute in New York. Within seven years, he'd worked at two prominent cutting-edge restaurants (Wylie Dufresne's WD-50 and Heston Blumenthal's Fat Duck), taken a year off to sail and cook in the South Pacific, then landed at Amaja. There, his willingness to "keep on failing without getting clinically depressed" and his experience cooking in the progressive kitchens of Dufresne and Blumenthal led him to become the resident R&D guy—"if the guys have a problem they want to solve, they send it to me."

Pareto maintained a close working relationship with the Amaja test kitchen but had moved on to become the founding head and sole full-time employee of the year-old Patagonia Food Lab—an independent culinary research lab set up by Amaja that shared the Amaja test kitchen's houseboat work space. "Tómas [Amaja's founder] wanted a lab that would have the freedom not just to have to come up with new dishes for Amaja every day but to think about other kinds of things," he said. "What we do eventually will be interesting to chefs cooking service, but not quite yet. Stuff like figuring out how to make miso from stuff like *arvejas* [yellow peas] that grow here, or cataloguing and running toxicology on all the different kinds of seaweeds here to figure out which ones can be used as food ingredients."

As we drove further north and into the forest, Pareto told me that "miso is one of those ingredients that helps define the flavor profile of a cuisine because it can be used everywhere, like salt, but has a distinctive flavor. If we can make misos from here, that gives us another strong anchor for Patagonian cuisine."

Miso is a traditional fermented product commonly used in Japanese cooking. Developing a miso made from Patagonian cultures and ingredients would be like a basic research program in cooking—an attempt to manufacture a new kind of uniquely Patagonian ingredient. Making miso is a complex multistage process that is hard to master. First, a starter fungus culture called koji (strains of *Aspergillus oryzae* originally isolated from rice) is grown under carefully controlled conditions of humidity and temperature. When ripe, this koji is added to a cooked substrate that can be made from a wide range of legumes and grains. The fungus colonizes the substrate and produces enzymes that break down its starches and proteins. Other bacteria and fungi can then colonize it too, changing its texture and flavor. The end result is an intensely flavored seasoning product whose flavor profile can be further influenced by aging it in containers made of different materials and for different lengths of time.

Traditionally, miso is made on substrates that consist of a combination of soybeans and other legumes and grains commonly grown in Japan. The culturing process and koji strains used in traditional miso-making have been gradually selected over many hundreds of years to suit these Japanese substrates. The subtleties of the different strains of koji, the composition of the substrate, the timing and temperature of the fermentations and aging processes produce the thousands of varieties of miso in Japan.[1]

A truly Patagonian miso would be made from native strains of starch- and protein-digesting fungi grown on native substrates such as the yellow peas (cultivated varieties of *Pisum sativum*) that have been grown in Patagonia for centuries.[2] The different enzymes would break down the native Patagonian substrates to produce flavor compounds different from those that would be found in a Japanese-style miso. But creating a truly Patagonian miso would require reverse-engineering a complex fermentation and culturing process—which at a high level is still deeply empirical and much guided by experience and instinct—to understand how to modify it for different substrates and different fungi. Pareto again: "The process understanding that's needed to develop a Patagonian miso will also open the door to creating miso-type seasoning products in many other parts of the world—that's what's really interesting."

Culinary R&D in most restaurants is about coming up with applications of culinary knowledge that are quite close to the end consumer, such as new dishes. By comparison, what the Patagonia Food Lab proposed to do with miso was relatively fundamental research, quite removed from the end consumer. As Pareto said, "The Patagonia Food Lab was set up to push backwards down the R&D chain, to do much more basic work on developing generalizable processes, new ingredients, that kind of thing. Eventually we want to be like a regular research lab—write grants to fund research, collaborate with university researchers, and develop intellectual property that we can sell or license."

On our way back to Amaja after picking up many gallons of dead yeast sludge, I asked Pareto what he was planning to do with it. "We thought it would be cool to try and make a Patagonian umami sauce. I think we just need to incubate it to get the proteolysis going and maybe salt it a bit. Like Marmite, but Patagonian. And one of our pastry chefs wanted some for an idea she has for a spent yeast and corn-smut dessert."

Despite the importance of culinary innovation today, R&D remains unusual in the food world because innovation requires failure in pursuit of success. Most people and organizations are conditioned to respond well to success and recoil from the possibility of failure—this is true for chefs as much as anyone else.[3] This means that what culinary R&D teams do is poorly understood, both outside the industry and inside it.

## A REVOLUTION IN HIGH-END CUISINE

Revolutions occur when customary ways of doing things change quickly and dramatically. These changes result from the combination of discovering new ways of working and re-examining how things have always been done. The first Industrial Revolution was driven by the development of mechanical power and mechanization combined with the shift from producing goods artisanally through piecework to specialized and mechanically powered production lines. The modernist revolution in painting in the nineteenth century was driven by the introduction of new paints and pigments combined with a desire to re-examine and challenge the figurative-realist mode that had dominated painting until then.[4]

In high-end cuisine, the revolution of the last decade brought innovation from the margin to the center. A handful of chefs and scientists, all interested in science and cooking but scattered around the world, found one another and discovered the creative and promotional possibilities of a systematic approach to innovation and applied science in the kitchen. More chefs recognized—and were forced for commercial and reputational reasons to recognize—these possibilities and began to work on their own culinary innovation projects. An appropriate metaphor here is that of a chemical reaction that starts unnoticed, grows barely perceptibly, then suddenly explodes. The group of innovation-oriented chefs grew and ramified; slowly at first, then more quickly, until it reached a critical reaction mass in the last decade.

Broad trends within high-end cuisine and communities that grew increasingly connected to it—outlined in part I—laid the foundation for this reaction and interacted to accelerate it. Cutting-edge, high-end cuisine emerged from people, knowledge, and ways of working moving from their home communities and recombining in new ways in a new one. However, culinary innovation would not have had a toehold for this reaction had it not quickly shown its value to many aspects of the production of high-end cuisine, few of which are visible to the guest in the restaurant. The most widely known form of culinary invention is the creation of a new dish, since that is what bloggers photograph, critics write about, and guests eat. But the invention and innovation embodied by cutting-edge cuisine today goes deeper than that.[5]

Though popular media focuses on technology innovation as embodied by large firms, innovation actually happens at different scales of analysis and in many different contexts. Culinary innovation is more like innovation in other industries (including software) than it may at first appear. Innovations fundamentally change how people, organizations, or industries do things,[6] and they exist on a continuum between being technical or sociocultural. At the technical end of the continuum are functional innovations grounded in material processes and discoveries. One example is the development of a slow, low-temperature process for fermenting bread dough to develop a mixed culture of yeasts and bacteria. This process, through its temperature, duration, and promotion of a mixed microbial culture, both leavens the bread and makes it more nutritious compared to one fermented quickly with a yeast monoculture. Fermentation by a diverse population of microbes has been found to have many effects. Among other things, it slows starch digestibility and thus reduces glycemic response, increases the concentration and bioavailability of a wide range of vitamins and minerals, and allows native enzymes to reduce phytate and phytic acid levels to make the nutrients in the bread more easily digested and absorbed.[7]

At the sociocultural end of the continuum are innovations that are aesthetic and that change social norms and preferences. An example of this is the invention of a new and counterintuitive combination of flavors that is nonetheless delicious, such as Alain Senderens's baked lobster with vanilla sauce, introduced in the 1980s at his restaurant, L'Archestrate, in Paris. Craig Claiborne, the influential *New York Times* food critic, described the dish as seemingly "one of the least compatible flavor liaisons conceivable. If the reflexive reaction to such a dish was a grimace, it was quickly dispelled. The combination not only worked, it was a triumph of taste over logic."[8]

Food is a good place in which to understand innovation generally, because innovations in food can be found—as these examples show—all along the continuum between technical and sociocultural innovation.

# 4

# FOUR TYPES OF NEW IDEAS IN FOOD

**H**IGH-END cuisine is an industry in which businesses (restaurants) manufacture products (dishes) for customers (paying guests). Customers usually see innovations that are the culinary equivalents of new products made of existing materials using existing processes and methods—new dishes made by combining known ingredients using known processes and methods. Developing new dishes is the most common form of high-end culinary innovation. But other types of more fundamental innovation are also possible, including the development of new concepts that enable many new dishes to be created.[1] These other approaches to coming up with new ideas in food are neither as common nor as easily visible to external observers of the industry. Three of the most important of these are the creation of new ingredients, new cooking methods, and new kitchen processes. Each of these four types of innovation in food (summarized in figure 4.1) poses different challenges for culinary R&D.

## NEW DISHES

A dish is a set of components—ingredients, serving ware—cooked and assembled, then presented to the guest as a coherent

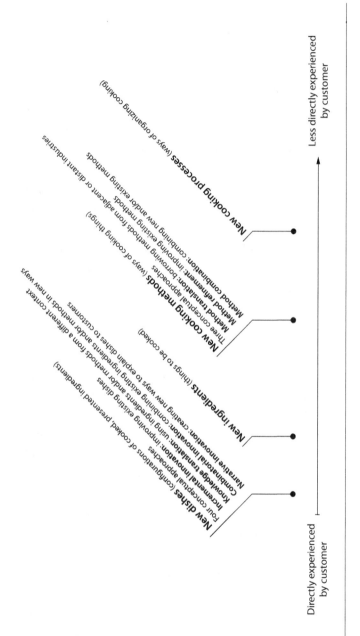

**New dishes** (configurations of cooked, presented ingredients)
Four conceptual approaches
Incremental innovation: improving existing dishes
Knowledge translation: using ingredients and/or methods from a different context
Combinational innovation: combining existing ingredients and/or methods in new ways
Narrative innovation: creating new ways to explain dishes to customers

**New ingredients** (things to be cooked)

**New cooking methods** (ways of cooking things)
Three conceptual approaches
Method translation: borrowing methods from adjacent or distant industries
Method refinement: improving existing methods
Method combination: combining existing and/or new methods

**New cooking processes** (ways of organizing cooking)

Directly experienced by customer → Less directly experienced by customer

FIGURE 4.1  Four common approaches to new ideas in food.

whole. Today, late in the history of cooking, few dishes called new contain entirely new components. That would be akin to defining a cellphone as new only if it uses solely materials and manufacturing processes invented specifically for its production. A radically new dish is rare when so much cooking builds on deep bases of ingredients, methods, and history. For high-end cuisine today, new dishes can be made using four broad strategies: improving existing methods (incremental innovation), applying methods or ingredients from a different context (knowledge translation), combining existing methods and ingredients in new ways (combinatorial innovation), or by creating a new way to explain the dish to the customer (narrative innovation).[2] Creating a new dish is often a protracted process that requires culinary R&D teams to use different combinations of these strategies at different times.

## *The Fat Duck travels to the Land of Nod (2015)*

The eight members of the Fat Duck Experimental Kitchen (FDEK) surrounded a grey canteen table, all in chefs' whites except for the resident engineer/project manager. Isabella Rodriguez, head pastry development chef, set down a tray with four small spoons. Each spoon's handle was covered in soft felted wool, and each spoon's bowl held a small scoop of a pale milk-flavored custard in one of four textures and shades of cream. This was part of a prototype: an early version of one component of a new dessert course intended for the Fat Duck, an internationally acclaimed restaurant in the town of Bray, outside London.

The Fat Duck's building was closed for major renovations at the time and the entire service team had moved temporarily to run the restaurant as a pop-up in Australia, leaving the FDEK team with the mandate to overhaul the menu for the reopening. One of the anchors of this new menu would be a completely new dessert. The team had decided that it would have to convey the feeling, as Rodriguez said, of being "dreamy, comforting, surreal. Like how you feel when you are about to fall asleep when you're small. You've been bathed, and you're feeling clean and tired, and everything smells like baby powder." They had taken to calling the dish Counting Sheep.

Rodriguez had principal responsibility for this dish. She'd been working on the concept for over a month, but had found the idea too vague to act on. The details a development team might consider in developing a new dish are so numerous it is difficult to count them. This profusion of possibilities can be crippling. Over lunch the previous week, she'd told me that "it is difficult to start like this. Comforting, the feeling of *abrazos* ["hugs" in Spanish] and 'a warm blanket in a slightly chilly room,' Heston [Blumenthal, the Fat Duck's founder] said. What gives you that feeling? There are so many ways to go that I am stuck."

Things began to coalesce over the next few days. Rodriguez found a few ideas that cohered enough for her to temporarily push the rest to the back of her mind. This initial winnowing down, she said, was crucial for her to be able to start visualizing what the finished dish might look like. This, in turn, was an essential first step for actually planning and then cooking the components of a prototype for the finished dish.

To get over the initial blockage produced by the profusion of options, Rodriguez focused on investigating only the serving-ware that would accompany the dish and the flavors and textures of the dish's edible components—just two of the many possibilities that might lead to a dessert with the psychological property of being both soothing and soporific. Rodriguez said, "Milky flavors and creamy textures, which is why the milk-flavored custards. But usually, the spoons you get feel cold and hard. If the spoons feel soft and warm when you pick them up, maybe people can get more into this feeling." Denby Marston, the FDEK's head chef said, "the soft handle is another version of an idea we've been trying to put into a dish. We've been working with a psychologist from Oxford to see whether engaging other senses can amplify the effect of a dish. The sense of touch seems to be very important even if you don't realize it consciously."

The tasting was quick. No one seemed convinced by the soft-handled spoon or excited about the custards, but this didn't seem to surprise anyone. The team decided that the driving idea behind Counting Sheep was good and that they would continue to explore vanilla and its related flavor notes, but they also agreed that a dessert with only custardy textures and milk/vanilla flavors wouldn't live up to guests' expectations for the Fat Duck's big reopening. Blumenthal said, "it's promising but there's got to be more. How do you make the dish interesting and surprising to eat, but still have it be soothing and comforting, like going off to bed after a long day on holiday? And it has to be delicious too. It's a paradox."

After the tasting, Gareth Henderson, the restaurant group's head chef, told me that, "Today's tasting was good, though maybe it doesn't seem like it. It's important to just start, choose some things to work on. There's no chance what we tasted today will make it to the final dish. But if you're not trying things out and tasting them, you can't know what will work and what won't. We sometimes get trapped because we have too many ideas and it stops us from just getting started somewhere. Starting somewhere—anywhere—is the most important thing."

Tolerating failure is crucial in culinary innovation. "Counting Sheep" was one of the few dishes the FDEK worked on that made it successfully all the way through the development process into something a paying guest would actually eat. Even then, its final form bore only a few similarities to Rodriguez's first version. Observing the team working on the dish for several months, I saw the idea meander through many treatments, some of which were dead ends, before eventually splitting into two dishes. The first was a meringue flavored with milk and cookies, served on a floating cushion (magnetically levitated on a custom-designed base) to create a sense of lightness and literally suspended reality. The second, served in quick succession, was an all-white exploration of soft, creamy, light textures: a white chocolate and vanilla sponge-encased panna cotta flavored with tonka bean (chosen for its powdery, vanilla-like scent from the chemical compound coumarin) and made more complex with the aroma of orange blossom—to be eaten with a fuzzy-handled spoon dusted lightly with baby powder.

In the course of developing this idea, the FDEK had to conceive of, design, and manufacture a cushion-shaped levitating machine (one of the team members was a mechanical engineer with an aptitude for electronics), commission a silverware designer to fabricate a fuzzy-handled spoon and then figure out how to clean and sanitize it for service, create a new combination of flavors (tonka bean, coconut, orange blossom, vanilla) that would be complemented by the scent of baby powder, develop a method for baking a panna cotta (usually set with gelatin that melts at body temperature) inside sponge cake, and work with the servers and a screenwriter to develop a storyline and script that would connect the two dishes to each other and to the rest of the meal but still be brief enough to not interrupt an already elaborate and carefully choreographed service.

After all this work, one might imagine that the FDEK would not want to change those two dishes. Soon after the reopening, though, Blumenthal said that they were "good enough but we're going to refine them a bit more. Now that we have them doing what we want, we have to rebuild the recipes from the ground up and strip away as many of the ingredients and processes as possible to make it simpler and more direct."

Plenty of work and hundreds, sometimes even thousands, of conscious and unconscious choices lie between the original impulse for a dish and its final version. R&D chefs make these choices to strike a balance between the dish's objective and the practical necessities of needing it to be safe and delicious to eat, while also accommodating the restaurant's budget, staffing, and space constraints. More often than not, this balance cannot be found. Because there are so many compounding possibilities to explore, a point of balance may exist but there may not be enough time to find it. The landscape of possibilities is vast, mountainous, and hidden in shadow—the culinary R&D team explores it with tiny flashlights as they experiment, seeing only a little of it at a time and often reaching an impasse. What the team finds, it then has to interpret and make sense of. It is due both to luck and skill that this exploration sometimes leads to the creation of a new dish that works. Many dishes are abandoned during their development, sometimes on the cusp of a breakthrough that some other chef or team of chefs might later make.[3]

The amount of time, energy, and resources the FDEK put into developing new dishes is not unusual among cutting-edge restaurants, nor is the low success rate—yet most high-end culinary R&D work done today is aimed at creating new dishes. This reflects how important dish-level innovation is for customers and critics who increasingly associate new dishes and constantly changing menus with a restaurant's quality.

## NEW INGREDIENTS

While guests consume new dishes directly, new ingredients are at least initially a step removed from their experience.

Ingredients are precursors or components of dishes; like tools, their most important characteristic is that they have affordances—properties that make it possible for them to be used in a range of ways to achieve different results. If you've made an omelet for lunch and then a mayonnaise for a sandwich, you have personally experienced two of the many affordances of the egg.[4]

Many ingredients have a wide range of affordances. For example, different apple varieties have different levels of sugars and acids and behave differently when baked in dry heat. Each variety behaves differently again when cooked in moist heat. To make a tarte Tatin, where apple slices are first caramelized in a pan holding quite a lot of butter and sugar then baked again under a layer of pastry, the cook should choose high-acid varieties of apples to balance the sugar, but these apples should also cook to tenderness—first in the moist heat on the stovetop, then in the dry heat of the oven—without collapsing into a mush. As Jane Grigson says, "for good food, one needs to understand that a Cox's Orange Pippin in a pie will give you a quite different result from a Bramley."[5] An intimate understanding of the affordances of different apple varieties (and of butter, salt, and sugar) distinguishes a merely competent tarte Tatin from a memorably delicious one.

The distinctions among the different affordances of an ingredient can be subtle. In fact, they are often hidden so that happy accident or systematic study is required to bring them to light. For this reason, most ingredients we cook with are not new. Cooks have taken generations to either intentionally or accidentally learn how they should be used.

To investigate an ingredient's affordances means focusing attention on it and spending time and resources testing it. For instance, learning that the flavor and texture of yellowtail (Japanese amberjack, *Seriola quinqueradiata*) changes over the course of its six- to ten-year lifespan requires tasting and cooking with yellowtail of different ages. Where this kind of close attention has been paid to ingredients for a long time, systems arise within some cooking professions for understanding subtle differences in the affordances of ingredients. Sushi chefs, for example, recognize yellowtail as one of a group of fish species called *shusseuo*, in which each species of fish is given several different names to clearly distinguish among its different flavors and uses at different ages.[6]

Because developing new ingredients is time-consuming and difficult, attempts to create them are rarer than attempts to create new dishes. Newness in the context of ingredients is about finding affordances that no one else knows about yet. Culinary R&D teams do this either by finding a new ingredient (a material not currently used as an ingredient) and learning its affordances, or by finding new affordances for an old ingredient.

## *Mahogany Clams at Amaja (2011)*

Amaja holds a preservice briefing for the kitchen and front of house staff before the first guests arrive for lunch each day. On this midsummer day in 2011, the briefing started at 9 a.m. because it was going to be longer than usual. In addition to the usual review of guests with dietary restrictions and special occasions, Amaja's R&D team was planning to introduce and explain a new dish coming onto the menu for the first time. To ease the dish into service, it would initially only be served to a few tables during each service instead of being added to every guest's menu. The three R&D chefs would join the service kitchen to work out the last kinks in the recipe before eventually handing first the cooking, then both the cooking and the preparation, to the appropriate stations in the service kitchen. The dish in question was built around, and intended to highlight, a new ingredient that head chef Tómas Irigoyen said no one else had yet figured out how to cook: mahogany clams (*Arctica islandica*) that were two centuries old, individually hand-harvested by Amaja's shellfish provider from feral stocks in cold, deep waters at the very southern tip of Patagonia.

Irigoyen stood at the pass with Gustavo Terzan and Martín Varela (Amaja's R&D chefs) behind a series of translucent plastic tubs and aluminum trays. He passed around a tub that held a few raw clams in their shells, each a rough dark brown and the size of a human fist. The other tubs and trays on the pass held the prepared components of the finished dish: a tub with a few shucked clams that had been cooked at a very low temperature and then cooled in their own juices supplemented with some dried seaweed stock, a flat tray with three leeks that had been grilled over live coals for just long enough to char the outside but leave the inside a softly crisp bright green, a few small cups holding washed herb flowers for garnish.

Terzan took one of the leeks and began to slice it into centimeter-thick rounds, placing each round on a plate. "These clams come from Rodrigo, and we're going to serve them with this charred leek that's still a bit crisp. Gustavo is beginning the assembly now," Irigoyen said, taking a prepared clam meat onto the cutting board in front of him. "The texture and flavor of the clam, you will see for yourself, is not like a normal clam because it is so old and takes so long to grow. You cannot treat it like a normal clam or mussel. It is like rubber when it is totally raw, but you cannot cook it like a normal clam because it gets powdery. They used to just throw them into stews if they found one in the trawl and cook it to death. It took us a long time to figure out how to treat it right."

Dan Camarata, the executive chef, said "We've spent three months trying many different cooking times and temperatures, and then we realized that it's also how the meat is sliced for presentation. Rodrigo's clams are so big and old they have even more texture difference than most shellfish, so you have to treat it like meat. Figure out the grain and slice correctly."

"So we are doing the clam with a very short cooking time at low temperature just to open up the clam and firm up the meat a bit, then we cool it down in its own juice. Gustavo and Martín will show the prep team later. If we got it right," Irigoyen said, beginning to slice, "the meat will be firm outside like properly cooked lobster, and inside it will be creamy. We slice across the clam like this so every slice has both textures and is thin enough to eat in one bite. Watch how the slicing goes; if you cut it this way, it's fucked. There will be too much firm texture." He placed samples of the clam sliced the right way and the wrong way on another plate and sent it around. Each glistening slice was mottled dark pink and brown, not resembling shellfish at all. "Try it to see how different the textures are. And remember that each of these clams is about 150 kroner [about sixteen dollars], so please treat it with respect. We lay about five slices of clam on the plate around the leek pieces, and then it's ready for sauce and garnish."

After lunch, Irigoyen said, "These clams are amazing, yes? But we have to spend the time and money to know how to cook them. It's a lot. We went through months of these expensive clams. We do the research and we get the permits and find the best suppliers and everything, and then after us everyone just has to pick up the phone and call and get it. But this will be the first time these clams have been cooked to bring out how they are supposed to taste. One table today told me it was one of the best things they'd ever eaten, and no one else will have them yet."

Amaja's three-month investigation of the mahogany clam, a new ingredient not used elsewhere in high-end cuisine, yielded just one affordance. But this was enough for them to build a dish around the clam that no other restaurant—at least in the short term—would be able to produce. A program of developing new ingredients, while costly and time-intensive, is one way ambitious restaurants can distinguish themselves from competitors. Restaurants like Amaja, DOM in Brazil, Attica in Australia, and Noma in Denmark are distinctive and able to create new dishes frequently partly because they have found ingredients in their home regions that other chefs aren't using, and they have invested the time and effort to learn how those ingredients can be used.

## NEW COOKING METHODS

New cooking methods are even further removed from the guest's experience than new ingredients are. Cooking methods are fundamental and generic processes—sequences of actions a cook takes on ingredients and equipment—that can be applied to a wide range of ingredients. Almost all the cooking methods chefs use for transforming ingredients are extremely old: blanching, baking, boiling, sauteing, searing, steaming, braising, frying, and the like were all invented generations ago.

There has been relatively little radical innovation in cooking methods in high-end cuisine. Developing a new method in today's culinary context usually consists of translating a cooking method from outside high-end cuisine, refining an existing cooking method, or combining existing cooking methods. Method innovation of late has been translational, incremental, or combinatorial. As the following three cases illustrate, developing new cooking methods allows chefs to achieve results that were previously too difficult or too impractical.

## *Method Translation: Spherification at El Bulli (2003)*

Spherification exemplifies the translation of methods (in this case from industrial food chemistry) into a high-end culinary context. Spherification encapsulates a liquid within an edible and visually indistinguishable skin of the same flavor—an effect which was previously practically impossible. The method the team at El Bulli initially devised for doing this entails dissolving sodium alginate (a texture-modifier often used in industrial food chemistry) in the liquid to be spherified, then immersing droplets of the liquid in a calcium chloride solution. Calcium ions replace the sodium ions in the sodium alginate dissolved in the liquid to form calcium alginate, which is a gel. This gel layer forms the skin; what's inside the skin remains liquid.

The larger the droplet, the larger the sphere; the longer the droplet is left in the calcium bath, the thicker the skin. The first dish El Bulli's R&D team built around the spherification method was a liquid pea ravioli first served in 2003: a bright green sphere of pea purée that burst in the mouth much as a ravioli would do, but without a pasta skin. Nowadays, even fairly unambitious restaurants can spherify liquids with off-the-shelf, easy-to-use reagents. Back in 2003, though, this was a revelation for chefs. As Lars Williams from the Nordic Food Lab said, "imagine you go to dinner and they give you a spoon with a green blob. Just by looking at it, you know it isn't purée because it isn't pooling on the plate. You know it's not gelatin or agar because it's wobbling about a lot but not falling apart under its own weight. Then you bite it and it explodes like a ravioli. The inside is definitely liquid. It's got this skin that is so thin. It's literally a shock. It's like if you've never heard of fire and someone gives you a piece of roast pork. Your mind is blown."[7]

Sodium alginate and other alginates had been used for decades to adjust processed food textures by the time the El Bulli team discovered them while visiting the Spanish offices of an international food development and production company called Griffith. Alginates had always been used to thicken liquids such as sauces, or to produce flavored solid beads to add textural interest to a liquid. Until El Bulli, they had never been used for spherification because this required unprecedentedly fine control of the method to achieve two distinct textures in the same item.

To obtain a delicate but sufficiently stable skin without noticeably changing the base flavor of the liquid being spherified, the amount of sodium alginate in the liquid and the concentration of calcium chloride in the calcium bath must both be carefully calibrated against composition of the liquid and the time the droplet is left in the bath. Just as there is considerable embodied knowledge, mostly tacit and difficult to describe, required to correctly manipulate a pan when making a good French omelet, El Bulli's R&D team had to develop—through repeated trial and error—a physical understanding of the myriad details of how to introduce the liquid into the calcium bath so the resulting sphere would appear smooth and unblemished, and how to detect when the skin on a sphere had formed to the right extent. They eventually designed perforated, specially shaped spoons that would allow them to remove the spheres from the calcium bath without damaging them.

El Bulli took alginate chemistry out of the industrial food setting and translated it for high-end culinary use, experimenting with the method until they understood it with the level of detail and sophistication needed to produce the delicate textural effects they sought, in the process creating a new method that they (and many other chefs thereafter) refined and expanded upon.[8]

## *Method Refinement: Agar Clarification* at Ideas in Food *and* Cooking Issues *(2009)*

Methods for clarifying liquids are important for high-end cooking, and they're more important the more effective (the clearer the resulting liquid) and the more efficient (the less waste is generated) they are. A relatively recently discovered, highly effective way to clarify a liquid is to set it with gelatin, freeze it, then allow the gelled mass to thaw slowly under refrigeration. The gelatin forms a matrix trapping the suspended particles that make the liquid cloudy. Freezing, then slowly thawing the solidified mass breaks up the matrix enough to release only clear liquid, leaving the suspended particles behind trapped in a collapsed pile of gelatin. However, gelatin clarification takes many hours and ties up valuable refrigerated storage space because the gelled block needs to thaw slowly and at a low enough temperature for the gelatin matrix to not melt and contaminate the clarified liquid by releasing its particulates. This makes the process inconvenient and unusable for clarifying liquids, such as fresh juices, whose flavors change rapidly.

In 2009, Alex Talbot at *Ideas in Food* (an independent culinary R&D team) wrote a blog post describing a faster, less equipment-intensive clarification method that replaced the gelatin with agar, a vegetarian hydrocolloid derived from seaweed that sets quickly into a solid at room temperature.[9] Talbot's method put the agar-gelled liquid inside a vacuum bag and evacuated the air from the bag to disrupt the gel matrix and encourage faster draining of the clarified liquid. His post and method led Dave Arnold from *Cooking Issues* (then the technology and innovation department in the French Culinary Institute in New York) to the insight that agar gels could be disrupted as soon as they formed, by hand with a whisk, without being frozen or vacuum sealed. Arnold also realized that the clarified liquid could be even more quickly and inexpensively pressed out of the broken-up agar gel by wrapping it in reusable cheesecloth and squeezing it out. Arnold wrote two blog posts describing his method that same day: it was a refinement of Talbot's method (in turn a refinement of conventional gel clarification) that allowed room temperature clarification (thus not tying up freezer and refrigerator space) in a small fraction of the time needed for gelatin clarification.[10]

Arnold's refined agar clarification method quickly became widely used because it was both more effective and more efficient than gelatin clarification. More types of liquids can be clarified with this method, the clarified liquids preserve better flavor because the process is faster, and the process requires both less time and less equipment.

## Method Combination: Sous Vide and Sear (2004/2005)

For most of the history of cooking, it was inconceivable to cook a tough cut of meat to tenderness while keeping it rare or medium-rare. Tough cuts of meat (like short rib), have deep flavor compared with tender cuts (like filet) because they have been worked extensively during the animal's life. For the same reason, they contain a lot of intramuscular connective tissue, which produces the sensation of fibrousness and toughness. These cuts have traditionally been cooked using long wet braises at relatively low temperatures. This causes the collagen that makes up much of the connective tissue to first hydrate and then break down, reducing the toughness of the meat. A correctly traditionally braised short rib will be tender and unctuous, but will also have a distinctly well-done appearance. A new combination of existing cooking methods that became coherent around 2004 allowed high-end chefs to achieve the previously impossible outcome of a visually rare (i.e., pink) yet texturally long-cooked (i.e., unctuously tender) short rib.

This combinatorial innovation was the development of a method of cooking a tough cut of meat sous vide to achieve a rare appearance, then searing it for service. Sous vide processing had been used in industrial cooking since the 1960s, initially to pack and pasteurize foods and extend their storage lifespans. By the 1970s, chefs working in high-end cuisine, like Bruno Goussault, Pierre Troisgros, Georges Pralus, and Joël Robuchon, began experimenting with modifying sous vide and combining it with other methods.[11]

In the late 1990s, high-end chefs such as Alain Ducasse and Heston Blumenthal began to experiment with the possibilities of finely controlled temperature when cooking meat, with the aim of producing slow-cooked tough cuts that were tender but still appeared pink and medium-rare. This is only possible by holding the meat at a temperature below 57°C (135°F) so that the red myoglobins that give rare meat its pink color don't denature into the tan-colored hemichromes that turn well-done meat grey. However, too low a cooking temperature would prevent the collagen in the connective tissue from breaking down within the cooking time, leaving the meat tough. Conventional wisdom held that collagen would only denature and melt above 70°C (158°F), but those who tried cooking meats for extended periods around 57°C (135°F) found that collagen breakdown did occur, though it took much longer. Eventually, through trial and error across a large number of kitchens, chefs found a way to thread the needle by cooking a cut like short rib for many tens of hours at 56–57°C (133–135°F).[12]

Due to the long cooking times—the most consistently reproduced method, developed by The Cooking Lab, called for a seventy-two hour cook time for short ribs—the ribs would have to be sealed in a vacuum pack to reduce oxidation that would introduce off-flavors and discoloration. A short rib cooked rare sous vide would emerge from the vacuum pack pink inside and extremely tender, but pallid and unappetizing outside. The solution to this cosmetic problem was to keep the meat in a water or butter bath at the desired service temperature, then sear the already-cooked meat just before service to caramelize the outside. By combining two existing methods—low-temperature long-duration cooking in vacuum packs and searing—chefs were able to cook short ribs that looked and tasted rare or medium-rare but with the texture of traditional braised short ribs.

Because cooking methods can potentially be applied to a wide range of ingredients and dishes, method innovation is a powerful means of reaching, and then staying on, the culinary cutting edge. However, R&D specifically aimed at developing new cooking methods is relatively rare in high-end cuisine because it usually requires enormous investments of time and equipment. While organizations like El Bulli, *Cooking Issues*, and The Cooking Lab have invested in this kind of development work, new cooking methods more often emerge when an R&D team or a distributed set of groups and individuals accidentally produces or observes a phenomenon and experiments with it until it is understood well enough to be applied with predictable results.

## NEW COOKING PROCESSES

Processes are instructions for how to cook, and they explain which ingredients and methods should be combined, in what sequence, and in what way. Creating a new process in high-end cuisine can mean either developing a viable way to cook a new dish or part of a dish, or finding a new way to cook an old dish more quickly, more reliably, or less expensively. Recipes are the type of process familiar to most cooks, but they are not the only type: processes are also used to coordinate the many aspects of work that surround recipes.

## *The ThinkFoodTank's New* Canelones *Process (2011)*

In April 2011, Ruben Garcia—then ThinkFoodGroup's head of R&D—let me join him on one of his periodic walks through each of the group's restaurants, this time at a restaurant called Jaleo in Washington DC. Because Jaleo serves through a long lunch and starts dinner service early, the kitchen is in active use for much of the day and late into the night. Lunch service had just started and ingredients were being prepared for the dinner service, so we walked around the crowded kitchen looking at cooks jostling for space to prep ingredients or to cook and plate dishes.

When we rounded the corner to the cold store, we ran into a prep cook, Luis Silva, draining a pot of pasta sheets next to a tray of finished canelones. At Jaleo, each canelone is a four-inch square sheet of house-made pasta, parboiled, drained, cooled, then rolled around a moist but not liquid filling (that day, it was finely shredded braised pork mixed with duck liver). To serve, two canelones are placed in a serving dish and baked under a layer of bechamel until the sauce browns appealingly. The dish is quite delicious. Garcia told me that Jaleo sold a hundred to a hundred and fifty servings of canelones every day.

Garcia glanced at the tray as we passed, then stopped. He called Silva over to point out that the canelones were of many different sizes and were lumpen instead of being smooth, uniform cylinders—it would be okay for today, but the consistency of the shape and size would have to improve. Then he spotted a trail of rust-brown liquid emanating from a canelone. A closer look revealed that many of the cylinders were either already broken and leaking or had hairline cracks. The weakness of the shells,

Garcia said, would make it difficult to quickly and neatly transfer the prepared canelones to individual serving dishes, or they might result in the canelones leaking while on their way to the guest—both unacceptable.

It turned out that Silva was following Garcia's recipes for the pasta sheets and filling precisely, but still producing inconsistent or defective canelones each day. It was assembling the canelones that was messy; this made him run far behind in preparing them each day.

Silva told us that he normally began assembly by parboiling some pasta sheets, then drying and laying them out on trays so they wouldn't overlap. Working one-by-one, he would add the filling with a spoon, roll it up, and transfer the finished canelone to a storage tray. The standard pans Silva was using only held about ten sheets each. Parcooking hundreds of sheets before beginning assembly tied up counter space and storage pans, which were also used by other cooks in the kitchen. He did his best under the circumstances: he parboiled as many sheets as would fit in two to three pans, made canelones with them, then repeated the process for the next batch. Assembling a day's worth of canelones might take up to two hours—he had to boil a fresh pot of water to cook each batch of pasta sheets (there's no room for pots of pasta water in cramped busy restaurant kitchens), and prepare extra canelones to make up for defective ones. Garcia asked Silva to finish the day's prep but keep aside a tray of pasta sheets and a tub of filling.

Some of the ThinkFoodTank team met in Jaleo's private dining room later that afternoon to update each other about their respective projects. Garcia sat with Aitor Lozano, Rick Billings, and Joe Raffa at a cluster of tables cluttered with notebooks and laptops, a stack of empty trays, a cling-wrapped tray of pasta sheets, and a tub of canelone filling. After the others had given their project updates, Garcia described the canelones problem; he noted that the issue was with the assembly process, and that it resulted from lack of kitchen space and equipment. As Garcia framed the problem, he rejected as "inelegant" the obvious, easy solution—buying more sheet pans.

Raffa (Oyamel's head chef and an advisor on restaurant openings and special projects) identified the main issue as laying out the sheets so they wouldn't overlap. Each sheet took up too much space. "They don't look like they're that sticky if you drain and dry them well," he said, "maybe we can overlap them and save some space." He laid out a few sheets and the whole team gazed at the tray.

Rearranging the sheets, Lozano said, "we can actually roll them directly from this." He had overlapped the sheets slightly in the order in which they'd be filled, making it possible to fill, roll, and store the finished canelones on the same tray on which the sheets were originally laid. This saved space but also eliminated the need to transfer finished canelones to a separate storage tray, which often led to cracks in the pasta.

"This is good," Garcia said, "we can actually overlap the sheets even closer. We only have to leave enough space for the filling to go on. And I think we should pipe the filling in, not use a spoon. It will be more consistent." He arranged the sheets even more closely, leaving only an inch and a half of each sheet exposed, while Lozano went for a piping bag fitted with a 1.5-inch nozzle into which he scraped the tub of filling. "We can make it even faster by piping every sheet before rolling them all together," Garcia said. He piped one sheet and tried to roll it up, then realized that the stacking order was wrong: the sheets would have to be overlapped in the opposite direction that they were rolled in.

Raffa and Billings (the group's head pastry chef) laid out an entire tray of pasta sheets in the right order, eventually fitting nearly sixty sheets on the pan. Garcia then piped filling onto all of them and rolled each canelone all the way down to the bottom of the tray, revealing the pasta sheet under it. The entire pan of canelones was assembled in just under seven minutes, each canelone an identical, smooth, unbroken cylinder. Raffa said, "This definitely works. You can prep an entire day's production of canelones with the same number of trays, in literally a tenth the time, with no breakages, zero waste, and perfect consistency, without having to go back and forth in batches."

Guests almost never experience process innovation directly and good restaurant staff improve processes constantly without necessarily thinking about it, because each incremental innovation seems so trivial compared to the obvious failure and stress that usually attends new dish development. However, restaurants that systematically and intentionally pay attention to process innovation—like ThinkFoodGroup did—become more consistent and efficient in their production and in their use of resources.

I've described these four kinds of culinary innovation separately for clarity, but they shade into each other in practice. Learning a new affordance for an ingredient is equivalent to learning a new process for cooking that ingredient. Creating a new cooking method that can be applied to many ingredients almost inevitably creates new affordances for many existing ingredients. Developing a new affordance for an ingredient might be the stimulus for creating a new dish. A new process might allow a chef to create a new ingredient out of existing ingredients and methods.

## THE PEOPLE

High-end culinary innovation is generally difficult, prone to failure, and time-consuming, no matter whether the innovation is in creating dishes, ingredients, methods, or processes. Even something as apparently simple as creating a good new combination of flavors is hard. New combinations of flavors are common, but combinations that are both new enough to be memorable and delicious enough to be enjoyable are rare. Tools help, but only a little. Books like Karen Page and Andrew Dornenburg's *The Flavor Bible* catalogue flavor combinations[13]—traditional ones from around the world as well as novel ones created by prominent chefs—to give chefs a framework for creating new flavor combinations. More recently, both IBM's Watson supercomputing division[14] and a Belgian food consultancy called Foodpairing [15] have offered services that generate novel combinations of ingredients based on the theory that ingredients that share flavor or aroma molecules go well together. But identifying a theoretical match between chamomile and strawberries isn't enough. High-end culinary innovation requires insight from trained cooks with broad exposure to flavors and cooking techniques, combined with much experimentation and adjustment.

In high-end cuisine, an R&D chef therefore performs a fundamentally different role from a service chef who cooks for paying guests. Service chefs have to cook fast and accurately, and become as good as possible at consistently producing the same dishes every service while minimizing waste—they focus on optimizing toward well-understood, clear goals. R&D chefs are also motivated to become as good as possible but at coming up with good problems to solve and then solving those problems. This often means walking a long, looping path littered with failed projects and other dead ends. R&D chefs have to confront uncertainty constantly. The goals they must pursue are neither as clear nor as well-understood as those that service chefs pursue, and the goals themselves often change over time. Unsurprisingly, chefs attracted to R&D work often have a fundamentally different mindset, one more oriented to exploration and amenable to uncertainty and failure than the mindset of chefs primarily attracted to the rush of service.

Many R&D chefs started working in a restaurant service kitchen, worked their way up, eventually realized that they were particularly good at coming up with new dishes, and found jobs doing that. But culinary R&D has also benefited from the growing attraction of culinary work more generally to a wider range of people. José Andrés told me one day, as we walked between two of his DC restaurants, that "when I was an apprentice, being a cook was something I did because I didn't know how to go to school. Nowadays, I have people who come from university to cook."

The media appeal of cooking and especially its recent portrayal as a venue for creative expression and technical sophistication means that high-end restaurants are these days increasingly filled with people who are much more diverse in age, background, gender, nonculinary education, and aspiration than they used to be—often people like César Pareto or Joe Raffa who are in their second or third careers. Among the people I met in the course of fieldwork: an ex-music video producer, an English PhD, a biochemistry PhD, a ex-software product manager, an anthropologist, a physicist. Each person brought some element of that previous career to the culinary R&D work he or she did.

Media portrayals of culinary work may have drawn some of these diverse and unconventional people into the industry, but it is the growth in the importance of R&D and innovation work in high-end cuisine that has created the exploratory roles that hold their interest.

## THE TEAMS

Because culinary R&D work is so failure-prone and time-consuming and the nature of R&D work is so profoundly different from that of routine kitchen work, restaurants that want to be innovative frequently invest in dedicated R&D teams—the chefs who work in the service kitchen cooking for paying guests seldom have time to seriously engage in innovation work.[16]

High-end culinary R&D teams operate in different organizational contexts. An R&D team can serve a single high-end restaurant (like Amaja's test kitchen), be part of a group of restaurants (like ThinkFoodTank), or be entirely independent of any restaurant (like The Cooking Lab). This range of different business and organizational models for doing high-end culinary R&D has developed in tandem with a growing number of ways to make money from innovation work.

Finding ways to pay for expensive R&D is a crucial prerequisite for a sustainably innovation-led restaurant or culinary laboratory. Guests at restaurants who see the dish-level innovation that results in constantly updated menus are often surprised by how expensive meals at cutting-edge restaurants are. Nonetheless, guest revenue at one of these restaurants is rarely sufficient to pay for dedicated culinary innovation teams. Culinary R&D has to be subsidized.

The Fat Duck Experimental Kitchen pays for itself by developing dishes for the more casual dining restaurants in the same group where volume and margins are higher, developing a range of branded products for a premium supermarket chain and an electrical appliance producer, and producing cookbooks and television series. Mugaritz's R&D team sells its gastronomic expertise to packaged goods companies trying to develop new consumer products. The Cooking Lab makes money by developing, self-publishing, and selling a growing range of lavishly produced and profitable cookbooks. The Patagonia Food Lab writes grant applications to fund its staff and specific projects.

There's no single model for making a cutting-edge culinary R&D team financially and operationally viable, and culinary innovation seems to happen through the same kind of creative scrounging for and use of resources that marks highly innovative groups in any context.

These R&D teams are often relatively small and organized quite differently from teams we're accustomed to seeing in conventional businesses. The more time I spent with them, the more convinced I became that these differences gave them the ability to continually innovate and adapt—the chapters to come focus on these aspects of their work.

## INNOVATION LESSONS FROM CUTTING-EDGE CUISINE

High-end culinary R&D work is different from traditional high-end kitchen work. It requires a mindset, approach, and work process analogous to that needed to design a new piece of consumer electronics or software. Creating new dishes, ingredients, cooking methods, and cooking processes is difficult and unpredictable, the more so because the whole industry—both driven by and hotly pursuing constant change—itself changes rapidly and unpredictably. Both the state of the art and what is considered new keeps changing, so the rules of the game keep changing as well.

In the rest of this book, I show how these teams were able to innovate and adapt to unpredictable change because they had an unusual mindset that embraced true uncertainty. This uncertainty mindset changed how they worked, from how they found new members, to how they taught each other the crucial knowledge needed to innovate, to how they motivated themselves to do the difficult work of innovation.

# PART III

Innovation Is Uncertainty

# 5

## A NONDELUSIONAL WORLDVIEW

B Y my second visit to Amaja, I could already see that it worked differently from what someone steeped in conventional management wisdom would expect. These differences helped Amaja continually create new dishes that won it critical acclaim.

Early in that visit, I asked Amaja's head chef and owner Tomás Irigoyen how he'd built a team that was so successful at reinventing the menu so frequently. He said that there hadn't been any strategic plan at the beginning. Amaja had been driven by the realization that whatever they did would likely only be relevant for a brief instant, and that the key was to get things "right for now" because "everything would change anyway." At the time, I did not understand what he meant. I thought he was being evasive. I came to comprehend Irigoyen's offhand remark gradually, as I became immersed in how these research and development (R&D) kitchens worked.

Until 2011, Amaja's identity was New Patagonian, which is to say that it distinguished itself by discovering or reinterpreting foods and cooking techniques unique to the southern extremes of South America. Amaja's uses of these ingredients and techniques were thus frequently the first time they were exposed on an international level in high-end cuisine. Amaja's dishes—and Amaja itself—presented critics and guests with flavors, ingredients, and cooking methods that they had never encountered before.

By then, social media had become an important communication channel in the culinary world. Twitter, especially, was well on its way to supplanting blogs as the way information spread among and between restaurants and their customers, just as blogs had largely taken the place of the forums that existed before them. Amaja staff (junior and senior chefs, front of house, and Irigoyen himself) were active on Twitter, using their personal accounts to share new menu items, ingredients, and techniques, often while they were still in development. This drew both guests and critics to the restaurant and contributed to its quick climb up the 50 Best list.

At Amaja, social media was a two-way channel. Amaja broadcast the innovation work that it did through Twitter—but it could also see, almost in real time, how the high-end restaurant industry worldwide was shifting. As Amaja surged up the 50 Best list starting in 2008, it became clear to the team that a growing number of restaurants worldwide had become aware of New Patagonian ingredients, methods, and of the distinctive culinary style that Amaja had created. As César Pareto said to me, "There's a sell-by date on this stuff." Put plainly, the team had their ear to the ground and they were driven by the realization that just retaining and refining their New Patagonian identity alone would not keep Amaja permanently distinctive.

## SEEING THE WORLD CLEARLY

Each of the innovation teams I spent time with had this same urge to try to stay one step ahead. Joe Raffa at ThinkFoodGroup referred to it as "a sort of itchy feeling" that things in the world of high-end cuisine were changing, accompanied by a desire not to be left behind. As I came to see it, this "itchy feeling" was because these teams saw that they would not be able to predict the future and plan for it in the conventional way. In chapters 1–4, I've shown how social media, trends in criticism, cross-pollination among different fields, and the increasingly dense professional networks among chefs made it undeniably clear that the cutting edge in high-end cuisine would continue to change unforeseeably.

Superficially, these teams looked different from one another. They were of different sizes, they worked on different kinds of R&D projects, and they were in different countries. Nonetheless, all of them had the same uncertainty mindset.[1] This undeluded view of the future was foundational; it had broadly similar, wide-ranging effects on each team. The uncertainty mindset led them to work in similar ways despite being so different on the surface, influencing how they designed themselves and chose what to work on. Put plainly, the uncertainty mindset made these teams work unconventionally—these differences were visible in how they found new team members, how they set and pursued goals, and how they motivated themselves. These counterintuitive methods of organization, founded on a view of the future as being dominated by uncertainty, were in turn responsible for their success in innovating continuously.

This chapter prepares the ground for rest of the book by clarifying the difference between *uncertainty* and *risk*. These words are too often used interchangeably to refer to situations in which the future is unknown. However, there is a fundamental difference between the two that must be understood for the rest of this book to make sense.

## CERTAIN VS. UNCERTAIN WORLDS

Explaining the difference between risk and uncertainty is easier when certainty and uncertainty are clearly defined. In a certain world, you have all the knowledge necessary to know exactly how the future will be. Certain worlds are easy to describe, as the following scenario illustrates.

*Certainty.* Suspend disbelief and imagine that you are a U.S.-based manufacturer of a carbonated drink. You are sure that demand for your product will grow steadily at four percent a year. You own your manufacturing and distribution facilities, have long-term price contracts for all the materials you use to make your products, and have no desire to introduce new products. Current regulations also mean that you can be sure no competitors will enter the market. In this world, your business decisions—such as how much and when to invest in equipment, when to hire production staff and how many of them to hire—are straightforward and easy to analyze and plan for.

This scenario sounds almost caricature because such absolute certainty is nearly unheard of. We live in worlds that are uncertain in that we don't know (and often cannot know) enough to be sure about how the future will work out.

### *Uncertainty takes two forms: risk and true uncertainty*

The future can be unknown in different ways, because different types of unknown-ness are possible. Risk represents one of these types of unknown-ness, in which the world is not completely known but is fundamentally knowable.[2]

*Risk.* The world of complete certainty described above remains except for one detail. There is now a chance that bad weather affects harvests in the countries where your sugar producers are located. If this happens, even with long-term price contracts, there is a chance that some of your sugar suppliers will be unable to deliver as much sugar as you will need. Specifically, your infallible analysts have put the chance of a 1,000-ton sugar shortfall at 20 percent within the next two years. Your production will be affected by such a shortage, reducing profit in that period by $2 million. Given current sugar prices of $220/ton, you protect yourself by buying 1,000 extra tons of sugar for $220,000 and renting additional warehouse space to store it for two years at $24,000. The risk here is the 20 percent chance of losing $2 million in profit in the next two years (i.e., $400,000), which exceeds the cost of buying and storing the emergency sugar stockpile ($244,000). Deciding to stockpile some sugar is clearly sensible.

The word *risk* here means that the exact future that will result is unknown, but the different possible futures are knowable in a way that allows you to plan by calculating how likely different possible futures are and taking clearly sensible actions based on those calculations. To be clear, this requires a type of certainty about the unknowns (in this case, being certain that there is a 20 percent chance of a 1,000-ton sugar shortfall in the next two years). In other words, risk is a type of uncertainty that can be measured, quantified, then eliminated by a calculated strategic action (in this case, by stockpiling sugar).

R&D teams in cutting-edge cuisine saw the world in a fundamentally different way—not as risky, but as truly uncertain. True uncertainty is a different form of uncertainty that cannot be measured and cannot be eliminated using strategies chosen based on likelihoods of outcomes.

*True uncertainty.* The world is again slightly different. This time, you're uncomfortably aware that no regulations prevent competitors from entering the market and introducing new drinks that will compete with your product. You're profitable, but not so profitable that you can be certain competitors will enter the market attracted by those profits. But you're aware that competing products that do enter the market will probably affect not only how much you sell but also how much you can charge. However, you're not sure how likely this is or how it will affect your business. Your company's exact future is unknown, but you know neither all of the possible futures nor how likely each of those possible futures is. You aren't able to calculate how likely the different possible futures are (as you could in the risk scenario) and make sensible decisions about what you should do based on such calculations.

In fact, this third scenario introduces only one element of uncertainty—whether another company will introduce a competing product into the market. Realistically, in a complex and interconnected world many other things are likely to happen to your soft drink company that would make its future difficult to foresee and thus to plan for.

## TRUE UNCERTAINTY IS *FUNDAMENTALLY* DIFFERENT FROM RISK

The unknown is existentially threatening, which is why people and organizations act both rationally and instinctively to reduce or avoid it.[3] Confusion arises because unknown-ness is not monolithic. Risk and true uncertainty are both unknown (and thus often conflated), but the scenarios above highlight how true uncertainty represents a fundamentally different type of unknown-ness than risk. Truly uncertain worlds are unknown in ways that make it impossible to decide how to act based on calculations that can be done in advance. True uncertainty thus has quite different implications for people and organizations compared to risk. For the rest of this book, I use *uncertainty* to mean true uncertainty as opposed to risk.

Uncertainty became more widely understood as a concept in 2002 when Donald Rumsfeld (at that time the U.S. secretary of defense) described the problem of uncertainty in terms of "unknown unknowns—the [things] we don't know we don't know" (in contrast to risk, which he called "known unknowns") during a White House press briefing about weapons of mass destruction in Iraq.[4] Nonetheless, we continue to think of risk and uncertainty interchangeably, though we have seen increasingly often in the last few years that the world is more often truly uncertain than it is risky. The more interconnected and interdependent a system is, the more likely that events in one part of the system affect the rest of it. The larger such an interconnected, interdependent system is, the more likely that more of these events happen and that their unexpected effects mutually amplify and ripple throughout.[5] Complexity and interconnectedness thus increase the likelihood that a system behaves in a truly uncertain way.[6] This was and is true in cutting-edge cuisine and, to give just one example from recent memory, in the financial mechanics that produced 2008's global financial crisis.

The overwhelming majority of people—even experts deeply embedded in the parts of the financial system that had developed the asset-backed securities that triggered the crisis—did not predict its onset and progression. In fact, many of these experts believed that the global financial system was stable and asset-backed securities were reliable until just before Lehman Brothers collapsed, precipitating the crisis. They believed that the global financial system was comprehensible and knowable, that it was a situation of appropriately managed risk.[7] Hindsight has since revealed that what had been perceived then as risky was actually uncertain. Where a situation is uncertain in reality, believing it to merely be risky—and thus susceptible to planning—is to believe in a form of false certainty and to be, in a real sense, deluded about the state of the world. It is perilous to mistake true uncertainty for risk.[8]

The existential threat from true uncertainty can undoubtedly be terrifying, but it also represents opportunity for innovation. Where the future is uncertain, people and organizations have the freedom to influence what it becomes. Apple Inc. is one example. Steve Jobs gave a talk in 1983, before Apple became a household name and when barely anyone owned a personal computer or thought they were necessary. Despite having little concrete evidence to support his conviction, Jobs told the audience that "in a few years people will be spending more time interacting with personal computers than with cars." Uncertainty about the future in 1983 meant that great things were possible. With hindsight, Jobs's talk should be interpreted as the kind of entrepreneurial imagination that resulted in the stream of design and technical innovations Apple eventually produced in the following decades.[9]

As of 2019, the same uncertainty about the future exists for quantum computing, blockchain technology, cryptocurrencies, genetic engineering, drone technology, and space exploration— to name just a few. These fields are still developing basic technical understanding. The limits of what is technically possible are unclear, to say nothing of the uncertainty about how each of these fields will evolve. The wide range of entrepreneurial ideas emerging within them attests to how true uncertainty produces the open space that encourages both entrepreneurship and innovation.

# 6

## THE UNCERTAINTY MINDSET

U NDERLYING the chapters to come is the idea that individuals and teams have mindsets that affect how they see and interpret the world, and thus influence how they act.[1] Cutting-edge cuisine developed as an industry in ways that not only made it truly uncertain but also made it unavoidably clear that it was uncertain instead of simply risky. The R&D teams I spent time with therefore had the uncertainty mindset: the belief that what happens in cutting-edge cuisine's future is uncertain, not risky. Perceiving the world as uncertain motivated these teams to explore and seek new information in an attempt to change the world and guide how it would change.

The uncertainty mindset also affected how they acted and how they organized themselves and their work. It drove their methods for finding new members, shaped the kinds of goals they pursued, and influenced how they motivated themselves. The rest of this chapter briefly introduces these teams and outlines their unconventional ways of working.

### CONTINUALLY ADAPTIVE TEAMS

When I first came across the ThinkFoodGroup at a talk at Harvard in 2010, it had two full-time R&D chefs—Ruben Garcia and Aitor Lozano—but their work was frequently supported by a group of about ten people (collectively, the ThinkFoodTank) drawn as needed from other restaurants and operating units across the entire ThinkFoodGroup organization. José Andrés, the cofounder and head chef of ThinkFoodGroup, called the ThinkFoodTank his "Delta Force," a team he could send in anywhere. They could reliably, he said, "parachute in, work fast together to figure out the problem, create an elegant solution," whether the problem was an inconsistent dish at one of the ThinkFoodGroup restaurants or opening a new restaurant with all the conceptual and logistical complexity and uncertainty that entails. The ThinkFoodTank sounded like an innovation dream team: flexible enough to be deployed across a wide range of situations, comfortable even in situations of high uncertainty, with individual team members working independently and interdependently as needed.

I eventually spent several months in 2010 and 2011 with the ThinkFoodTank, both in their Washington DC homebase and in Las Vegas as they handled the simultaneous openings of three new ThinkFoodGroup restaurants in the Cosmopolitan Hotel. From what I saw, Andrés had undersold the ThinkFoodTank's capabilities. Despite having members who drifted into and out of the group, and lacking fixed roles for any member, the Think-FoodTank could coordinate its members with tremendous precision and work extremely quickly without extensive planning or management oversight. I saw this first-hand when I joined them for three weeks in Las Vegas. One of the new ThinkFoodGroup restaurants would be another branch of an existing innovative tapas restaurant; another would be a small tasting-menu restaurant; and the third would be a new concept (Chinese-Mexican) with a menu, preparation methods, and kitchen layout quite different from anything the group had done before.

A well-functioning restaurant provides great service and makes money only if thousands of moving parts work in alignment with each other each day; achieving this level of coordination takes great sophistication in planning. Frequently, collisions and misalignments result from unknown and unanticipated interactions among different parts of the operation; these only get discovered over time. A new restaurant opening is thus one of the most challenging things a restaurant team can do, because only a limited amount of planning and preparation can be done ahead of actually moving into the space and readying it for operation.

Once moved in, the weeks before actually opening are filled with myriad problems that must be found and solved for the restaurant to provide a good guest experience. At first almost nothing works because so many systems are all slightly broken. Recipes fail because the ingredients are slightly different from when they were tested in a different city, the kitchen is built to plan but works slightly differently than anticipated, the supply chain functions slightly differently in an unexpected way. Above all, the new restaurant team (the kitchen and the front of house) hasn't had time to learn the complexities of working together yet.[2]

In Las Vegas, the ThinkFoodTank was dropped into a high-uncertainty situation. When simultaneously opening three restaurants, thousands of emergent and potentially interacting problems must be discovered and resolved. This complexity produced uncertainty about what actions to take to solve these problems so the restaurants could open. In this situation, the ThinkFoodTank behaved in a way that seemed self-organizing, analogous to how a swarm of bees explores a new landscape.[3] Each team member scoured part of the terrain of the overall problem for new information and brought that information back to the group. It seemed as though individuals worked on problems independently and autonomously. However, the team as a whole seemed to be collectively aware of these problems and how they individually related to each other. When the problems being discovered or solved were beyond the capacity or the skills of the individual member, the team escalated into interdependent work.

The team seemed to effortlessly—and with barely any active management—scan this uncertainty-filled environment, absorb, process, and integrate the problems and information it found, then balance independent and interdependent work to solve those problems. Each team member seemed to know what needed to be done and what part of the overall task was his or her individual responsibility. It seemed even more like the ideal type of an innovation team than Andrés had made it out to be. How did everyone know what to do and how it fit in with the rest of the group without a detailed plan at the outset, or a leader doing a lot of complex coordination as the situation developed, or discussing things at great length?

I gradually came to understand how this was possible when I connected the team dynamics I saw in Las Vegas with an unusual hiring process I'd observed several months earlier in 2010 when I spent time in the ThinkFoodTank's DC homebase. Several months had passed between my meeting them at Harvard and my DC visit. In that time, ThinkFoodTank had brought on a new member. Rick Billings had been hired with the title of group head pastry chef, a senior R&D position responsible for developing desserts for all ThinkFoodGroup restaurants. I followed Billings around a lot because he mostly worked out of a semipermanent pastry station (a small prep counter in the basement of one of the restaurants) and was easier to locate than Garcia or Lozano, who were often zipping between the five ThinkFood-Group locations in DC and nearby cities.

Billings was working on developing new desserts—including some for the restaurants opening in Las Vegas—and training cooks in the restaurants in preparing and plating them. But he spent what seemed an inordinate amount of time reflecting on what he should be doing, and running these ideas by Garcia, Lozano, and some of the other senior chefs who were part of the extended ThinkFoodTank team. It seemed as though Billings was going through many little tests constantly. It also seemed odd that he was so tentative about his work considering he was a senior hire. This would have been more understandable if it had been Rick's first weeks on the job, but he had been on the team for several months by then. Conventional management practice emphasizes how important it is to be as detailed as possible about a job specification then to find the person best matching that specification to fill the job. Though not often mentioned, the implicit assumption is that the job specification shouldn't change.[4]

Midway through my two weeks in DC, I finally felt comfortable enough with the team to broach the question. I was having lunch with Joe Raffa, head chef of one of the DC restaurants and one of the core ThinkFoodTank members. I asked him why a senior hire like Billings, who had been in the job for a few months, still appeared so tentative about his role. Raffa said: "We hire people when they have the skills we know we need for the job, but working on this team is not just about skill. Getting the job and the title is the first part and the most straightforward. It's important, but what's more important is that each of us has to understand what everyone else likes and is good at doing. How do we all think and approach problems? Rick and Aitor and Ruben know that they have to figure each other out before they can work well together, and that is what all this back and forth with Rick is about."

Months later, in Las Vegas, the two parts of the puzzle came together. I saw that the ThinkFoodTank was able to work together without appearing to communicate much because they understood in intricate detail not only what skills each team member had but also how they would approach problems. This understanding emerged from the long periods each member spent working out and negotiating his or her role with colleagues. It allowed members to put themselves in each others' shoes often without even really thinking about it. The unconventional provisional roles they took on gave them time to figure out their role's parameters and how it fit with the roles of other team members. Consciously deciding to invest in spending this time and effort paid off in the form of a team that could work interdependently like a dream—something like how a perfectly integrated jazz ensemble or basketball team might play together. And this payoff seemed to last over the team's lifespan.

Every team I spent time with used similar extended trial and testing periods. In contrast with conventional hiring practice, which treats the role as scoped as being stable and complete, this approach to negotiated joining treated the role as provisional, unstable, and open to change. It was always clear on both sides that the title was one thing and the actual role—in Billings's case, what part he would play in relation to others in the team—was another thing entirely. Numerous little and big tests gradually filled out these roles in a way that ensured an uncommonly deep and functional knowledge of each member's skills and inclinations.

## LEARNING HOW TO
## MAKE INNOVATION FEEL FAMILIAR

My first visit to The Cooking Lab was in early 2012 during a rare sunny spell in late winter in the Pacific Northwest. I'd been visiting friends in Seattle and rented a car to drive to Bellevue, a neighboring city grown wealthy from the inflow of well-paid technology workers at the nearby headquarters of Microsoft and Amazon.

After crossing the pontoon highway across Lake Washington, I followed the instructions Wayt Gibbs, then *Modernist Cuisine*'s editor, had emailed me and went down a series of roads walled with lush conifer forests. Eventually, I popped out by a cluster of long, low, anonymous-looking industrial buildings with few windows. The reception area felt like what I was used to at Google—furniture in primary colors, a cheerful gatekeeper politely demanding photographic identification, a mandatory-to-sign nondisclosure agreement. Soon after the thermal printer gave me an adhesive visitor badge, Gibbs emerged to take me in.

Back then, The Cooking Lab worked out of a few thousand square feet of double-height laboratory and workshop space carved out of a much larger development facility owned by the intellectual property company, Intellectual Ventures. The core team consisted of six development chefs, a photographer, a graphic designer, an ex-technology product manager, and an editor. It had slowly grown over the course of preparing *Modernist Cuisine*, as the project's scope and the demands it imposed on the team grew.

As we moved further into the building, passing projects Intellectual Ventures had in progress (space radio antennas, mosquito-killing lasers, that kind of thing), Gibbs said that *Modernist Cuisine* had begun as "a quick, short book about sous vide cookery." As the initial team (comprising a chef and an editor) worked on the project, they realized that explaining sous vide adequately would also require explaining a lot of chemistry and physics. The project gradually expanded in scope, complexity, and difficulty to become a wide-ranging general research project.

The challenge was compounded by the need to present this body of knowledge, unfamiliar to most professional chefs, in ways that would make it easy for them to understand and use.

*Modernist Cuisine* satisfied what had been a hidden demand in the market for books on food and sold unexpectedly briskly for a book listed at $650. It has been a strong seller since, both in English and in translation. This was partly because much of the knowledge it collected had never been easily available before, being dispersed across numerous specialist journals and publications. The book put it all in one place.

More importantly, it succeeded because of its distinctive approach to presenting comprehensive and technically sophisticated information. This approach might be—incompletely—described as translating such knowledge to be appealing and useable to chefs through clear writing, visually distinctive graphics, and extensively tested recipes. In particular, the recipes were designed to both illustrate scientific principles and show how such principles could extend the range of the professional or home kitchen. The Cooking Lab's books since then have been aimed at different audiences and investigated different areas of cooking, but always with the same distinctive approach.

Back in 2012, having quickly become well-known for this singular style, The Cooking Lab had to figure out what to do after *Modernist Cuisine at Home*. Their challenge was that the next project would have to be something that was simultaneously new *and* infused with the distinctive style that had made *Modernist Cuisine* so successful. "The flavor of it has to be right," Gibbs told me. "The next project will sell based on our reputation from *Modernist Cuisine*."

Innovating within a distinctive style matters. In cutting-edge cuisine, a restaurant succeeds when it can provide guests with new dishes or experiences that nonetheless feel familiar in ways that are unique to that restaurant. Each cutting-edge culinary team thus has much in common with an author like Margaret Atwood, a major animation studio such as Pixar, a film director like Quentin Tarantino, a fashion house like Issey Miyake, or an artistic practice like the Olafur Eliasson Studio—new work must be produced, but consumers only pay a premium if it feels stylistically consistent with what came before.

Making products that are consistent with a particular style is relatively easy if those products don't have to be novel. The essence of style is that it makes a product feel familiar because it has some continuity with previous products. Creating novel products is difficult even if those products don't have to be consistent with a particular style. The Cooking Lab faced a double challenge. It had to create new products that combined novelty and familiarity in a kind of style that was consistent with what it had become known for but also open-ended enough to permit new things to be infused with it. Open-ended style thus goes beyond simply creating a one-off signature dish or song or movie. It requires knowledge impossible to put into words that nonetheless produces new things that consumers perceive as consistent and familiar.

Understanding and using open-ended style is hard enough for creative individuals working alone. It becomes an even bigger challenge for innovation teams working interdependently. Conventional wisdom holds that teams need clear and stable shared goals to coordinate their work effectively, so that they don't work at cross-purposes.[5] Aiming to produce novel work interferes with this because team goals become impossible to fully and clearly define in advance. Requiring new work to be consistent with open-ended style adds a further challenge: every team member must have a similarly detailed understanding of the team's style to be able to work effectively together.

Understanding open-ended style is like knowing how to ride a bicycle—possible to do but impossible to put fully into words. This kind of tacit knowledge of open-ended style is hard to share between team members.[6]

Open-ended style introduces uncertainty about what the group should work on and how it should be evaluated. An innovation team can only use open-ended style effectively if it has some way to train its members so they have similarly accurate understandings of its style. The Cooking Lab and the other R&D teams I visited pursued open-ended style in their work, and their members seemed to have accurate shared understandings of each team's style. At first, I could not see how they managed it. I had expected the teams to have what conventional wisdom would advocate: systematic training programs that took style knowledge and articulated it so team members could learn it. Because I was looking for these programs, I initially missed a counterintuitive but effective approach to teaching and learning style knowledge that was hidden in plain sight.

It was the inadvertent result of what seemed a haphazard innovation process in which members in each team had enormous autonomy in defining or modifying projects but interacted and consulted with their colleagues repeatedly in a loose, largely unprogrammed way as they prototyped their individual projects. What was hard to see was that learning happened as an unintentional result of how team members gave and received prototype feedback during these interactions. Instead of isolating teaching and learning in formal training programs, these teams spread it across almost every piece of work each member did. Microteaching and microlearning happened all the time in the course of daily work. Continuously exposed to learning opportunities, members developed an accurate, detailed, and shared understanding of their team's open-ended style remarkably quickly.

## MOTIVATING PEOPLE TO STAY UNCOMFORTABLE

The Fat Duck was a pioneer in cutting-edge cuisine and one of the first restaurants worldwide to engage in systematic culinary R&D. As of 2019, a meal at the Fat Duck is between fourteen to eighteen courses of technically sophisticated cooking, which also includes a significant personalization component in which the overall narrative of the meal and sometimes specific courses make references to details that are relevant to individual guests.

R&D at the Fat Duck happens in the Fat Duck Experimental Kitchen (FDEK). When I first went to visit the FDEK in 2011, it consisted of three chefs in a separate building across the road from the Fat Duck. The Experimental Kitchen developed and refined dishes for the growing number of restaurants in the group, as well as developing content for its numerous cookbooks, TV shows, and partnerships.

I eventually returned to the Fat Duck several years later. The restaurant, housed in a sixteenth-century cottage, was being renovated to expand the kitchen and update the dining room. The service kitchen and front of house teams had relocated for the year to run the Fat Duck as a pop-up in Melbourne. This temporary closure gave the FDEK a strictly delimited period in which to reexamine the Fat Duck's menu and update it by removing many classic dishes and replacing them with completely new ones. They also hoped to change the menu more fundamentally by introducing a new narrative that would connect all its dishes more coherently than before.

Creating new dishes and then training service kitchens to prepare and cook them to a high standard is often a drawn-out process. Restaurants rarely replace the bulk of a menu all at once, especially one as technically complex as the Fat Duck's, instead preferring to switch dishes out one or two at a time. This gradual approach is more comfortable—it gives the R&D team time to troubleshoot each new dish and figure out how it will work under the pressures of service before sending it into the kitchen. Putting in multiple dishes at once while redesigning the menu to be driven by a new narrative was not comfortable. For the R&D team, by then six people including a project manager who also served as a mechanical engineer, it was akin to being thrown into the deep end.

The radical menu redesign—made irrevocable by early PR-driven announcements of a brand new dining experience when the Fat Duck reopened—created a feeling of palpable desperation in the team. In spite of itself, the team was energized by needing to create so many new dishes and to conceptualize and execute on a new narrative structure for the meal itself, all before a specific date for which prepaid reservations were being taken.

The team began to explore previously unexplored avenues and reach out to adjacent disciplines (including screenwriters and narrative specialists) that they'd never seriously engaged with before. When the Fat Duck eventually reopened in September 2015, the menu contained more new dishes than had come on in the preceding decade—twelve in all. Further, the menu and entire experience was given coherence by being embedded in a single-day narrative of an holiday excursion, and dishes and entire menus were also personalized for individual guests. To the team, it seemed that they only pulled the whole thing off at the eleventh hour.

Such an ambitious overhaul of the menu and dining experience had clearly been beyond the FDEK's ability when they committed to doing it. Conventional wisdom might interpret that decision as poor judgment. Yet, the result was both unexpected and desirable. The pressure of the task brought the team together. It also pushed them to learn to work in new ways and seek new information, ultimately allowing them to design a groundbreaking menu and experience. Desperation pushed them to achieve something they had previously thought impossible.

This illustrates one of the paradoxes of innovation work. Innovation teams know that failure is essential for innovation, yet human nature makes them reluctant to try things that might fail. Moreover, good innovation workers need the stimulation of learning new things in order to feel engaged with their work. Innovation teams need to be forced into doing things they don't yet know how to do to keep their members happy and engaged *and* to be effective at innovation. Counterintuitively, projects that create desperation by design can help overcome this problem.

## A MAP OF WHAT'S TO COME

The culinary R&D teams in this book were able to continually innovate because they had a clear view of the world as an uncertain place. This made them more attuned to developments at the frontiers of food and more receptive to new information and resources. But that was only part of how they were able to innovate so effective. The other part was that this perspective gave them a mindset that treated the world as uncertain rather than risky.

This uncertainty mindset led them to organize how they worked in counterintuitive ways. These teams thought about how to bring in new members, what types of goals to pursue, and how to motivate themselves in ways that largely eschewed the conventional pursuit of stability and known routines. And these unconventional approaches to organization allowed them to change quickly and relatively painlessly, to absorb new ideas and resources so that they could interact with existing ones and swiftly become productive for innovation work, and to continually motivate themselves to do the cognitively and emotionally uncomfortable work innovation requires. For the eating public, this has produced the tremendous vitality of high-end cuisine over the last decade or so.

However, these teams also hold valuable lessons for designing and managing innovation teams outside the world of high-end cuisine. I've briefly described what these R&D teams did—but simply imitating them won't work outside the cutting-edge culinary industry (and probably won't work even for other teams working in cutting-edge cuisine). To understand how other teams can benefit from this unconventional approach to organization design, we need to understand how it works in the first place.

This haphazard-seeming, highly unorthodox approach—featuring unstable roles and shifting goals, fraught with desperation—should have led to chaos and failure.[7] But as I spent more time with the teams, I saw that though it was unorthodox, this approach worked because it was far from haphazard. On the contrary, it was systematic but in ways that were obscured by the lens of conventional management wisdom. The rest of this book takes a deeper look into each of the teams to understand the methods behind the apparent madness.

Part IV of the book is about designing ever-changing teams, because innovation implies continual change. Chapter 8 argues that these culinary R&D teams hired new members into malleable, open-ended roles that could adapt to changing demands. Though roles in these teams were provisional and constantly changing, the teams had a systematic way of negotiating and experimenting with such roles. Chapter 9 explains how this led to innovation dream teams that were richly interconnected, constantly changing, and highly adaptable. This adaptability gave them the ability to seek out new problems, work well in unfamiliar environments, and integrate members with new and needed skills.

Part V is about how these teams created familiar innovations: products that were new but nonetheless felt familiar to customers. Chapter 10 argues that open-ended style permits teams to create familiar innovations but also introduces uncertainty into team goals and creates a management challenge because it is difficult to teach and learn. Chapter 11 explains how these teams designed their work routines to help their members teach and learn open-ended house style quickly and effectively.

Part VI is about how these teams motivated themselves to stay in the discomfort zone. Chapter 12 argues that innovation teams are simultaneously energized (in the long term) by innovation work and repelled by it (in the short term) because the work is viscerally difficult and its rewards are perceived as distant and uncertain. Chapter 13 explains how these teams used projects designed to inject uncertainty into their work and induce real desperation as an effective way to force themselves to do uncomfortable innovation work.

This book concludes with part VII. Chapter 14 describes the wide-ranging new projects these teams have worked on in the intervening years, while chapter 15 explains how innovation insights from these teams can be applied in other industries.

# PART IV
Building the Ever-Changing Team

# 7

## INNOVATION IMPLIES CHANGE

I WENT to the Fat Duck for the first time in 2011, at the height of summer. I took an early train from London to Maidenhead. It being a warm, clear day, I walked from there to Bray, where the restaurant is located. Delivery vans, kebab shops, and liquor shops faded out during that half-hour walk, gradually replaced by old trees, carefully pruned green hedges humming with insects, large houses set well back from the streets, and expensive sports cars. Bray's short high street is where most of the town's commercial activity is located. Almost the first thing I came across was a pub owned by the group of restaurants of which the Fat Duck is the crown jewel. Next to it, in a merchant's house several centuries old, is the Fat Duck. A cluster of buildings down an alley across the street from the main restaurant houses prep kitchens, storage, and other functions—including, in 2011, the Fat Duck Experimental Kitchen (FDEK).

I arrived right at 9 a.m., when I'd arranged to meet Gavin Stuart (then head of the FDEK) and Michael Rylan (his right-hand man). The prep cook who answered the door said that I could go up to the lab but the FDEK wasn't in yet. They had gone off early that morning to a shoe factory and were running a bit late. The principal lab space turned out to be a small but high-ceilinged room with a bank of windows looking into trees on the first floor. It had been fitted with an induction range and a large central island. Other than a large whiteboard covered in a thick layer of brightly colored sticky notes and marked-over lists, it looked nothing like a conventional lab.

Stuart and Rylan got in about forty-five minutes later. Almost immediately, someone came over from the pastry prep kitchen with a problem: the chocolate for that day's batch of the restaurant's iconic Black Forest Gateau-inspired chocolate dessert—a precise, thin-walled, sharp-cornered prism of dark chocolate filled with chocolate and cherry mousses—was setting up blotchy and unsightly instead of glossy as expected and required.

Chocolate's texture and appearance is determined by how the cocoa butter in the chocolate crystallizes. Cocoa butter has multiple crystallization states, one of which results in a glossy surface and crisp snap.[1] Tempering is the process of manipulating a batch of chocolate so that the cocoa butter it contains solidifies in the correct crystallization state. Tempering chocolate correctly is important not only because gloss and snap are associated with great chocolate but also because proper tempering makes chocolate more stable and suitable for finely detailed structural work.

Tempering requires melting chocolate and then holding it at a series of specific temperatures for specific periods of time. This allows the correct crystallization state to propagate through the cocoa butter in the entire chocolate mass. The process is finicky and affected by even small changes in temperature and humidity—getting it right is as much a science as it is an art. The pastry team had retempered the chocolate three times already, without success. Stuart, an award-winning chocolatier, zoomed off to help.

Meanwhile, Rylan and I went to get a coffee in the prep kitchen downstairs. I asked the question that had been at the top of my mind. Why had they just visited a shoe factory? A tall, sardonic young chef from Iceland, Rylan had transferred to the experimental kitchen soon after joining the Fat Duck and was now a senior R&D chef. He told me that the FDEK had been asked some months earlier to rethink the experience of dining at the Fat Duck. This included redesigning the uniforms and footwear worn by the front of house team and thus a visit to the factory contracted to make the new shoes.

The tanning process (using vegetable and mineral extracts to transform animal skin into leather) had reminded Rylan and Stuart of how cooking methods like roasting and drying transformed ingredients. They had no specific plans for the idea but thought it might be possible to apply an analogous process to fish skin to transform it into a new type of product that might anchor a dish they were working on. Their follow-up visit that day was a meeting with the head tanner who, Rylan said with a sharp laugh, had been bemused by the improbability of the idea of tanning something meant to be edible. "He thought we were bonkers." Rylan's overt cynicism failed to hide a profound earnestness about the project of culinary creativity.

Apparently outlandishly long-shot connections like this were not uncommon for the FDEK. Its remit was wide and vague at the time, which gave them the psychological latitude to make such leaps. They were also exposed to a wide range of types of problems to solve and situations in which those problems and solutions were embedded. They were brought in to develop new and technically challenging dishes for the Fat Duck, like a drink that would be cold on one side of the cup and hot on the other. They worked on producing the group's books and TV series, which meant finding and working with anyone from cinematic riggers to the European Space Agency's R&D team. They were involved in research collaborations with universities and other institutions. Rylan and Stuart both attributed the Fat Duck's ability to innovate in great and unexpected leaps to the wide-ranging nature of the FDEK's work, and therefore the broad exposure to many sources of stimuli that could then be connected or hybridized in new and unexpected ways.

By the time Rylan and I got back up to the lab, it was time for the daily morning meeting to go over the day's work. Stuart had returned from his chocolate mission. He'd started out as a potwasher in restaurants in rural Scotland before moving up through the ranks at a succession of hotels and restaurants (including the then two Michelin-starred Inn at Little Washington in Virginia). He eventually became an internationally respected pastry chef and master chocolatier. Stuart had been with the Fat Duck for over a decade by the time I met him, working on R&D projects for much of that time. Compact, intense, and fast-moving, he was quite different from Rylan. Nonetheless, they were a good team for dealing with, as Stuart said, "the crazy shit we do everyday."

Glenn Webber, a junior chef from Australia who had just transferred into the FDEK from the Fat Duck's service kitchen, had written up and printed out the work plan, a listing of individual projects that each member would work on. The three of them went through the list quickly. Numerous adjustments were made. A project to redesign a fried potato dish for one of the pubs had to be delayed because the desired potato variety hadn't been delivered. A scheduled tasting would have to be postponed because they had finally succeeded in luring a scriptwriter down for a much-anticipated meeting. The updated version of the Fat Duck's classic liquid nitrogen-poached cocktail was literally falling to pieces during service. And so on. By the end of the short meeting, most of the original list had been crossed off or modified, and many new items had been added.

Rylan told me that this level of unpredictability was normal: "This list is just what we start with. Every day, something will happen that ends up bumping stuff off the list, like Gavin getting stuck in the chocolate just now. You never end up doing exactly what's on the list, not even close. But this is part of how we can come up with so many new things." The unavoidable tradeoff for the innovation and the ability to make great leaps from one area to another was that the FDEK's work was unpredictable in both nature and scheduling. The reality of what each FDEK member did was largely emergent and therefore mostly unclear, even to the members themselves.

The contrast between this approach to managing work and conventional management best practices was stark. On my second day in Bray, I met the FDEK's new R&D director who had been brought in a few days a week. She had come from a large consumer goods company where she'd run the R&D operation. Rylan said that one of her first actions had been to ask every FDEK member to write out detailed job descriptions and work to them. The goal was to make the apparently haphazard, chaotic work planning more efficient. "That's when everything really began to go to shit," Rylan said. "It's very satisfying at first to have these long lists of roles and responsibilities. It definitely feels very efficient and like you're getting something done. But does it work in real life? No. There's no point being efficient and hiring for a very detailed job description if the job changes every day. That's being efficient about the wrong things."

## THE PEOPLE PROBLEM IN INNOVATION

Well-understood, predictable processes and outputs—like the step-by-step production of an already designed car—can be automated. But it takes a creative and sophisticated individual or team of people to think up something new and then develop it into something that makes sense in the context of existing markets. Innovation work is fundamentally different from other kinds of work because it requires coming up with new things. By definition, you cannot predict fully what innovation work entails and what innovation teams will have to do.[2] This makes finding the right people and building them into an effective innovation team extraordinarily difficult.

If innovation work itself is different, then the way the team is built and the way new members are brought into the team should be different, too. Yet, as the new R&D director had done at the FDEK, the same logic of hiring and thinking about team member roles used in conventional hiring and recruitment is usually applied to innovation teams. Teams built this way are rarely innovative.

This chapter explores a different way of thinking about how teams are built. Instead of roles designed to be stable, these teams kept their members' roles intentionally provisional in that they were explicitly open-ended and malleable.[3] The provisionality of these roles built adaptability into these innovation teams from the level of the individual member. Provisional roles also forced individual members to do things that improved team dynamics, making the teams both highly effective and highly responsive.

## RESPONDING IN REAL-TIME

Remember Ruben Garcia's discovery of a tray of malformed, structurally unsound canelones? While leaky pasta isn't an earth-shattering catastrophe, the episode nonetheless illustrates the unpredictable nature of innovation and R&D work. The canelones were subpar though the prep cook had followed the recipe and directions as written. Either the recipe or the directions was flawed. ThinkFoodTank would have to revisit both;

this was urgent since the canelones were already on the menu and were a popular item. This immediately created a new and unanticipated task for the ThinkFoodTank.

Where a less imaginative team might have done the obvious thing and developed a more robust pasta sheet (sacrificing the delicate texture prized in canelones), the ThinkFoodTank instead developed a process innovation that responded to the problem in context. The canelones from the new process were robust with almost no leaking or malformed pieces (in fact, the new canelones were almost preternaturally perfectly cylindrical), the new process took up significantly less space in a crowded kitchen, and it took a tenth of the time it used to. This was elegant because it improved the restaurant's operations overall but not at the expense of any of its parts.[4]

The type of swift, elegant process innovation work ThinkFoodTank did is analogous to what production processes often need. The trigger for the work was an unexpected task. However—like the FDEK—the ThinkFoodTank saw these unanticipated tasks as opportunities instead of undesirable interruptions to their scheduled work. Their members were able to work together to use these triggers as stimuli for developing and implementing real process innovations.

## OPEN-ENDED ROLES MAKE CHANGE POSSIBLE

Conventional wisdom urges managers to make each person's job as clear and well-defined as possible.[5] This push for predictability and certainty in job descriptions takes both obvious and insidious forms. The team's leader may not be thinking, "Let's make this all predictable" when she asks every team member to write down his or her job description and for the team to work to those descriptions. Nonetheless, what she is doing is forcing each member to capture a static snapshot of his or her work. The insidious assumption, never voiced, is that these job descriptions are stable and therefore that the work will not change in the future. This veneer of apparent predictability is often desirable because nearly everyone instinctively wants the certainty of knowing what to do and when to do it.[6]

Innovation work makes stable roles impossible because the end goal of innovation definitionally can't be known with certainty until the team reaches it. Innovation teams face changing and emergent demands that make it impossible to know in advance how team members will have to respond. This is true both in cutting-edge cuisine and in any industry experiencing unpredictable change. The film manufacturer Kodak detected but failed to respond appropriately to the shifts in markets and technology that gave rise to digital cameras.[7] Many believe the same was true for Digital Equipment Corporation (an early and influential mainframe computer manufacturer) and the rise of the personal computer.[8] More recently, similar things have happened with traditional newspapers and the rise of internet advertising, publishers and the emergence of e-books, and retailers and the rapidly growing dominance of online retail. The list of companies that have been extinguished because they failed to innovate in response to changing market environments (or innovate in order to create change beneficial to themselves) is a long one.

Teams facing uncertain demands and environments are more likely to be able to respond successfully and innovatively if they can adapt as things change. For a team to be adaptable, its members have to be willing and able to adjust what they do as demands on the team change.[9] Being told, as conventional management practice would have it, that their jobs are and should be predictable pushes them in the wrong direction.

In contrast, the cutting-edge R&D teams I spent time with assumed that their work would be changeable because they would have to respond to any changes in their environments that they discovered. In turn, their members understood and accepted that their job roles—their responsibilities on the team—were provisional at best and could change at any time. These open-ended roles were the foundation of team adaptability because they made it both possible and easy for the team's role structure to change.

## MODULAR—NOT MONOLITHIC—ROLES

Joe Raffa did not fit the media stereotype of the shouting, egotistical head chef. Level-headed and apparently unfailingly cheerful, his frequent reaction to a stressful situation was to close his eyes, turn up his palms, touch his thumbs to his forefingers, and emit a low, "Om." In his forties at the time, Raffa was one of the most senior and trusted chefs in the ThinkFoodGroup when I met him in 2011. His career illustrates several unusual things about how jobs work in cutting-edge cuisine that are so normal for people in the industry that they take them for granted. He'd become a chef after a decade working as a public servant in the U.S. Government Accountability Office. After working at a series of DC-area restaurants, Raffa joined ThinkFoodGroup's first restaurant, Cafe Atlantico, in 1999. After a few years away to help open a restaurant with his first chef-mentor, Raffa returned to ThinkFoodGroup to run the team relaunching a failed concept: a restaurant called Oyamel that would serve innovative Mexican regional cuisine.

Raffa had no real experience cooking Mexican food then. There was an entire cuisine (methods, flavor combinations, menu compositions, logics of dish assembly) to learn, in addition to the already formidable challenges of designing a kitchen and hiring and training a new restaurant team. He described his learning curve as being steep, "sort of like a bridge abutment." Nonetheless, when Oyamel opened in DC, it rapidly became one of the most lauded restaurants in the city core. Raffa stayed at Oyamel but was often pulled into ThinkFoodTank work because of his management expertise, long tenure with ThinkFoodGroup, and his equanimity in the face of uncertainty.

"I do a lot of different things for ThinkFoodGroup," he said, "my job has lots of pieces and they've changed a lot over the years. At first, it was a bit unnerving to realize that I couldn't just figure out what my job would be, get good at that, and then coast. But once I got over that, having a job that never gets old is what keeps me here. I think that's true for most of us."

Most managers and workers think of jobs as monolithic things, each one a set of responsibilities and expectations that come together in a job description and cannot be pulled apart and recombined. Perhaps it's better instead to think of a job like Raffa did: as a collection of role-components, each representing some responsibility or ability, the composition of which can and should change over time. "If what we as a team need to do changes," Raffa said, "then what we do individually should change too."[10]

It wasn't only Raffa who thought of his job this way. Everyone at ThinkFoodTank and, in fact, everyone at the R&D teams I spent time at simply accepted that pieces of their job might fall away or new pieces might be added when new members joined their team, when they learned new things, or when the demands on the team changed. They took it for granted that the role-components that made up their jobs could change at any time. This sounds daunting, yet they treated it as an unremarkable part of work life. The next chapter explains how these open-ended roles were the building blocks for highly effective innovation teams.

## Insight 1

*Modular, provisional roles lead to adaptable organization members.*

# 8

## BUILDING INNOVATION DREAM TEAMS

RYLAN had told me that (again) almost everyone would be out of the Fat Duck Experimental Kitchen (FDEK)— "we have to be in Oxford for a meeting about some experiments we're running"—on my third day with them. I went to Bray anyway. When I arrived, I found Eugene Nolan, who was doing a couple of unpaid months there as a stagiaire before going back to Sydney to open his own restaurant. His project for the day was to fix the Welsh rarebit at one of the Fat Duck group's gastropubs located in Bray.

The group's restaurants innovate in different ways. The Fat Duck itself is known for whimsy combined with science. Other restaurants in the group are known, among other things, for using modern techniques to build dishes inspired by historical recipes. Welsh rarebit is an old English recipe, recorded in the first popular cookbook published in English—Hannah Glasse's *The Art of Cookery Made Plain and Easy* from 1747.[1] Its original form is something like a sophisticated open-faced grilled cheese sandwich. To make a traditional rarebit, cook some sharp cheese, possibly a well-aged Cheddar or Lancashire, into a thick sauce with a bit of ale, spread the sauce onto a robust slice of grilled bread, then apply high heat from above until it bubbles and chars here and there. Properly made and fresh from the broiler, a rarebit is a marvel of crunch and unctuousness. It is nearly a perfect drinking snack. Let the rarebit cool even a little bit, though, and the sauce on top congeals and loses its luxurious texture and the bread goes cold and soggy. The emulsified ale and cheese sauce can also be finicky, especially for inexperienced cooks. If the emulsion breaks, the sauce becomes a greasy, curdled mass, neither attractive to look at nor good to eat.

Nolan's was a two-pronged project. He was to reformulate the recipe to make the rarebit reliably delicious even in the hands of the most inexperienced cook. ("Basically, nowadays you hope for the best and expect the worst from cooks in restaurants," Rylan later said. "After all, everyone has to start somewhere.") That was easier than the second part, which was to rethink the recipe so that the rarebit would be delicious both freshly made and after it had cooled. At first, I thought that Nolan had been assigned this project as a stagiaire because it was relatively trivial. In fact, he said, "remaking an existing dish to fix stuff behind the scenes is really hard. It's going to be much harder than it looks." He had volunteered to take on the project to test his own ability and out of a mix of professional pride and ambition.

He worked on his first prototype for a couple of days, tuning the flavor by having Rylan or Stuart taste versions of it whenever they were in the lab and adjusting it based on their comments. He finally presented his first attempt at one of the regular FDEK meetings where team members gathered for feedback on completed dishes or parts of dishes. As was often the case, the tasting happened at the end of the work day just before the team cleaned down the lab. Rylan, Stuart, Webber, and Nolan stood around its central island, on which numerous prep boxes and trays were arrayed (Webber and Rylan were presenting prototypes, too).

Introducing his prototype, Nolan said he'd decided to begin by focusing on solving the problem of reliability, leaving the question of texture until he got the flavor profile right. To do this, he converted the cheese topping from a sauce that had to be cooked to order and spread onto the grilled bread into a solid block that could be premade and presliced into portions, only needing to be assembled and broiled when the order came in. "I wanted to front-load the skilled prep as much as possible," he told the team, "so that it will be easier to control the quality." To make the topping mixture both solid enough to slice and unctuous when broiled, he had looked up how prepacked cheese slices that melt easily (like Kraft Singles) are formulated. Based on this research, he'd added a small amount of sodium citrate to the topping mixture to make the proteins in the cheese untangle more easily, making the solid topping slices silky smooth instead of grainy when heated.

While talking, Nolan took a piece of previously grilled bread and set it under the broiler to reheat, then added a slice of the topping and returned it to the broiler. A few minutes later, the rarebit was ready. He cut it up on a board and put in on the island. Everyone leaned in and took a piece. Stuart took a bite and pronounced the flavor delicious, needing only more acid—"boost the sharpness to cut the grease a bit, or else people won't want to eat the whole thing." The tasting moved on remarkably quickly.

When Rylan's and Webber's prototypes had been tasted, Rylan picked up a leftover piece of now thoroughly cooled rarebit. The previously silken and molten cheese topping had become hard and crumbly. Rylan said, "this is the problem with all hot cheese sandwiches. They're fantastic when they're hot, but terrible cold. The fat in the cheese has coagulated so the texture is all wrong. That's what really needs to be fixed." In a gastropub setting, Stuart said, it would be common for a table to come in and order the rarebit and a few other snacks to share, so that the rarebit often would not be consumed quickly enough to avoid it being disgusting—not a good customer experience. Serving a smaller portion would partly solve the problem but would look stingy, not in keeping with the gastropub's intended atmosphere. As he packed down to go home, Nolan said, "that was incredibly discouraging. And all for a sandwich!"

After the tasting, I went for a post-work pint with Rylan and Stuart. Rylan said that the challenge of making a version of the rarebit that would be good cold required "a special way of thinking. We end up having to do this a lot, make very specific changes that won't even be obvious to the person eating it. It's almost harder than coming up with a brand new dish, and there's not the same kind of ego boost either. You have to really understand the problem before you can break it apart and solve it. It's really to see how Eugene thinks, whether he's got the way of thinking for R&D."

Nolan spent a few more days working on his next attempts. Understanding the desired flavor and texture profile was the first step—he knew that from the first prototype. The goal was to achieve this flavor and texture even when the rarebit had cooled. One morning, after cooling a promising potential topping alternative and finding it dispiritingly grainy, he said to me, "I mean, it's a cheese toastie, right? How hard can it be? But nailing it is not straightforward at all. There's a lot more food science than I thought. I think there are basically two ways to go about this: make a normal-style topping based on cheese that will be liquid when cool or make a topping with the same flavor but where the texture isn't from the fat in cheese. Is that even possible?"

Nolan and Rylan talked about the problem over staff meal that day. The traditional rarebit topping's silky texture comes from the dairy fat in the hard cheese used in the recipe interacting with water and milk protein. When the mixture is heated enough, the milk proteins unravel and form an emulsion with the water and now-liquid fat; this emulsion has a luxurious mouthfeel. However, the emulsion falls apart when the protein-fat-water mixture cools. First the proteins clump together again, then the fat solidifies. The result is a grainy, often greasy mass.

To get around this, Nolan had tested his recipe on some cheeses that are almost liquid at room temperature because of some combination of high moisture content, low acidity, or protein breakdown by enzymes or micro-organisms. The problem, Nolan said, was that these cheeses (like Camembert or Pont l'Évêque) had a different flavor profile—often either mild and mushroomy, or very pungent—from the clean sharpness that was the result of aging heavily salted traditional English cheeses to the point where they became hard in texture. The soft cheeses made the rarebit taste wrong, and the hard cheeses always went grainy when cool. "It's always worth trying the straightforward approach," Rylan said to him, "but I'm pretty sure you'll have to really tear the thing apart to make it work." Back, in other words, to the drawing-board.

Nolan stayed after everyone else had left that night, trying a different strategy. I stuck around with him until I had to leave to catch the last train home. He seemed energized by a new direction he'd thought up. The next morning, he showed the team a rarebit that had been reconstructed from the ground up. His new strategy abandoned the cheese-based topping (an unstable emulsion affected by temperature) and replaced it with a cheese-flavored bechamel sauce. Bechamels are emulsions of fat and water-based liquids cooked and sufficiently thickened with starch that they are stable even at room temperature. Bechamel sauce (*besciamella* in Italian) is often used to layer lasagne, giving them a lush creaminess even when cooled to room temperature.

Getting the bechamel sauce to the right consistency was a matter of experimenting with different ratios of fat, water, and different kinds of starch. Replicating the flavor of the original cheese and ale topping was harder. Nolan ended up replacing some of the water with a dark, more deeply flavored ale than the original recipe called for. Because the bechamel was not primarily based on cheese, he also had to boost the sharpness by using an extra long-aged cheddar (with lower water content and more intense flavor) and adding some powdered mustard and vinegar. Rylan said, "this is surprisingly good. You can probably make the bechamel even smoother if you replace some of the flour with cornstarch and cook it very slowly to make sure you fully gelatinize the starch molecules. But I think it can go to Heston [Blumenthal, the Fat Duck's founder and head chef] after that." The bechamel topping could be made in advance, spread onto grilled bread and broiled to order, and remain fluid even after the rarebit had entirely cooled to room temperature. Serving the rarebit on a very hot plate prevented condensing steam from making the rarebit soggy. The final result, while not precisely replicating the flavor and texture of the original, was good enough for both Stuart and Rylan to approve it for a tasting with Blumenthal.

I went for another pint with Stuart and Rylan to discuss the rarebit problem again. The assignment had been, as Rylan had alluded to before, a sort of test. But it wasn't the kind of monolithic test where it only mattered whether Nolan managed to create a workable fix for the rarebit—for Rylan and Stuart it was much more important to watch his strategic moves and how he thought problems through. It was a test designed to give him an opportunity to demonstrate his approach to defining and solving problems. It was about showing thought processes instead of just the final answer. "Some chefs have a very straight, one-direction approach to things which is not very good for R&D work," Stuart said. "You have to watch people as they work to understand how they think. Every project we work on is a lot of little tests where we get to see little pieces of someone's approach. You see enough of those pieces and you know how someone thinks." "And," Rylan said, "when you really know how someone thinks, that's when you can really start working together."

## MICROTESTS FOR MICROCHANGES

The way Stuart and Rylan thought about routine work is one of the keys to understanding how these R&D teams managed to work with changeable provisional roles. They treated routine work not only as the work itself but also as an opportunity to continually test and expand their knowledge of what team members could do. Each task became a test of ability and an opportunity to demonstrate competence.

These tests could be significant, with much at stake (as was the case when Raffa took on the project of relaunching Oyamel for ThinkFoodGroup). However, they were mostly almost trivially small microtests. Watching someone receive and inspect a shipment of leeks was a chance to see how detail-oriented that person was. Listening to someone presenting their thinking behind a new dish they'd come up with was a chance to understand their approach to problem-solving. Asking someone for help on a problematic bread recipe was a chance to see how much they knew about fermentation. These microtests of different parts of a member's role were important because roles in these R&D teams were modular instead of monolithic, so role-components could be added or subtracted as needed. Frequent microtests and modular, provisional roles meant that each member's role could change constantly but in small ways.

For the most part, individual motivation drove these attempts at change. These were personally ambitious people in a team situation in which their ambitions for more responsibility could find a useful outlet. Knowing that their roles could be modified, people in these teams actively sought out new responsibilities that they wanted to take on and worked to identify new abilities that they wanted to be known for among their colleagues. They demonstrated these abilities to their colleagues through routine work, as Nolan had done. Danny Gledhill, the Fat Duck's head chef at the time, said, "the ones who come with ambition, they look out for the least opportunity to move ahead. Which sounds bad but it isn't. We want people to keep looking out for ways they can do what they want to do while doing what we need."

The team-level adaptation Raffa had talked about happened almost automatically and in small increments instead of the big movements I'd expected. It was only after my conversation with Stuart and Rylan that I understood why it seemed so unforced. The low stakes, trivial nature, and sheer volume of the microtests involved in routine work were the key. The low stakes involved in each test meant that people were less stressed about the implications of the outcome for their careers and simply worked as they normally would. Each microtest was an honest signal of the person's ability that other team members could rely on and act on.[2] Microtests therefore allowed each job to evolve gradually. If someone showed over a series of microtests that she understood fermentation more than anyone else, other team members would gradually start going to her for advice and help with their fermentation projects: a natural evolution of that person's job.

It was just as important that team members dropped responsibilities that they were not very good at fulfilling or that a new member could do better. This happened so fluidly that it appeared effortless. This was surprising given how easily turf wars—conflicts within organizations based on competition for tangible and intangible resources—seem to erupt in conventional organizations.[3] I realized that this was an unanticipated effect of a work environment where tests were small and trivial, and jobs were treated as a collection of many responsibilities and abilities. If a series of microtests showed that someone was not detail-oriented enough to write good recipes, her responsibility for recipe-writing might fall away though her other responsibilities might persist. Due to the low stakes involved in most tests, few people seemed to resist dropping responsibilities that the tests suggested they weren't very good at.

This continual stream of tests affected not only individual member roles but also the structure of the team itself. Each team, through its members, was able to add and drop responsibilities or reallocate them within the team. These daily tests changed the team's structure—each one, big and small, modifying the shared mental map of who did what.

Because the tests were often held at group tastings or discussions like the ones Nolan had done with his colleagues, the team also had concrete, collectively validated evidence of each member's ability. The resulting changes in team structure were therefore seldom questioned internally. It helped too that, apart from at the FDEK, none of the other teams worked to formal, written job descriptions. And the FDEK, to be honest, didn't work to those written job descriptions either. Roles could adjust as demands on the teams changed, without individual team members wanting (or needing) to stick to job descriptions that had become outdated.

What had seemed at the outset like an unprofessional, haphazard way to manage jobs and responsibilities turned out to be one of the keys to understanding why these teams could adapt in the first place. Adaptation was driven by team members motivated by the changeability and modularity of their roles to explore and evolve what they did. The adaptation was possible because the teams had processes for identifying, testing, and confirming changes to the sets of modules that made up team member roles. These processes looked superficially like regular work, and they were effective because team members treated them as tests of ability.

## IN THE GROOVE

I went to Las Vegas in early December 2010. Even at 5 p.m. in winter, the desert glare and baking heat radiated through the window of the air-conditioned shuttle from the airport terminal to the car rental complex. The sun sank below the horizon as I crawled through rush hour traffic to the off-off-Strip apartment I'd rented. When I reemerged after a shower, it was to drive out into a city ablaze with neon. My destination was the soon-to-open Cosmopolitan of Las Vegas, a casino-hotel with over 3,000 rooms and 300,000 square feet of restaurant and retail space located on a mature section of the Strip.

With less than two weeks to go to the official opening, the Cosmopolitan was still a twenty-four-hour building site. I joined a line of cars and trucks to sign in for a site access pass, then another line for parking. The 3,800-car, four-level underground parking complex was nearly full with construction workers' vehicles; I drove down into the furthest corner of the deepest level before finding a spot. Once in the building itself, it was difficult to imagine the Cosmopolitan opening any time soon. Most of the elevators and escalators weren't working, and the corridors and open spaces of the hotel and casino were covered in protective sheeting and building dust. Panels in walls and ceilings everywhere were open, revealing ductwork and electrical infrastructure. Painters, electricians, tilers, and plumbers swarmed about on overtime, going through the structure to finish construction.

I was in Las Vegas because I had convinced Andrés and Garcia to let me join the ThinkFoodTank as they simultaneous opened three restaurants in the Cosmopolitan. One would be a new outpost of ThinkFoodGroup's Jaleo concept (innovative tapas), the second would be a new Chinese-Mexican restaurant called China Poblano (named for Asian immigrants to Mexico in the New Spanish period), and the third an eight-seat tasting-menu restaurant called é bar, nested in the Jaleo space. Each restaurant concept and menu had been mostly designed from scratch, the operating teams hired in Las Vegas but anchored by trusted chefs from ThinkFoodGroup's restaurants in Washington DC. Opening a new restaurant is a challenge even with a thoroughly tested concept and in a familiar city with established relationships with workers and suppliers. It's much harder to open three restaurants simultaneously in a new and unfamiliar city. These would be the group's first restaurants in Las Vegas.

The Cosmopolitan's restaurants are spread over the four lowest floors of the complex, mixed in with the retail shops and part of the casino—they were due to open on the same day as the hotel and casino. Jaleo and é bar are close to China Poblano, but a floor apart. I was to check in with Andrés at China Poblano. When I found it (most of the wayfinding signage had not yet been installed), the dining area was almost unnavigable. Tables and chairs had just been delivered and were stacked just inside the entrance in drifts of packing material. Pots, pans, and pantry products were piled up in a corner. Amidst the disarray, two technicians on tall ladders were installing an array of projectors that would cover the walls and the central twelve-foot high sculpture with video art. One of them pointed me to the kitchen.

At one end of the long kitchen space, two plumbers and an electrician were at work; at the other end, a team of riggers was moving a bank of high-heat stove units into place. Andrés, Garcia, and Raffa were standing in the middle looking at a station. When designing this part of the kitchen, they had overlooked how the station's undercounter fridge doors would open into a frequently used rack intended to hold trays of prepared food: a hazard during the service rush. The station would have to be redesigned and reinstalled.

We left China Poblano to go up a level to meet Lozano and Terri Cutrino (ThinkFoodGroup's special projects chef) at Jaleo. On the way, Andrés and Garcia said that the general disorder had been compounded by cascading construction delays. Equipment and supplies had to be held in temporary locations while their final locations were made ready to receive them. They were working out of the banquet kitchens and storage spaces many levels below in the subbasements. Elevator rides between floors took twenty to thirty minutes per trip because so many other businesses opening in the Cosmopolitan were using them to move supplies between floors.

As a result, the ThinkFoodTank team ended up doing a lot of enforced waiting and thinking between bursts of intense activity. More problems were being discovered with every passing hour. Many of the ingredients they'd hoped to use weren't yet available as supply chains were still being built, and supplier options were limited by the Cosmopolitan's procurement service. Two of the three kitchens were only partly fitted out. Serious cooking couldn't be done in them until the major equipment and infrastructure (gas lines, electricals, plumbing, stoves, and ventilation systems) had been installed, tested, and passed inspection.

Their first task, as soon as the kitchens were usable, would be to cook through the three menus to validate recipes and begin training the new kitchen teams. Recipes that had been tested in DC kitchens on familiar equipment with ingredients from

DC suppliers might not work in a different kitchen with different equipment and ingredients sourced from different suppliers. Even seemingly trivial things, such as the lower water content and different flavor of a desert-grown vegetable, can throw a recipe off. All this testing and any menu redevelopment would have to be compressed into the increasingly short time between the kitchens being ready and the scheduled opening day.

The ThinkFoodTank had anticipated the need for having, as Cutrino said, "all hands on deck in the last mad dash to the finish line." Expanding on that, Raffa said, "The opening rush is when you need your best people. There's not going to be time for a lot of management, so you have to have a team who don't need to be managed to take the initiative, spot problems, deal with them." They had arranged—as they always did in these situations—to bring in an ancillary team of trusted chefs from across the company.

We were at Jaleo for a team catch-up led by Cutrino. In addition to Cutrino, Garcia, Raffa, and Lozano, there were six others all of whom had worked together on ThinkFoodGroup restaurant openings. Greg Basalla was a sous chef at Zaytinya in Washington DC. Josh Whigham was the head chef of Bazaar (a ThinkFoodGroup-run restaurant in the SLS Hotel in Los Angeles). Charisse Dickens, Jorge Hernandez, Justin Olsen, and Michael Turner worked with Garcia and Lozano cooking and doing development for Minibar. At the time, Minibar was a six-seat restaurant in DC serving a tasting menu of thirty or more dishes. Due to its small size and unusual service model (each chef cooked for and served only two guests), Minibar could experiment with cutting-edge recipes and challenging preparations that the larger restaurants could not handle—it was the ThinkFoodTank restaurant. This extended ThinkFoodTank team had been dropped into a rapidly changing, highly uncertain situation in which they had relatively little control and where the many problems to be solved were often not yet apparent.

For the first few days before the kitchens were usable, I watched as the team scoured the three sites for problems to solve: anything from redesigning kitchen layouts to figuring out optimal arrangements for temporary and permanent supply storage. They split up to find and then tackle these problems, recombining as needed when they found that any particular problem demanded the abilities of more than one person. There was little central control from Garcia, Raffa, or Cutrino other than brief group check-ins at the start and end of each day. Yet, as Raffa had said, the team had a remarkable collective ability to adapt and respond to each situation despite light management supervision and the uncertain and emergent nature of the work.

When the kitchens finally opened and the ThinkFoodTank began validating recipes, I saw that their adaptiveness was matched with extraordinarily competent execution. At the brief catch-up meetings, the team split work up between members with almost no discussion. They moved through the testing at great speed, identifying recipes that would have to be redeveloped. When expertise from another ThinkFoodTank member was needed, that person was quickly identified and seamlessly pulled in. It felt like watching chefs working the way great basketball teams or ensembles of improvisational musicians played.[4]

Some of the smaller restaurants in the Cosmopolitan had managed to open early and were cooking for anyone who was working in the building as a way to get their staff up to speed for the opening. We ate together on days when there was a brief lull at the right time. On the day Jaleo's kitchen passed inspection, I went to lunch with Garcia, Lozano, and Whigham while the Jaleo team prepared for an afternoon of recipe testing. As we headed back to Jaleo, Whigham told me, "We've done openings as a team before, and you feel alive when you have to think on your feet together. It's just not the same once the restaurant is up and running. All the chaos of opening is one of best things about working at ThinkFoodGroup. What makes it even better is we've all worked together enough that when we're together in this kind of situation, we get into a real groove."

## A DIFFERENT WAY TO BUILD TEAMS

This chapter described a different way to build a responsive and adaptable team. Provisional roles generate internal uncertainty that, when combined with specific management processes, makes teams more likely to be able to adapt to whatever is thrown at them.

These R&D teams were frequently faced with unpredictable changes to what they had to do, and they were able to respond gracefully to this uncertainty. These teams and their members did not try to avoid or suppress this uncertainty, as most teams in conventional organizations would. Instead, they acknowledged it, treated it as opportunity, and worked with it. This adaptability allowed them to handle uncertainty whether it was trivial (on the order of having to redesign the process for making canelones) or significant (on the order of opening multiple new restaurants simultaneously). This adaptability seemed to persist and in fact increase in the face of having to do things that they had never done before.

These teams were adaptable because of the unusual structure of job roles they had evolved. Everyone knew what everyone else was good at. No one expected to always do the same thing because formal job descriptions were minimal and it was taken for granted that roles would change. Their members worked independently or interdependently as needed, changing what they did by mutual adjustment and with little management or coordination overhead. These were dream innovation teams.

One level deeper, these teams were able to work this way because each member's role was constantly being tested and validated by everyone else. Each member ended up doing more of the things he or she was good at and fewer of the things he or she was not so good at. Team members were alert for new responsibilities that might be simultaneously useful and relevant to the changing demands on their team. Because these teams managed their role structure like this, they became self-adjusting and self-adapting.

Stepping back from the specific context of cutting-edge cuisine, what these innovation teams did was, at base, remarkably simple—simple enough that the underlying principle likely generalizes to innovation teams in other industries. They simply ignored the conventional management wisdom of making job descriptions stable and clearly defined in advance. In fact, they went against this conventional wisdom by setting clear expectations that members' roles would be continually tested and possibly changed. This seemingly trivial decision made it possible for individual roles to change and adapt. It also drove adaptation by motivating team members to seek out changes in their roles.

These responsive, adaptable teams were founded on rejecting traditional stable job descriptions in favor of provisional, open-ended ones. However, this decision was supported by processes that made testing new roles not only easy but something members took for granted. The R&D teams I've described created these processes by setting expectations among their members that all work, especially routine work, would potentially be an opportunity for a test in addition to the work itself. Being explicit about this led team members to regard their work—including apparently trivial work—as opportunities to demonstrate their own ability and evaluate that of their colleagues.

Treating all work as a testing opportunity sounds inefficient, but it isn't. As these teams show, it is in fact extraordinarily elegant to use work that would have been done anyway as a way to continually monitor and update how the team is structured and what its members do. It also works quickly. While most microtests were trivial, they were numerous and swiftly added up. A multitude of microtests quickly created detailed, accurate, and validated understanding of each member's numerous and often inarticulatable skills and inclinations.

Two other apparently trivial details about how testing was set up are noteworthy. First, tests were done in public because multiple team members participated in them and saw their results. This ensured that there was socially validated, shared evidence of individual competence. Team members' roles weren't built out of individual assertions; instead roles developed out of shared history and knowledge. Testing in public was essential for team members to have an accurate shared understanding of their colleagues' abilities and responsibilities, even as those changed from test to test. The shared and public nature of the tests was also essential for individual members to definitively accept the results of tests that affected their own roles.

Continual testing and role-change sounds brutal, exhausting, and dramatic. But in reality it was banal because it happened in the context of routine work. Using routine work for testing ability instead of specially set-aside test situations meant that most tests seemed trivial, with little at stake. This was true both for the individual member and for the team as a whole. Reducing the potential for individual and collective damage from each failed test made it easier for team members to be willing to try new things in each test. This made it more likely that useful new skills were discovered. Small, low-stakes tests also made it less likely that members resisted dropping role-components that the tests showed they weren't good at. Through gradual, tested addition and subtraction of role-components, each member's role eventually ended up far more stable than this description might imply, with only role-components that were on the margins continuing to change. To be clear, this way of thinking about building innovative teams doesn't come cheaply. It entails considerable effort and investment of time from team members. The payoff is that the teams that resulted were remarkably adaptable and effective at what they did.[5]

There was another payoff however, which was visible in the intense and pleasurable engagement the ThinkFoodTank's members reported as they worked on the openings in Las Vegas. The other R&D teams highlighted this, too. The same processes that built adaptable teams out of collections of members with open-ended roles also ensured that their members knew each other at a remarkable level of detail—both what their colleagues were good at and also how they worked. This deep knowledge meant that team members could operate at a high level and be energized and completely absorbed by the experience of being thrown into uncertain situations. When this happened, they seemed to enter a sort of collective flow state, their members working at a high level of ability with energy, joy, and intense focus.[6]

### Insight 2

*Continually adjusting member roles leads to responsive, adaptable, high-performing organizations.*

# PART V

Creating the New Familiar

# 9

## THE POWER OF FAMILIAR NOVELTY

**T**HE ThinkFoodTank stood around a stainless steel counter in Oyamel's basement kitchen, tasting soup. Joe Raffa said, "Doesn't feel like one of ours yet." Michael Turner, the research and development (R&D) chef working on the soup, nodded as he took notes.

Ruben Garcia, the head of R&D, said, "The flavor is too powerful, the dish is not refined enough. The whole thing has to be very elegant and not too intense, but at the same time have strong and clear flavors like you would get at Jaleo. You can go in a few ways for this dish, but it definitely doesn't work like this."

It was yet another prototype for an updated version of a traditional Spanish almond soup called *ajo blanco*. It was being developed for é bar, the small tasting-menu restaurant soon to open inside the new Las Vegas branch of Jaleo. Like Minibar in DC, é bar would be a place where guests came to experience menus that captured ThinkFoodGroup's unique perspective on food. This made even the soup an unexpectedly complicated proposition. After the tasting, Turner said to me, "it's a challenge to get this ajo blanco right. It's just bread, almonds, garlic, oil. It sounds trivial that we're obsessing about it, but even this ultrasimple dish should reflect a point of view that is uniquely ours."

As with every other new dish development project the Think-FoodTank worked on, one of the priorities for ajo blanco was to make sure that it bore the ThinkFoodGroup's distinctive stamp. Garcia said, by explanation, "If you know the food made by a great chef, you can taste his hand in every dish, like a signature." Having a recognizable signature even in new dishes implies that the house style is open-ended (more on this later). Open-endedness in style can be a liability. It introduces uncertainty into standards of quality within the team and makes it hard for members to learn what they have to do and when their work is suitable. Without learning this distinctive style, team members cannot work effectively. On the other hand, a team that can teach its distinctive open-ended house style to its members can turn this liability into a competitive advantage because it can create dishes that are both new and consistently familiar. Novelty combined with distinctive familiarity makes for loyal customers—and is nearly impossible to copy.

## DISTINCTIVENESS AND FAMILIARITY

Distinctiveness is important in cuisine because it confers familiarity, and familiarity is important in deciding what we choose to consume.

Before your first sip from, for instance, a bottle of Richard Leroy's 2014 Les Noëls de Montbenault, you might suspect that you'd enjoy it because it has characteristics you've enjoyed before. It is made from the chenin blanc grape variety (you've liked chenin in the past), grown in Anjou (you've liked Anjou chenins before), and made by Leroy (you've liked his other wines in previous vintages). But only after you've experienced the wine directly by drinking some of it can you can say *for sure* whether or not you actually do enjoy it. Products like wine, music, art, books, and meals in high-end restaurants are things that must be directly experienced before we can decide with certainty whether we like them.[1]

Nearly everything we eat or drink for pleasure is too complex to fully measure in numbers or describe in words. A bottle of wine may be described as having characteristics you like but still turn out to be not so nice, for reasons that are impossible to articulate. Conversely, it may be described as having characteristics you know you hate but still turn out to be delicious, again for inarticulable reasons. Even after experiencing the wine, it is impossible to say precisely and completely why you liked it. You might have words to describe some parts of your enjoyment (perhaps it had "good structure" or "rich fruit"), but those words will be both imperfect and incomplete descriptions, a pale shadow of what you actually enjoyed about it. What we enjoy in any particular food or drink is a type of tacit knowledge: a complex of interacting characteristics that we know but are unable to say.[2] Fortunately, though we may be unable to say what we like about a particular food or drink, we can still appraise these enormously complex products once we've directly experienced them. We can make up our minds about whether we like them or not, and we can remember that when we make future consumption decisions.

If you did enjoy the wine, you have a good reason—anchored in direct experience—to buy the same wine again in the future (or the same brand of tortilla chip or bar of chocolate). But this is only true if what you liked when you experienced it stays the same from bottle to bottle. If that's true, every bottle will be both distinct (from other types of wine) and consistent (with previous bottles of the same wine). This consistency is what makes the wine familiar and makes each bottle enjoyable for the same reasons as the first one.[3] This style that the producer infuses into the wine is what the consumer perceives as a familiar imprint. Lovers of Burgundy (to take just one example) can identify the imprint of a specific winemaker on grapes grown on a specific plot of land across multiple vintages of a particular wine.[4] Good producers—whether winemakers, cellphone designers, architects, authors, or chefs—are able to infuse a complex, unique cluster of characteristics into what they make, and to keep those characteristics consistent over time.

Once a consumer experiences a product directly, that experience becomes a foundation for deciding whether or not to consume it again. If that experience encompasses something that is distinctive and repeated in other things the producer makes, then this distinctive style allows customers to come back again and again and enjoy these products for the same reasons each time. In other words, the familiarity that comes from distinctive style helps transform a first-time consumer into a repeat customer.

## STYLE IN HIGH-END CUISINE

In high-end cuisine, technical mastery—a kitchen's ability to cook meat to the right level of doneness, to prepare correctly emulsified sauces, to prepare vegetables for cooking with the appropriate knifework—is a nonnegotiable baseline. However, technical mastery alone isn't enough for greatness. Greatness comes from being able to go beyond this, to develop a distinctive house style that guests can detect and become familiar with.

ThinkFoodTank was not unique in its drive to produce food that was consistent with its own house style. Particularly in high-end cuisine, style is the distinctive thread that connects everything a particular kitchen produces—when guests experience and enjoy a restaurant's identity, this familiar thread is what they want to return to experience again and again.

However, high-end restaurants are usually small and expensive, making it difficult for customers to experience them directly. Most customers experience high-end restaurants initially through proxies—reviewers of all sorts. Potential first-time customers of high-end restaurants (always in the vast majority compared to repeat customers) will usually decide where to go based on reviews. In the past, the reviews were from professional critics and published in prestige media (largely newspapers and magazines). These days, the reviews that drive consumer behavior come from a much wider range of critics: bloggers, social media celebrities, and such.[5] So much high-end restaurant business comes through reviewer endorsements that they have no choice but to compete for critical attention.

Standing out is therefore crucial. One approach to differentiation is for a restaurant to develop a distinctive style in the form of a suite of signature dishes that don't change often. The distinctive house style here is essentially closed-ended—guests come back for the same set of signature dishes, not for new ones. Developing the signature dishes that embody closed-ended style is difficult, but once that's done the main creative challenge is over. It's hard to train a service kitchen team to repeatedly execute the same dishes to the same high standards, but closed-ended style isn't *conceptually* difficult.

House style works in a fundamentally different way for cutting-edge restaurants. Like a traditional high-end restaurant, the cutting-edge restaurant's success rests on creating an experience that draws critics and guests to come back. But for cutting-edge restaurants, this enticement is the implicit promise of new dishes or experiences at every visit. A prominent European food critic captured the sentiments of chefs, restaurant staff, and industry observers when he told me that, "There is a tension at these [high-end, cutting-edge] restaurants. The critics and writers who are influential will eat at a restaurant several times, sometimes many times, over a few years. They will want something new every time but also a consistent experience that expresses a unique aesthetic."

Critics return to cutting-edge restaurants when their innovations feel familiar and consistent with their respective house styles. What critics (and consumers who are guided by them) come to expect from cutting-edge, high-end restaurants is a distinctive house style embodied in a continual stream of new dishes—open-ended instead of closed-ended style.

## BUT THEN WHAT NEXT?

When I first went to The Cooking Lab in 2012, they were in the middle of promoting their first book, *Modernist Cuisine*, arranging for translated editions of the book in Europe, and finishing development on their second book, *Modernist Cuisine at Home*. But there were no major new projects in the pipeline yet. The Cooking Lab isn't part of a restaurant or restaurant group. Without a stream of future projects, the team's future was itself uncertain, and they had to ask themselves what would come next. I joined them for several of the meetings they had to discuss this existential question.

*Modernist Cuisine* made an enormous amount of rigorously assembled and synthesized technical information palatable to chefs. The Cooking Lab had achieved this by illustrating the science through rigorously clear writing and a uniquely appealing style of informational graphics based on ground-breaking photographic techniques, and by developing sophisticated recipes that illustrated scientific cooking principles and approaches. This distinctive style of research and communication had created the problem they now faced.

Maxime Bilet, then one of the senior chefs there, said that the challenge was "like being at a restaurant like the Fat Duck and trying to figure out what new dish to put on the menu. It has to be new, because guests are expecting something new. But it has to also give them what they expect. Now that *Modernist Cuisine* is out, people will be expecting our next projects to have the same approach. We're confident that *Modernist Cuisine at Home* will do that. But then what next?"

The challenge was, as Bilet said, to innovate within the constraints of a distinctive house style. The possibilities on the table ranged widely and included opening a restaurant that would serve dishes that illustrate the science of cooking, becoming a consulting company for developing new dishes and cooking equipment, or working on more books on different topics.

"Our problem is that there are too many directions we could go in," Sam Fahey-Burke, one of the development chefs, said, "because what we do is a way of looking at things which could apply to lots of different things." The openness of The Cooking Lab's style left room for the subsequent projects to be novel and surprising but therefore also injected uncertainty into the team. The Cooking Lab members had a good sense of what would be consistent with the team's style while still being uncertain if it would be possible to infuse it successfully into any particular project. As Johnny Zhu, another development chef, said, "The next new thing might break the magic." Uncertainty permeated the team's discussions about its future.

## OPEN-ENDED STYLE

The Cooking Lab's existential crisis illustrates how open-ended style is fundamentally different from closed-ended style that faithfully replicates what has come before. Open-ended style is the externally recognizable imprint of a group (a particular restaurant or R&D team) that results from that group's particular configuration of priorities and problem-finding/-solving approaches.[6] As figure 9.1 shows, the distinctive property of

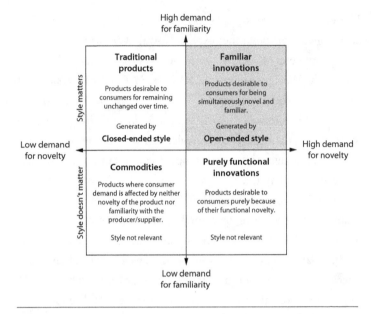

FIGURE 9.1 Open-ended style paradoxically combines familiarity with novelty.

open-ended style is that it is recognizable even in something new, no matter whether it is infused into a new dish or a new project. Open-ended style is the reason why someone who's eaten at El Bulli many times can recognize a totally new dish as one created by the El Bulli team. Or why someone who read and loved *Modernist Cuisine* would preorder the next The Cooking Lab book even before publication. It is an inescapable part of the dynamics of cutting-edge, high-end cuisine.

Style knowledge is always complex. Where style is closed-ended and doesn't need to admit new things—where the things which embody that style need only be repeatedly replicated—the difficulty lies in practicing until replication of that complex knowledge is perfect. Open-ended style is different. It must admit new and unexpected things but somehow make them familiar. This kind of style is alive, and its living nature is what makes it unpredictable and impossible to put fully into words. Though open-ended style is conceptually simple (make something new that feels familiar), actually creating new things infused with any particular open-ended style is difficult. Open-endedness makes style inherently uncertain. Only the best restaurants and R&D teams can keep distinctive familiarity and novelty productively in tension against each other for any length of time.[7]

The inevitable uncertainty introduced by open-ended style creates a problem for open-ended style in a group setting. Producing novel work infused with open-ended style is hard enough for individual creators. The challenge of innovating with open-ended style is compounded when it is a team, not an individual, that must do the work. Chapter 10 explains what this challenge is and how these culinary R&D teams surmounted it.

**Insight 3**

*Choosing to pursue open-ended goals permits and encourages familiar innovation.*

# 10

## LEARNING HOUSE STYLE

C ÉSAR Pareto at Amaja said to me, "I'll know when I see and taste something if it's right, but it's impossible to write it up and put it in a manual like some kind of recipe—there's no way we can describe what a dish we haven't even made yet should look like or taste like." Rick Billings, ThinkFoodGroup's head of pastry R&D, told me about a restaurant he knew where "they tried to lock down the style by documenting the hell out of it. They locked it down all right, but it destroyed the spark. They've stopped making really new things there." Understanding open-ended style in sufficient detail to create new things that are infused with it requires knowledge that cannot be articulated. Moreover, attempts to put this tacit knowledge into words seemed to destroy it. Knowledge of open-ended style is inherently tacit: knowledge that cannot be put into words for easy communication.[1]

The tacitness of open-ended style creates a problem for innovation teams that creative individuals who work alone don't face. A team cannot work interdependently unless its members learn its open-ended style accurately enough to create new things that are consistent with that style. At the same time, conventional approaches to learning implicitly assume that the knowledge to be learned can be put into words.[2]

The teams in this book managed to solve this problem. Their members were able to teach and learn open-ended style surprisingly quickly, and accurately enough for them to work interdependently to produce innovative output that felt distinctively familiar to guests. Consequently, they benefited from it: the same tacitness that makes open-ended style hard to teach and learn also makes it almost impossible for competitors to imitate. "I don't mind sharing techniques or tweeting about new discoveries," Tomás Irigoyen said, "because no one can do Amaja except us." Open-ended style forced other restaurants to develop their own styles and thus created a huge barrier to entering the high-end, cutting-edge culinary industry.

## STRAWBERRY/BEET

In early November 2011, Patagonia was transitioning from spring to summer. Outside the long winter, seasons in the southern high latitudes are short and intense, often changing abruptly. The seasonal peak of any particular product, say a variety of berry or cabbage, lasts a correspondingly short time. Amaja's commitment to seasonality and only using ingredients from the southern extreme of South America meant that its menu at that moment in the year was evolving swiftly from dishes based on the foods available in late spring to those available in high summer. The menu as a whole was also changing to reflect how the feeling of the seasons was changing from spring's light freshness to high summer's intensity.

Naturally grown products come into and go out of season unpredictably. Too little rain early on might bring the first radishes a few weeks later than expected; a heatwave near the end of the season might make all the forest berries ripen at once, with few or none left for the weeks to follow. In the restaurant, service must go on nonetheless. To keep pace with the menu's evolution and be prepared for unpredictable changes in ingredient availability, Amaja's R&D work had to look ahead of the present by at least a few weeks.

In the houseboat test kitchen, a large whiteboard listed the team's current projects. At any time the list might be twenty to forty projects long, each at a different stage of development. Back then, one early stage project was to add a course to the menu that would be a bridge from the lighter, smaller courses at the beginning to the heavier main courses. The asparagus dish that was serving this function felt a bit "too light and bright and cool," Martín Varela, one of the Amaja test kitchen chefs, said, "too much like a spring thing. Plus we're going to lose the asparagus soon." The team had decided to try to change this dish to be more appropriate for summer by making it feel deeper and warmer, and using products that would be in their prime in November. The idea they started from was to combine beets and strawberries for a sweet but distinctly savory course. I'd arrived in time to see them develop this idea from the beginning.

Each project was usually driven by one member of the test kitchen, and Varela was in charge of strawberry/beet (the team's shorthand for the dish). He'd be primarily responsible for developing it until it was ready to go onto the menu, involving his colleagues where their particular skills and insights were needed. Initially, Varela was guided primarily by what the dish would have to do (be a warm bridge between the light early courses and the heavier mains), so he didn't have a solid plan. He started out by "just trying out a bunch of things just to see if something works." His goal at the outset for strawberry/beet was to make a sort of warm root and fruit salad: cool, ripe strawberries contrasting with warm baked beets, the whole dressed with juices from beets and strawberries. Instead of using the strawberries as the sweet component and the beets as the savory, he wanted to invert convention ("our usual M.O."). He planned to roast some small beets in a salt dough wrapper "to seal it all in and bake it low to intensify the sugars while still keeping the texture very soft and not all dehydrated and leathery like how beets can get."

Varela began by making the two dressings. He juiced some large, very sugary beets and some underripe strawberries separately. The beet juice got boiled down fast to reduce the water content and produce a sweet, earthy, highly concentrated beet syrup. He blended the underripe, green-tasting, and acidic strawberry juice with a neutral oil to form a tart sort-of-vinaigrette, then aromatized it with anise-scented herbs and seeds: "Amaja's profile is usually quite low sugar but the feeling has to be very bright [in this case from the acids in the juice and the high-toned aromatics]."

Pareto and Gustavo Terzan (then Amaja's head of R&D) were working on the houseboat as usual, and Varela called them over for an informal tasting just before lunch. They came over to Varela's makeshift station on one of the counter spaces and dipped spoons into small plastic containers, one holding the beet reduction and the other the strawberry vinaigrette.

"The beet is simple," Pareto said, "but really good, not too earthy. It has this pure beet flavor that's in line with how we treat vegetables. Definitely keep the level of reduction here. The vinaigrette is nearly there too. Maybe amp up the green anise to make it smell sweeter but keep the acidity as it is."

Terzan agreed: "The flavor is nearly there. The beet reduction maybe can be done so it tastes even fresher. These are new [freshly harvested, newly mature] beets so they should taste like it. Did you boil it hard? [Varela had.] But the idea [of the warm salad] should be good. I think the hard thing will be to plate differently from the strawberry dishes we've done before."

After lunch, Varela made a new version of each of the two dressings. He tried them out on Terzan and Jeff Weston, a test kitchen stagiaire. This time, Terzan said that the beet reduction (cooked for longer at a lower temperature) had good flavor but seemed too viscous and thick in texture on its own. However, he also added the caveat that this texture might work when combined with the more fluid strawberry vinaigrette in the finished dish—"the dressings taste very well together, but you won't know if everything works until you try it all out. Can you get some ripe strawberries and try a plate-up?" Varela quickly made a batch of salt dough to create a sealed wrapping for the beets to steam-roast in.

Around 8 p.m., just before they began to close up the test kitchen, the whole team (including Clara Gomez, Amaja's head pastry chef and also a test kitchen member) gathered around the central kitchen island for the usual project tasting. Two other chefs had prototypes to show; Varela presented a first full prototype plate-up of strawberry/beet.

This brought all the dish's components together—fresh strawberries cut into vaguely pyramidal shapes, slightly warmed thinly shaved beets that had been roasted in a salt dough wrapper, the beet reduction, and the strawberry vinaigrette. They tasted through, with Pareto, Weston, and Varela recording their colleagues's comments on their respective projects. After just one intense day of work, strawberry/beet seemed close enough to being ready to go on the menu, but it was missing something. Gomez said, "It almost works but something feels a bit off. The roasted beets don't work perfectly yet with the vinaigrette. It tastes good but doesn't feel like something that would be on an Amaja menu." There was a brief silence. "It might be," Pareto said, "the shape of the beets. The shape may be affecting the acid profile when eaten with the vinaigrette."

The next day, the test kitchen team dropped everything temporarily to work on an unexpectedly challenging photoshoot for Amaja's upcoming book. Varela didn't get back to working on strawberry/beet until a few days later. "I'm going to focus on the roasted beets and vinaigrette," he said, "since everyone thought that was the problem." For the next tasting of the dish, he prepared a tray of cooked but uncut beets as well as several boxes of the same beets cut in different shapes—thin and thick slices, prisms, shards, asymmetrical pyramids.

This time, Tomás Irigoyen joined in, having come over from the service kitchen to discuss a VIP table's special menu for lunch the next day. Varela's new plate-up showed that the shape of the beet slices did affect how they tasted with the vinaigrette, but none of the shapes he had prepared worked perfectly. The team spent over an hour slicing the whole cooked beets Varela had prepared in various ways, but nothing they tried worked with the vinaigrette. Irigoyen eventually said: "I think you'll have to change the vinaigrette. It smells too sweet and with the beet and the reduction also quite sweet, it takes the whole thing off balance for Amaja."

Strawberry/beet had seemed tantalizingly close to completion on Varela's first day of working on it. However, no one was surprised that the different dish components interacted unpredictably when brought together. At least seventeen more prototypes (to my count) were needed over the course of the next week and a half before the team began to feel that the dish expressed a style that was distinctively Amaja's.

## PROTOTYPING TOWARDS INNOVATION

As with strawberry/beet, innovations are rarely perfected on the first attempt. Most dishes in high-end restaurants consist of many components (sauces, proteins, starches, garnishes, and such), each of which must be developed separately and then combined in the final plated dish. Some attempts are needed to figure out the general direction—what components should be in the dish and how they should relate to each other. A few attempts for each of the components to figure out what their respective directions should be, and a few more to hone them to a satisfactory level of refinement. Yet more attempts to bring the components together so the plated dish tastes good, is easy to eat, and can be plated reliably. The development process Varela used for strawberry/beet was characteristic of how all the teams did R&D. They moved every project along by creating successive actual prototypes and evaluating them internally, using the feedback from each prototype to inform the next iteration. This was true regardless of whether the R&D was aimed at creating a new dish, a new piece of cooking equipment, a new ingredient, or a new cooking process.[3]

Spending so much time and effort on the interplay of textures and flavors in a single dish may seem overwrought, but is necessary for innovation in high-end, cutting-edge cuisine. Every R&D chef has at least one war story of a stubborn project that had to be permanently shelved because some component resisted refinement. Strawberry/beet was a relatively simple dish with only four components; some dishes at Amaja have ten to fifteen components, and those components themselves frequently contain multiple components. The more components in a dish, the more attempts it takes before a new recipe is ready for guests.

As strawberry/beet illustrates, iterative prototyping often involves running into apparent and actual dead-ends, usually unexpected. Chefs developing new recipes loop back and forth repeatedly between experimenting at the component level and the level of the finished dish. This is unavoidable because the components and the finished dish mutually affect each other. The overall direction of the dish might have to change if one of the components resists refinement, and vice versa.

For Varela, the two-steps-forward-three-steps-back quality of the process made the final successful prototype an unexpected moment of minor triumph. After the tasting several weeks later during which strawberry/beet was approved, I stayed with Varela to help him pack up and get ready to leave the houseboat. "After all those rounds and getting all that feedback, I thought I might have finally nailed this one," he said, "but I couldn't be sure until I saw that everyone else thought so too. A fucking relief is what it is."

## TEACHING AND LEARNING STYLE AS A SIDE EFFECT

Getting to a final version of each project quickly wasn't the only consequence of iterative prototyping. There was also a side effect: team members were teaching and learning open-ended style by making prototypes and giving feedback on them. And this teaching and learning happened remarkably quickly despite knowledge of open-ended style being impossible to articulate without destroying it.

Style knowledge is impossible to articulate because it is both diffuse and voluminous. It is the accumulation of hundreds, thousands, maybe more, of data points. What style of illustration feels right for this book? What acid balance feels right for this sauce? Which plating feels right for this dish? As this mass of data points accumulates, it becomes an increasingly reliable database for the individual team member to draw upon when creating something new that still complies with the team's open-ended style. This accumulating mass of knowledge in each member's head is essentially a database that informs every prototype he or she makes.

As with Varela and strawberry/beet, prototyping forced each team member to learn by putting his or her existing knowledge of the team's style to use, to express this style knowledge in the form of a concrete object that would embody it. Iterative prototyping repeatedly tested, validated, and refined team members' knowledge of their team's open-ended style.[4] Learning tacit knowledge by putting it to use happened in combination with effective though unconventional methods of teaching style.

Each strawberry/beet prototype gave Varela both an opportunity to test his own understanding of Amaja's open-ended style, and an opportunity to test it against what his colleagues understood that style to be. The teaching happened because every prototype was a concrete focus for Varela's colleagues to express their knowledge of Amaja's open-ended style. They did this by saying whether or not it felt right and highlighting areas where it felt especially right or wrong. With each prototype the team gave feedback on, it became a little clearer where and how far Varela's understanding of Amaja's style diverged from the team's understanding. With each feedback session, the team obliquely revealed more information about its style, allowing Varela to gradually build a clearer picture of it.

Teaching and learning about style happened across projects. For instance, while working on a snack course consisting of a plate of wild flowers accompanied by a vinaigrette, Varela tried and rejected eleven possible platings before settling on the first prototype he presented to the team. When I asked him why he was being so selective, he said "[these other platings don't] look natural enough [for Amaja] . . . look at how we plate all the new dishes with flower garnishes [that we've been tasting for the last few weeks]." He thought for a moment when I asked him to say more, and said "Or like what he told [another junior chef] about the dish [of raw clams, seaflowers, wild beach greens, cucumbers, and cucumber gel] he showed us last night. [The head chef said:] 'The sheet [of cucumber gel] looks too machine-made . . . everything else feels like it naturally washed up on the beach.' If you look at all our stuff, it has to look like it all just fell there by itself, naturally, you know? Without someone tweezering everything into place. Which is bullshit of course." Every test added to or refined the same mass of style knowledge. As a result, learning style knowledge happened both within each and across all projects any person worked on.

In these teams, teaching about style happened obliquely, through the feedback members gave on their colleagues' prototypes. Focusing on whether these prototypes were consistent with their respective team styles allowed them to share their style knowledge without putting it into words. For each member, every piece of feedback from across projects either confirmed the mass of style knowledge, added something new, or removed something inconsistent. Each successive confirmation, addition, or deletion drew team members's individual understandings of their team's open-ended style into closer, more accurate alignment. Teaching and learning house style was happening through iterative prototyping, though it wasn't the main or even conscious reason for prototyping.

## SANDWICH TALK

Las Vegas is a city designed to attract people and money, and it has become adept at dividing the one from the other. Unlike many other cities, nearly all of the high-end dining in Las Vegas can be found in the enormous casino-hotels on either side of the traffic-choked Strip. In the furnace-like heat of daytime Las Vegas, most visitors try to arrange their time so they spend entire days in the same place without having to go outside. Most will stay at a casino-hotel that offers enough diversion in addition to the casino floor to be a self-contained entertainment destination. Each of these casino-hotels is like a small town with thousands of rooms, numerous restaurants, shops, and entertainment. Destination restaurants and shops are central in the logic of the Las Vegas casino-hotel.

Most of the new casino-hotels have adopted approximately the same strategy: entice well-known restaurants and shops to open branches, then use these in combination with subsidized room rates to attract hotel guests and tourists who spend money in the casino. In 2010, the newest luxury casino-hotel on the Strip was the Cosmopolitan. Its crop of new restaurants by famous chefs—Andrés included—was much anticipated by locals and visitors alike.

At the triplet of ThinkFoodGroup restaurants, order was beginning to emerge from the chaos as opening night approached. With just a few days to go before the official opening, ThinkFoodTank was working long hours. The team recognized that the restaurants had to operate effectively so they could handle a sudden onslaught of customers but also that ThinkFoodGroup's distinctive style had to be infused into each restaurant's food so they would stand out from the other well-known restaurants that would open at the Cosmopolitan. As Rob Wilder, ThinkFoodGroup's cofounder, said, "These will probably be the highest-profile openings we've done so far."

Some of ThinkFoodGroup's kitchen space had finally come online, so the ThinkFoodTank had split up among the restaurants to begin cooking and recipe-testing. Michael Turner, one of the ThinkFoodTank chefs, was working on fine-tuning recipes for é bar (the tasting-menu restaurant inside Jaleo LV) and training the Las Vegas-based é bar cooks who would execute the dishes after opening. Style was important for each of the three ThinkFoodGroup restaurants but perhaps most important at é bar—it was to be one of the two flagship dining experiences in ThinkFoodGroup (the other being Minibar in DC). é bar's no-choice, tasting-menu format placed a great responsibility on the restaurant. Because they couldn't choose what dishes they received, ThinkFoodTank expected guests to come to é bar wanting a menu in which the individual dishes and overall sequence reflected what Andrés called "the essence of *our* approach to food." Turner was steadily working through the list of over twenty dishes that would be the opening menu. The team had finished developing some dishes in DC, and Turner had spent a few days testing those recipes to check that they would work as expected with the equipment, ingredients, and cooking ability available in Las Vegas. But many dishes still remained to be conceptualized and developed from the ground up. Turner was now focused on one of these—a small dish to whet the appetite and show off the high-quality uni (sea urchin roe) that they could get because of the restaurant's location relatively close to Santa Barbara, where the uni was harvested.

In discussions with the other ThinkFoodTank chefs, Turner had decided to try making a tiny uni-stuffed baguette sandwich. He brought his first plated prototype—fried, panko-crusted uni tucked inside a baked-to-order mini-baguette—to Garcia, Lozano, Hernandez, and Olsen just before they all broke for a quick lunch. After they each took a little bite, the feedback came rapidly.

HERNANDEZ: I like the baguette here but the crust on the urchin is too thick.

GARCIA: Why do you say the urchin crust is too thick?

HERNANDEZ: The urchin's too creamy and by the time you bite through the bread and the crust it's oozing everywhere.

LOZANO: Yes, that's a problem, but it's because the crust on the baguette is too tough. The crust on the urchin is too heavy also, but the more important thing is we should be using a different kind of bread.

GARCIA: The idea here is to have it be like our other courses, a two-bite with perfect textures and flavors. The crust on the urchin should be much more delicate, and you should be able to get the crust through the bread—

TURNER: —like the calamari fritti [a dish previously on the menu at another ThinkFoodGroup restaurant]?

GARCIA: Yes, but make sure it isn't overcooked, it has to be delicate. What are you thinking for the bread?

TURNER: Maybe like a brioche?

HERNANDEZ: Or one of the steamed breads? Those have barely any crust at all.

GARCIA: Good idea. Try to make the difference in textures [between the fried urchin and the bread] really big. What did you all think of the flavors?

LOZANO: More acid, and more bright.

HERNANDEZ: I thought it needed more salt, too. Maybe salt plus lemon zest after frying—

GARCIA: —and at service finish with a bit of [lemon] juice so the urchin doesn't get soggy. Done. Can you get the new bread ready by today?[5]

## LEARNING IN PUBLIC

Group feedback is, as César Pareto said, "a huge time suck," but the uni sandwich feedback illustrates how valuable it can be. The most obvious benefit was that feedback recipients saw many different perspectives on the team's style in relation to the same prototype. More importantly, the group context also compelled participants to go beyond simple, superficial feedback on whether or not a prototype fit the team's style.

Hernandez's first comment about the thickness of the uni's crust contained little useful information for Turner. Garcia's clarifying question pushed Hernandez to be more detailed about the thinking behind his feedback. It forced him to explain *why* he thought the crust was too thick. This opened up a new, broader discussion which then moved swiftly among the participants. The discussion expanded to include both the urchin crust and the baguette around it and held useful information about how textural balance was crucial to ThinkFoodGroup's style ("a two-bite with perfect textures and flavors"). The interpersonal dynamics of giving feedback with others present made it much harder to get away with giving only basic (and therefore less informative) feedback.

Across all the teams, participants in these sessions offered feedback regardless of seniority.[6] Giving feedback in a group often highlighted slight differences in team members' interpretations of what was good or bad about the prototype—in other words, it revealed the often subtle differences between members' understandings of the same team's open-ended style.

Making these differences explicit forced teams to discuss them and make arguments to support their respective points of view. Though contained in just a few sentences, Garcia and Lozano made strong arguments that the refinement that marked a ThinkFoodGroup dish came in part from the delicacy and precision with which the textures of the dish's components were calibrated against each other. For Turner and the other chefs present, this discussion was a valuable source of additional information about the team's style. Across the teams, group evaluations helped their participants refine their ability to identify their team's style by providing a source of additional examples of style and feedback on those examples.

This vicarious learning was especially useful for those new to their teams and still trying to learn the nuances of their respective styles. As Martín Varela at Amaja said, "I think I learn as much from hearing comments about other peoples' stuff as I do from getting comments on my stuff." Group evaluations were useful even for those already familiar with the house style. "Doing tastings in a group setting forces you to really think about your criticisms before you put them out there," Raffa told me. "After a while it gets instinctive, but sometimes you'll be asked to explain what you just said and then you realize after you've talked it out that your thinking about it was fuzzy before but is now much clearer." These teams had so many prototype evaluation sessions that tasting and giving feedback in a group setting became practically habitual; their members were continually exposed (almost at an ambient level) to a stream of information about their respective team's style.

## PRECISION SOUP

Three days before é bar was to open, Aitor Lozano was tying up loose ends. One of the early courses in the tasting menu was the ajo blanco Michael Turner had started working on in DC. Variations of ajo blanco can be found all over Spain. Traditionally, it is a cold soup made with stale bread soaked in milk or water, pulverized with almonds and garlic, and finished with olive oil, sherry vinegar, and a range of possible garnishes. Though the basic ingredients—stale bread, almonds, garlic, and water—are inexpensive, they can produce a soup of great richness and deep flavor. ThinkFoodTank was trying to make a dish that would capture the essence of ajo blanco with more intensity than a traditional one would, while still being more delicate, precise, and refined. Garcia said that it was even more important that the é bar version was infused with ThinkFoodGroup's distinctive style because it was so well-known in Spanish cuisine: "We cannot just put an ajo blanco on the menu. It has to be our version that no one else is doing, with our technique and finesse."

In setting out to reinvent a classic dish instead of creating a new one, the ThinkFoodTank had set itself an R&D challenge analogous to an artist reinterpreting a well-known painting, or a director making a new version of an old, well-loved film. Lozano had to create a version that would be familiar to those who had eaten a traditional ajo blanco while being both novel in form and approach and consistent with ThinkFoodGroup's style. As before, none of the ThinkFoodTank could say exactly how to express ThinkFoodGroup's distinctive style in the form of ajo blanco. However, Garcia told me that he would know it as soon as he tasted it.

Lozano had been put on the project in part because of his extensive knowledge of Spanish cooking. Like Andrés and Garcia, Lozano was originally from Spain. Both Garcia and Lozano had been recruited to ThinkFoodTank from working at El Bulli. (Andrés had cooked at El Bulli early in his career and regarded Ferran Adrià as a mentor.) As he worked on the next prototype version of the ajo blanco, Lozano explained the current state of the dish's logic to me. His initial attempts had largely taken a traditional approach to get the overall flavor direction right. For the previous prototype, he had blended soaked bread with almonds, garlic, sherry vinegar, and olive oil, and sweetened the soup with halved red grapes.

Feedback on that prototype had been that the flavor was approximately correct but the dish as a whole was too pedestrian. It was both "too heavy, it must be delicate" and "not intense enough." The texture, Garcia said, should be "smooth and creamy but not fatty and with just a bit of grain, like the gazpacho we did before." The seasoning had to make the soup "move and be alive," Andrés said. "The vinegar is now just a part of the soup. It should burst in your mouth—pop! pop! pop!—to contrast with the creamy soup." And the sweetness from the garnish had to be more evenly spread throughout: "There are only a few pieces of grape. Some spoons I have one, other spoons I don't have any. Every spoon of the soup should have that pop of a bit of sweet" (Andrés again).

After the tasting, Andrés told me that, "The simpler it seems, the harder it is to find a way to do it. Ajo blanco is only a few ingredients, so we must be even more creative with the technique to make something unique from it."

## DESIGNING TRULY USEFUL FEEDBACK

Step back and consider the type of feedback Garcia and Andrés gave Lozano. It had two characteristics that made it richer in style information and thus more useful to Lozano both in speeding his journey to a successful ajo blanco and in building up his knowledge of ThinkFoodGroup's style.

### *Outcomes, Not Processes*

The first characteristic was that the feedback focused much less on process than on outcome. Every dish is a complex and multidimensional product made up of many components, each with different characteristics that interact with one another. Even a single aspect of a dish—texture is an example—potentially depends on a huge range of things: the size of the particles that make up the soup, the types and amounts of starches in the soup, how much those starch molecules have been cooked and gelatinized, how much fat the soup contains, whether there is an emulsifier to keep the fat in suspension, the temperature of the soup, among many others. Such complexity means that you can get to the desired end result from many different starting points and by taking many different paths—what biologists and complexity theorists call equifinality.[7]

Because innovation work is complex and requires connecting formerly disparate bodies of knowledge or combining existing knowledge in new ways, teams that do it best have a wide range of skills and perspectives.[8] Effective feedback in a diverse innovation team clearly identifies the desired final outcome while leaving the recipient free to choose the path he or she will take to get there. Open-ended style is about getting team members to understand how to make aesthetic and practical decisions consistently at the team level, while giving them the freedom to make full use of their individual differences in skills, points of view, and ways of pursuing a project.[9]

In giving feedback, Andrés and Garcia focused on what they wanted the various aspects of the ajo blanco to be—what the texture should be like, how the flavor should be integrated into the dish, and so on. While they were as specific as they could be about the desired outcomes, they said almost nothing specific about how Lozano should go about achieving them. After the tasting, Garcia told me that, "Unless [the recipient of the feedback] is very inexperienced, I usually leave them to figure it out on their own . . . but I try to make sure that they know what the end result should be. That way, they can work out how to make the things to [ThinkFoodGroup's] style, but in their own way."

Outcome-focused feedback is necessarily vague and ambiguous about what the recipient should do next, whereas process-focused feedback tends to be quite clear and specific about this. Sam Fahey-Burke, one of The Cooking Lab development chefs, said: "It gets very easy to just go on very clear instructions about what to do next. If people tell you what to do, you're conditioned to do that and you won't really try to define the problem differently in a way that makes it easier to solve." Across the teams, members talked about the value of receiving outcome-focused feedback and of *not* receiving process-focused feedback. Ambiguity about next steps provides both freedom and motivation to explore a range of processes that might work.

After that feedback session, Lozano decided to pursue two strategies in the next prototype. The first was to move away from using traditional methods for making the soup base, and the second was to separate the ajo blanco into multiple individually cooked components before re-assembling it. Lozano used Garcia's comment about the gazpacho (which Lozano and Garcia had previously developed for another restaurant in the group) as a touchstone. Though the gazpacho was also made with bread, in the mouth, he told me, it was light and had barely any of the texture of bread. Garcia's comment gave Lozano a clear benchmark for the ajo blanco's texture because he had a concrete sense-memory of making and tasting the gazpacho.

For his next attempt at the ajo blanco base, Lozano modified the gazpacho approach by soaking stale bread in water as before, but squeezing the water out and blending only the bread-flavored water with blanched almonds and garlic. Leaving the bread out made the soup base lighter and more limpid in texture, without losing the flavor of bread that Lozano said was crucial to a traditional ajo blanco.

Making the seasoning and garnish more precise posed a different challenge. The feedback on the previous prototype was that every spoonful of the ajo blanco had to have the right level of seasoning and garnish, but that the seasoning and garnish had to somehow be discrete from the soup itself. They would be experienced together with the soup but distinct from it, to create the sensation of movement and liveliness in the mouth—the pop! pop! pop!—that Andrés had alluded to. Lozano's strategy for this was to take the soup and separate what had previously been a homogeneous amalgamation into many components, so that he would have more ways to control the soup's flavor, temperature, texture, and aroma. This, he said, would let him fine-tune the effects of the various ingredients and intensify or broaden some of them by layering different versions of the same ingredient together.

Here are a few strategies Lozano tried that didn't work: slicing the grapes into *brunoise* (sixteenth-inch cubes) instead of slivers; making a light gelée of manzanilla sherry vinegar and spooning it into the soup; replacing the grapes with tomato brunoise; making a sorbet of manzanilla sherry and manzanilla sherry vinegar and spooning that into the soup; adding cubes of reduced and gelled tomato juice. Each attempted to put a seasoning or garnish into a different format that could be uniformly dispersed through the soup without simply blending in—the difficulty, Garcia told me, was to get each little bit of seasoning to be intense enough to achieve the dynamic effect of flavor popping in the mouth.

It took four more rounds of prototyping and feedback before Lozano got to what Garcia said was "an ajo blanco that tastes like our own." In the end, the solution to the intensity problem lay partly in flavoring the garnishes and seasonings more intensely and partly in increasing the contrast in intensity between the soup and the garnishes and seasonings. The final version thus used a slightly less intensely flavored soup base that reduced the ratio of almonds and added a little bit of bread to bring up the texture. Lozano's earlier experiments with garnishes and seasonings ultimately paid off. In the end, much of the soup's flavor was added as garnish elements that remained separate from the base: dots of almond purée hidden under the soup, shavings of lightly toasted almond, tiny cubes of gelee made from a dark, syrupy Pedro Ximénez sherry vinegar, a scoop of tomato water sorbet, and small grape slices that had been marinated in manzanilla sherry vinegar.

The feedback Lozano had initially received left processes ambiguous enough that he was free to take advantage of equifinality—the possibility of many different fruitful paths to a solution—when working on the ajo blanco. He was able to use his unique set of skills and resources and his unique perspective to accommodate the working constraints he was aware of but that his colleagues might not have known about. It also encouraged active learning, in contrast with the rote learning that occurs through following process instructions.

Across the teams, focusing on evaluating outcomes and leaving processes ambiguous increased team members' freedom to use different approaches to achieve desired outcomes. As a result, they often ended up using processes that were not part of their team's regular repertoire. Ambiguity about how to achieve objectives provided not only the opportunity but also the motivation to explore a broad range of processes that might work.

## *Concreteness Beats Abstraction*

Intentionally leaving out process-focused feedback would be counterproductive if the feedback didn't also transmit to the recipient a clear idea of the desired outcome. The feedback Andrés and Garcia gave Lozano focused on concrete examples instead of relying solely on abstract concepts, thus providing him with a precise idea of what the desired outcome was (in this case, the ajo blanco's desired texture and effect).

Compare feedback anchored in an abstract concept ("I want the soup to be lighter in texture") to feedback anchored in a concrete example ("I want the soup to have the same lightness and slight graininess as the gazpacho you made last week"). Both are useful; they indicate that the soup's texture still doesn't pass muster. However, the feedback anchored in the abstract concept is not precise enough to give clear direction to the recipient about where and how far the soup's texture should go. In the context of inherently complex things, abstract terms like *texture* or *lightness* contain too broad a range of possibilities to contribute to precise understanding.

Feedback anchored in a concrete example—like the gazpacho above—circumvents the problem of having to break down and articulate something very complex because the concrete example is at the same level of complexity as the prototype. When we drink a spoonful of soup, the texture (which is the interaction of hundreds of factors) is perceived as texture, not as those hundreds of factors. Concrete examples are especially useful in the context of feedback because recipients don't need to pull them apart to recall how they perceived them overall. To understand the right texture for the ajo blanco, all Lozano had to do was recall the texture of the gazpacho and the specific ways the current prototype's texture diverged from it. Feedback based in concrete examples gave members of these teams a touchstone that both accelerated R&D work and enhanced their ability to learn open-ended style quickly.

But iterative prototyping alone wasn't what allowed these teams to teach and learn style so quickly. What also mattered was that they gave prototype feedback in ways that dramatically increased the amount of style knowledge members had access to: the way these teams designed their prototyping and feedback processes got them more bang for their buck.

## TAKING OPEN-ENDED STYLE FROM LIABILITY TO COMPETITIVE ADVANTAGE

Distinctive style is important in high-end cuisine but also in many other creative industries. In music, film, art, architecture, and fashion, making new products that nonetheless embody distinctive and consistent style is crucial for the kind of identity that leads to commercial success. People who have seen and enjoyed Wes Anderson's films anticipate new ones and expect them to have the same uniquely familiar look—in Anderson's own words, his own "way of filming things and staging them and designing sets. There were times when I thought I should change my approach, but in fact, this is what I like to do. It's sort of like my handwriting as a movie director. And somewhere along the way, I think I've made the decision: I'm going to write in my own handwriting. That's just sort of my way."[10] This is similar to how a client commissions Frank Gehry to design a new building expecting it to feel like his previous buildings,[11] or an art lover commissions new work from Richard Serra expecting it to reflect the same aesthetic approach of his previous sculptures.[12] Open-ended style is the reason why a new iPhone can be recognizable as having been designed by Apple, a new song as one performed by Adele, a new book as one written by J. K. Rowling—this recognizability derives from familiarity and explains why some companies have so much success convincing their customers to buy new things when they haven't experienced them yet.

Open-ended style fuses the familiarity of the old with the excitement of the new. It creates loyal customers and staves off competition. The downside is that it also creates uncertainty and is difficult to teach and learn. These culinary R&D teams intentionally pursued open-ended style despite the uncertainty it entailed. They managed to flourish with open-ended style because they found an effective way for their members to teach and learn style knowledge.

Their solution was not to try and codify open-ended style and try to teach it through dedicated training programs, as conventional wisdom about valuable organization intellectual property would recommend.[13] Instead these R&D teams embraced the inherently tacit nature of open-ended style. Teaching and learning about style became a side-effect of—and therefore suffused throughout—regular work rather than the focus of a training program done in time set aside for that specific purpose. Each team member accumulated a mass of data points about his or her team's style as expressed in various contexts before that knowledge became usable for creating new things infused with that style. Consequently, nearly everything done for work in these teams became an opportunity to teach and/or learn open-ended style. Embedding teaching and learning about style in routine work gave team members the chance both to see and to test their style knowledge in enormously varied contexts.[14]

Iterative prototyping was a helpful context for teaching and learning style. But it wasn't simply prototyping that was helpful—it was the act of prototyping (as a test of style knowledge) and of giving and receiving feedback on prototypes (as a mechanism for sharing style-relevant knowledge). Across the R&D teams, three principles for prototype feedback helped team members develop precise and detailed style knowledge surprisingly quickly: (1) ensuring that feedback was given in group settings, (2) emphasizing feedback on outcomes instead of processes, and (3) using concrete examples to anchor feedback on outcomes. These principles allowed these teams to transform open-ended style from a potential liability to a real competitive asset—something that differentiated them from their competitors and that attracted customers and made them loyal.

### Insight 4

*Organization members learn how to pursue open-ended goals by doing actual and consequential work.*

# PART VI

Staying in the Discomfort Zone

# 11

## THE MOTIVATION PARADOX

As the years passed, what had originally seemed to be a few isolated observations from my time with these teams became visible as a pattern. This was hard to see at first because the individual points making up the pattern were superficially diverse. They ran the gamut from Amaja deciding to tear out their kitchen and redesign it completely, to the Think-FoodGroup deciding to do three simultaneous openings in a city where they'd never operated before, to The Cooking Lab initiating a major book project on the science of bread when no one on the team had serious bread experience, to the Fat Duck deciding to fundamentally redesign its mode of service and menu logic.[1]

Every point in the pattern looked like this: commit to a project beyond the team's ability, freak out individually and collectively, work like mad, somehow pull victory from the jaws of defeat, breathe a massive sigh of relief. I ran into people from each of the teams periodically. When they were in the middle of one of these projects, they seemed desperate: emotionally and psychologically exhausted, worried (slightly terrified was often a better description) that things wouldn't work out or (worse) would be disastrous. The teams seemed unable to learn from their mistakes and avoid these desperation projects. In fact, they kept committing to doing them. They would heave a sigh of relief that they'd scraped by and then—the next month or the next year—find something else to do that would make them desperate again.

Eventually, I came to understand that they put themselves into these terrible situations as a way to force themselves to innovate, that the desperation was productive, not destructive. It was desperation, but by design.

## PUSHING HARD

"Do you know," Gustavo Terzan said, "what is very hard?" At 7:45 a.m., only Terzan and I were on the boat that housed Amaja's test kitchen. Terzan's white chef's coat and brown apron were still draped over the back of a chair at the long table. A big pot of water had just come to the boil on the induction range. Terzan is extremely tall and completely guileless. He hunched down slightly to pour ground coffee into a large stainless steel *cafetière*, added boiling water from the pot, then sliced himself a thick piece from a loaf of Amaja's sourdough left over from last night's service.

I took a piece, too—"No, tell me."

After a few days of grey clouds and persistent rain, it was back to intense sun and cloudless blue. On high summer days like this, when the sky is bright by 4 a.m., it was Terzan's practice to go for a five mile swim in open water and a twenty mile bike ride before coming in to the test kitchen. There was once a daily running component too, but he stopped that after developing shinsplints so debilitating he had to take several months off work because he couldn't stand all day.

"Making the new dishes to the point where it's good enough for the restaurant," he said. He spread a thick layer of butter on the slice of bread, then showered it with flaked salt from a little tub on the table. Terzan was one of the most senior chefs at Amaja when I met him in 2011. He'd joined a couple of years after the restaurant opened, starting out in the service kitchen that cooks for guests. A few years ago, he moved full-time into the test kitchen to develop new dishes and take care of the growing number of special projects that Amaja was involved in. Tomás Irigoyen told me once that, "Gustavo has one of the finest, most precise palates of anyone I know."

Terzan pushed down the plunger on the cafetière, then poured coffee into two bright orange plastic cups and handed me one. "In the restaurant, if it's something we have done before, I know we can just push." This was Terzan's word for the particular type of effort that allows a kitchen to make it through a difficult service.

Though calm on the surface, a high-end restaurant seethes with uncertainty from unpredictable guests being served complex menus and dishes. At Amaja in 2011, lunch or dinner began with a sequence of about twelve snacks, continued through six core dishes, and finished with two desserts and mignardises. At this level of cooking, even the so-called snacks are more complex than most dishes are at other restaurants. That summer, one of the snacks was a cod roe sandwich. The base of the sandwich was an ultrathin undulating layer of bread toasted on a wave-shaped form. To serve, the snack station chefs piped ten dots of smoked cod roe cream onto the toast and dusted the dots with hay ash and powdered trumpet mushroom. Then they tweezered on, one by one, various micro herbs and flowers to form a little carpet. Finally they laid a glassy, fragile, translucent wafer of dehydrated duck bouillon on top of the carpet and sprinkled the wafer with vinegar powder. Each of the sandwich's multiple components required delicate prep before service and it was fiddly to assemble during service. Nonetheless, this complexity was contained nearly entirely within one station in the kitchen.

Many of the savory courses that followed the snacks were more complex in composition and assembly, and they required input from multiple kitchen stations. Amaja's dishes are assemblages of anywhere from four to many tens of components. As in nearly every high-end kitchen, Amaja's solution to the problem of producing hundreds of complex dishes each day is to break the dishes down into components so that work can be serialized and parallelized. Each dish is inevitably the work of multiple hands at multiple stations. Dish components are handed off to other stations to be cooked further or combined, or to the pass where they eventually converge in the finished dish that goes out to the guest.

## FOUR TROUT

South Atlantic sea trout was on Amaja's 2011 summer menu. Prep for the dish involved gutting and fileting the fish; then skinning, deboning, and lightly salting the filets; then adding dill fronds before wrapping each portion in a blanched summer cabbage leaf. During service, the wrapped trout parcels were cooked by the outdoor station, a large Weber grill operated by one person and set up behind a windbreak in the open outside Amaja's service kitchen. A step out to the side during a lull, and the spread of the city as it stretched out to the South Atlantic could be seen over the waters of the inner harbor. On a clear day or night, this was probably the best station to be at. In the rain, the cook at this station was provided with a large golf umbrella a guest had left behind.

Trout came about two-thirds of the way through the progression of courses on the menu. For most tables, it came after asparagus (thick stems of grilled white asparagus with a green asparagus and pine sauce, warmed white pine branches, and an attractively fuzzy pile of new white pine needles concealing a heap of cultured cream). Out in the dining room, a table of four was almost done with their asparagus. Their table's server came by the kitchen to let Dan Camarata, then Amaja's head chef who was running the pass that night, know that he would probably clear asparagus off the four-top in five minutes.

Camarata was from San Diego and had worked at multiple Michelin-starred restaurants—Aureole and Le Bernardin in the United States, Le Manoir aux Quat'Saisons and the Fat Duck in the UK—before coming to Amaja as a sous chef. He'd then moved to Per Se in New York before returning to run Amaja's service kitchen. His surfer's demeanor had a calming effect on Amaja's hectic environment. He was tall enough that his characteristic posture was a wide-legged stance that brought him closer to the level of the service kitchen's counters. Now, he loomed over to scan the row of the tickets on the pass, each ticket representing one table's orders and tracking the table's progress through the menu. He found no other tables close to being ready for the trout dish, so he called out for "four trout."

Though the people in Amaja's service kitchen came from all over the world, the affirmative response in the kitchen was "si, gracias"—Spanish for "yes, thanks" and the equivalent of "oui, chef" in a French kitchen. A round of "si, gracias" came from those manning the hot and cold stations on either side of the pass, and Amaja's kitchen machine began to produce four trout. The stagiaire assigned to the pass went down the short hallway connecting the pass area to the back door, checked that the front door opposite wasn't open, then poked his head out to call for four trout. Outside in the drizzle, under his golf umbrella, Luis Orozco put four cabbage-wrapped parcels on the Weber grill.

A few minutes after that, Julio Molina, on the hot station where the main induction range was located, put the two small saucepots for the trout—one containing a ramson emulsion, the other a verbena fishbone broth—onto low heat to warm up. The sauces could not be allowed to get too hot for too long or they would break down. Meanwhile, one of the stagiaires checked the plate warmer to make sure there were enough of the correct plates at the right temperature, while another stagiaire took garnish boxes containing heat-sensitive beach greens, assorted foraged herbs, and flowers from the cold station's undercounter refrigerator. By this time the trout parcels were cooked, and Orozco was waiting with them on a steel tray outside the rear door. The rear door of the kitchen and the main entrance to the restaurant were aligned with each other; if both were opened at the same time, a windtunnel would form, spoiling the calm of the dining room and sending garnish flying in the kitchen. The stagiaire on the pass told Camarata that the trout was waiting. Camarata signaled to the host to stand by the front door to avoid a guest suddenly opening it, then the stagiaire opened the rear door to take the tray from Orozco and walk it to the pass.

Camarata prodded each parcel to confirm that they were cooked to the right doneness. He nodded, then slid the tray to the center of the pass that divided the hot stations from the cold stations. Seeing that the trout was ready to plate, Molina brought the two saucepots over to join the boxes of herbs and garnish on the pass while whipping the fishbone and butter broth into a frothy foam. Unbidden, Osvaldo Agresti (also on the hot station) and Héctor Ocampo (on the cold station) joined Camarata and Molina at the pass. Each took a warm plate from the stagiaire. The ramson saucepot began to circulate, each chef in turn taking a large spoonful of the sauce and laying down a loose, vividly green circle before handing the pot on. They each reached to the tray for a piece of cabbage-wrapped trout; this went onto one side of each plate. The second saucepot then went around, each chef taking a spoonful of the pale foam and pouring it over the fish.

The sauces laid on, each chef reached into the center of the pass for leaves trimmed from beach succulents, then for micro-herbs and flowers to finish the dish. Camarata took a quick look around each plate to make sure all the garnishes had gone on and that the plates looked consistent with one another. He nodded, and Agresti and Ocampo took two plates each and walked them out to the table. Just over a minute had passed between the trout parcels coming in through the kitchen's rear door and the finished plates leaving for the table. Other than Agresti and Ocampo, everyone else's attention had already turned back to the next dishes that were in various stages of being prepared to come up to the pass.

The stations of the service kitchen worked together this way, differently for each dish, and changing in response to what else was being cooked at the exact moment, for lunch and dinner five days a week. On a good night, these interstation actions meshed seamlessly with one another. Seamless handoffs required the different stations to judge their timings precisely. This gave the best results in the food the guest eventually received, but it also left little room for slip-ups. In a kitchen aiming for this kind of perfection, when things go slightly and then very wrong, the mistakes and mistimings swiftly pile up until there is no way to undo them. The kitchen first "gets in the weeds," then "goes down in flames."[2]

Stations in a kitchen don't mesh seamlessly because of habit and practice alone. At the individual stations, recipes and work are usually designed to be as predictable and learnable as possible. However, the sequence of orders, the makeup of the kitchen team, and how quickly guests eat will all be different with every service. Exactly how the different stations will have to work with each other also changes with every service. Achieving seamless handoff between stations requires people working in the service kitchen to focus intensely and concentrate on what's going on at any given moment. Just as sports teams do drills to make individual physical actions habitual, becoming habitual at the station in fact frees a chef in the kitchen to spend her conscious energy, her focus and concentration, not on the routine work of cooking but on a deep awareness of the state of her own station, the stations around her, the movements of people in the kitchen, the ebb and flow of dishes in their various stages of completion.[3]

This level of intense focus is hard to initiate and even harder to sustain over a six to seven hour service—mustering the energy and discipline to maintain focus in an already physically demanding setting is what Terzan meant by "pushing." Kitchens push so that they can work at the edge of their ability without going down in flames. The reward for pushing is the exhilaration born from stealing a victorious service from the jaws of defeat. Camarata again: "As a cook you want the excitement of the kitchen. Most of the time, you're just doing the same thing over and over again, and it's the adrenaline from staying one step ahead of getting in the weeds that gives you the rush. Without it, things get boring fast."

In the service kitchen, tedium and comfort were constantly in tension with fear and exhilaration. The exhilaration kept the tedium at bay, the comfort kept the fear tolerable. The point, as Camarata said, was not to eliminate one or the other but instead to somehow keep them in tension against each other. Agresti told me, after one especially difficult dinner service, that "you can't survive in a kitchen like this unless you get off on the rush. Otherwise it just eats you alive. But if you manage to pull it off, it's the best feeling." Pushing created the tension that energized the service kitchen and its team of chefs.[4]

## INTO THE DISCOMFORT ZONE

Back on the boat, Terzan cut himself another thick slice of bread. "What we do is not like what they do over in the restaurant. When we are trying to come up with something really new, pushing doesn't help." He coated it with butter and a shower of salt. "The feeling is not nice." He put on his chef's coat. "If we are only doing things where we know it will work, then we are not doing anything really new. There is no learning. It is not hard but after a while, you become very bored. This feeling is also not nice."

Like Terzan, members across the research and development (R&D) teams said that real innovation—coming up with really new ideas rather than something derivative or incremental—was inseparable from doing something they had never done before and weren't sure how to do. What Terzan described seemed like the R&D analogue of the service kitchen's balancing act between fear/exhilaration and tedium/comfort: the discomfort of doing new things balanced against the excitement of learning; the comfort of familiar and easy work balanced against boredom from not learning.

In the service kitchen, the immense effort required to push through a busy dinner was immediately rewarded by the adrenaline rush if it had been seamless. As I visited each team, I realized that the particular balancing act the R&D teams experienced was subtly but importantly different from what the service kitchen faced: in the R&D kitchen, there was no such immediate gratification to motivate the teams to enter the discomfort zone. This was the great challenge of innovation work.

My understanding of this crystallized when I overheard a passing comment Heston Blumenthal made after he left the Fat Duck Experimental Kitchen (FDEK) after a particularly frustrating tasting. During the tasting, it seemed as though every project the team was working on had come to a dead end. A senior chef at another restaurant in the group had asked if things were going well, to which Blumenthal replied, "The problem with the guys in the FDEK is that they know in their heads that they have to fail before they can get anywhere—but in their hearts they can't help being scared to fail. This is the biggest thing blocking us from real creativity."

Chefs across the different teams had expressed similar sentiments. They all described the same situation: knowing intellectually that they had to do something they weren't yet good at but being blocked by a deep-seated emotional fear of not doing it well. People, whether individually or in groups, generally hate the discomfort of uncertainty and love the comfort of doing something they know how to do.[5] More than that, as the individual or the team becomes better and better at doing any particular type of work, it becomes harder and harder to justify abandoning comfortable and predictably good performance for discomfort *and* unpredictable performance.[6]

The problem for R&D teams, as Blumenthal pointed out, is that they can only innovate effectively if they can force themselves to repeatedly learn how to become good at something and then throw away that hard-won skill and start over. R&D teams and those who work in them hate going into the discomfort zone but have to do it nonetheless. If they do manage to force themselves to do this, the reward is profound: the excitement of learning new things and new sets of problems to create and solve.[7] Unfortunately—unlike the service kitchen—the R&D kitchen rarely experiences the immediate adrenaline rush from having to enter the discomfort zone and the immediate feedback from seeing success shortly thereafter. Innovation workers need motivation to enter and then stay in the discomfort zone for long enough that they make it to the payoff from learning. This motivation needs to be applied continuously for the team to be continuously innovative. In the long term, growth through learning is what keeps R&D teams from falling apart.

Though these R&D chefs knew that discomfort was a necessary part of innovation, the native human aversion to discomfort stopped them from the kind of uncomfortable exploration and mistake-making that would result in real innovation. However, what some cutting-edge culinary teams had figured out was a way to trick themselves into entering the discomfort zone.

## FROM THE FRYING PAN INTO THE FIRE

In 2011, I went to Copenhagen to volunteer for the first MAD Symposium. I went back to Copenhagen several more times for some of the subsequent MADs, and eventually got hired to help program MAD5 in 2016. The MAD Symposium began as René Redzepi's idea and was from the beginning intimately connected with his restaurant, Noma. Watching how the MAD organization worked over the years led me to realize how an innovation team might benefit from intentionally getting into a desperate situation.

While getting ready for MAD1, one of the chefs I was working with told me how Noma rebuilt their kitchen in 2010, reconfiguring the spaces and the different cooking stations, changing the heat sources to induction, and cooling down the pass at which dishes are plated before going out to the tables. Layout and equipment are so intimately tied to what high-end kitchens can produce and how they produce it that the kitchen redesign changed the Noma menu and how the kitchen worked during service. Noma's platings often involved dramatic contrasts of temperature and often featured many cool or very cold components combined with warm and hot components. (Most kitchens are designed around keeping plates and the food on them hot.) The Noma kitchen redesign allowed them to preserve temperature differences on the plate for longer and made these kinds of platings easier to achieve. However, it also meant that their previous menu logic and the internal interactions of the kitchen team during service had to change.

In 2011, Noma made it to the very top of the World's 50 Best Restaurants list again. Even then, I thought that the kitchen redesign in 2010 had been partly responsible for their surge to the top. Though the transition to the new kitchen had been challenging, Redzepi told me that it had also made it possible for Noma to develop and cook dishes—and whole menus—that were even clearer expressions of its distinctive style.[8] In any event, after the 50 Best announcement that year, bookings had gone crazy and some weekend nights had over a thousand people on the waitlist for a table. Years of hard work had finally paid off and it was time to bask, at least for a moment, in the glory.

Instead, this chef told me, the Noma team decided (in addition to preparing an ambitious book and holding down their regular schedule of new dish development for Noma) to also organize a conference for cutting-edge chefs, having never put on a conference before. This was the idea that grew into MAD1. They had decided to shake things up just as the dust from the last shakeup had finally settled.

MAD1 took a growing community of innovation-oriented chefs from around the world and helped bring them together into a densely connected network. The symposium was not a new dish, nor a new cooking process, nor a new piece of equipment—it was an entirely different kind of innovation for the Noma team. They were trying to create a new kind of experience for chefs, and what they put together ended up playing a major role in bringing together the cutting-edge high-end culinary community.

In subsequent years, a separate MAD organization would be formed, consisting of a small team of people to run the main symposium in Copenhagen and a growing list of projects and other gatherings that emerged from the symposium. That first year, though, MAD1 was run by a cluster of people anchored by the team from Noma and its test kitchen. This team had worked together before, but the work they did in running Noma was very different from the work of organizing and running a conference. Conceptually, the R&D chefs on the MAD team had been used to the kind of knowledge-work necessary for producing books and new dishes, not convening what Redzepi called "a symposium to provoke chefs to have finally some new ideas." (MAD1's theme was Planting Thoughts.) MAD1 thus represented a qualitatively greater level of uncertainty and a set of demands that was beyond the team's abilities at the time.

MAD1 was meant to break the mold of chef conferences where speakers were mostly chefs and sessions were usually glorified cooking demonstrations. This urge to innovate on the substance of the conventional culinary conference drove the entire project but was also a source of difficulty. The team found that they faced a major challenge in finding and convincing speakers to come to a new and unusual symposium with no track record. Their mission to find nonchef speakers with interesting and relevant things to say made the job even harder. They quickly saw that they needed perspectives that could not be found within the existing team. At one of the team meetings that followed, Redzepi said, "To make a new kind of symposium, we must have a different way of thinking." The team needed these new perspectives to help identify thinkers who could stimulate new types of discussions among chefs and to strategize about which of these to invite so that the symposium would have a coherent group of speakers. One of the earliest actions the team took was to search for and then reach out to other people who had very different backgrounds—like historian and philosopher Tor Nørretranders and writer Harold McGee. They became adjuncts to the team, advisors who could offer different ways of thinking about the problem of organizing MAD.

The project's scope expanded as the weeks passed. At the most basic level, the team had never organized a conference before, so they continuously discovered things that they hadn't even thought about at the outset (such as the need for a conference program, which in turn required them to confirm speakers and their topics far in advance of what they'd expected, gather biographical snippets, hire a graphic designer, and so on). Meanwhile, interest in the symposium was growing. It was an unusual conference for the high-end food industry, being the first to explicitly be focused on ideas rather than on cooking demonstrations. MAD seemed to have tapped into a growing desire in the cutting-edge culinary community to articulate and grapple with bigger issues. This desire was unfulfilled at the time, so the initial enthusiasm of the response to the MAD1 announcement far surpassed what the team expected both in terms of the caliber of the speakers and of the guests. As the weeks progressed, more and more young and ambitious chefs from Europe and North America registered to attend. The team also began getting inquiries from influential journalists and chefs at some of the world's most well-known, cutting-edge restaurants and culinary R&D labs. In part, this was because of Noma's reputation for pushing the frontiers of food—growing already in the years before 2010 as it gradually climbed the 50 Best list and then cemented by its surprise emergence at the top of the list that year. People in the industry knew that Redzepi and Noma were capable of interesting and unexpected things, and this reputation transferred to MAD.

As the symposium grew in size and scope, the team began to run into logistical and practical challenges. From the beginning, they had rejected a traditional conference center location. Redzepi's instinct was that, "We won't do something grey and boring like that." But as interest and the attendee list grew, this initial commitment to not holding MAD at a conference center added considerable complexity to the organization. To accommodate the nearly three hundred speakers and attendees in an unconventional setting that they hoped would stimulate discussion, the team eventually decided to rent a big top circus tent for the speaker sessions. They planned to raise it in a disused field forming part of an old shipyard in Refshaleøen, an industrial area on a tip of land relatively far from central Copenhagen. This red circus tent would, in the years to come, become iconic and symbolic of the experience of MAD and how different it was from other conferences that had come before—fun, quirky, uncorporate, dramatic, earnest, and intimate. But the tradeoff was that Refshaleøen had none of the convenient infrastructure that comes with venues designed to host conferences for hundreds of people. The team would have to arrange everything from power, to toilets, to a catering kitchen, to transport for attendees.

MAD1's logistics quickly grew to the point where the Noma kitchen team and front of house team were also involved. Very soon, the team expanded the envelope of involvement again to also include friends and ex-colleagues who ran restaurants in Copenhagen, enlisting their help to provide hospitality for the presymposium program for speakers, opening night events, meals during the symposium itself, and the symposium afterparty. As new demands presented themselves, team members were pushed to take on new roles for the symposium that were often very different from their normal roles in the Noma organization. An R&D chef became one of the conference producers, service kitchen chefs coordinated internal and catering for hundreds of attendees, front of house staff developed transportation plans and ran evening events outside of the symposium's schedule.

Among the team, there was a growing and uncomfortable sense that Noma's reputation would suffer if MAD1 didn't go well. The growing scope and the increasing reputational consequences of the symposium fed on each other. Reputational fear led the team to put more and more effort into building the symposium up from a small, mostly European gathering into a much larger and more logistically complex conference. During an unguarded moment in July, a team member said, "It might be a total disaster. I can't believe we thought we could pull it off." At the same time, there seemed to be a dogged, almost fatalistic determination to see it through. Lars Williams (then head of the Nordic Food Lab and a key MAD1 organizer) told me, "We're totally committed. There's no way we can wimp out now."

By the end of August, the team was clearly desperate. The night before the symposium officially opened was crunch time. Nearly every Noma team member who could be spared from the restaurant was working on the symposium. Washing baby carrots received from a biodynamic farmer for a morning snack. Printing and checking the final ticketed attendee list. Organizing the teams of volunteers who would run the site. Prepping ingredients and putting together cooking equipment for a field kitchen to cook lunch for three hundred people on the first day. Sorting out accommodation for the last-minute guest of a speaker. Some of the team had not really slept for several days.

A rainstorm blew in from the Atlantic that night. Back at Noma, Torsten Vildgaard, Sam Nutter, and I packed prepared ingredients into boxes to be driven out to the tent, to the sound of increasingly heavy waves of rain and gusts of wind. Well after 3 a.m., Vildgaard's cellphone rang. It was the security service at Refshaleøen, letting him know that the tent appeared to be collapsing in the rain. Within a few minutes, we had all piled into one of Noma's cars and were speeding to the tent.

The field on which MAD1 would be held was (and still is) a thin layer of soil laid down over a layer of mostly unbroken concrete from its shipyard days. The full-size circus tent which would hold the symposium had been secured to the field with straps attached to stakes that had not been driven far enough into the ground to be firmly bedded into concrete. In the middle of the night, with the soil softened by a few hours of rain and the wind up, the stakes had begun to loosen. We arrived at Refshaleøen to find the strapping loose, the tent sagging slowly, and the central pole askew. Eventually, the tent riggers arrived with pneumatic hammers and sledgehammers to drive the stakes further into the ground. The worst of the storm passed just after the sky became bright enough for us to see that the entire field had become swampy with standing water that would not drain in the few hours remaining before several hundred people arrived for breakfast.

By this time, other Noma staff had begun to trickle in by car and bicycle. They had been scheduled to get to the site several hours later to set up the reception and breakfast areas, and to check in and welcome guests from the ferry service that would bring them from central Copenhagen—but had been called in early to help deal with this latest unexpected problem. They huddled together to take stock of the situation. The tent riggers had placed plastic walkways and sheets of plywood at the highest-traffic zones around and inside the tent to prevent those areas from being churned into a muddy morass—there were some spare sheets of plywood. Haybales had also been set up in low walls to act as area dividers. There wouldn't be time to bring in any more equipment or material.

The team decided that they would lay down the extra plywood and walkways in the wettest parts of the area where the breakfast tables would be set up, then cannibalize the haybales to break them apart and put down thick layers of hay in the other parts to at least attempt to prevent people from sinking ankle-deep into mud. Though called together at the last minute and confronted with an unanticipated situation with few resources to spare, the situation's urgency led the team to self-organize to respond to the urgent and emergent problems it posed.

When the first guests arrived at the ferry point at Refshaleøen several hours later, they were greeted by a wet, exhausted, and mud-covered welcoming party standing in front of a bright red big top circus tent. MAD1 worked far better than the organizing team had dared hope. The two days of the symposium felt, one of the attendees told me, like a "truly great jazz performance—you never quite know what's going to happen next, and you have the feeling they don't fully know either." The speakers spoke in the tent over the drumming of rain on canvas. Everyone got and stayed wet. There was a palpable sense of exhilaration among the guests for having been part of something alive, something that could have failed but had been pulled from the brink of failure by an act of collective will. "For the first time, this feels like a real meeting of people," a chef from Paris told me during a lunch break, "not just some networking thing. You don't want to miss the speakers but you also don't want to stop talking to the other people who are attending." Though MAD1 was unexpectedly successful, what's more interesting is how this desperation project affected the team.

## Insight 5

*Innovation work is best motivated not with carrots but with well-chosen sticks.*

# 12

## DESPERATION BY DESIGN

**H**ow do innovation teams motivate themselves to do uncomfortable, unfamiliar innovation work? The R&D team members I spoke to knew that they would find their work fundamentally unsatisfying if they didn't learn by putting themselves into the discomfort zone. But they still found it difficult to bring themselves to do this. As Joe Raffa said, "The mind is willing but the gut is weak." For innovation teams, this is a conundrum. These teams don't succeed in being innovative unless their members push themselves into discomfort zones. And if they don't do this, their members grow dissatisfied and the teams become even less effective—they fall apart as individual members leave to pursue more exciting projects elsewhere.

MAD illustrates a counterintuitive solution to this motivational paradox. Committing to a project that was clearly beyond the team's collective ability induced desperation that created a beneficial nexus of mutually reinforcing effects and behaviors that forced them to learn new things and ways of working. The desperation was essential.[1] While it was stressful, it also unlocked many aspects of team and individual behavior that can stifle innovation. To various degrees, each of the R&D teams used this strategy of inducing desperation by design. However, the characteristics of a desperation-inducing project were especially clearly visible in how the MAD team came together around organizing that first symposium.

MAD1 was publicly announced early, before it became clear to the team how much organizing the symposium would push them beyond the limits of their current ability. The public announcement, the immediate expressions of interest, and the increasing sense that Noma's reputation was on the line, made the project one from which there was no psychological possibility of turning back even after it became clear how much, as someone said, "in the shit" they were. The fact that there was no turning back was instrumental in creating a sense of productive desperation.

Nearly immediately, committing to a project the team lacked expertise in led members to realize that they could not succeed simply by doing business as usual with existing resources. They were each forced to look beyond their current knowledge base and to search for people with different perspectives and abilities outside the team. In the months leading up to MAD, the team repeatedly discovered sets of skills that they needed but did not possess, and things they had to do that they had never done before and didn't know how to do. MAD was thus an enforced opportunity for the team to seek out and bring in new knowledge and perspectives, and to learn how to work with them effectively.

Desperation led to other innovation-supporting behaviors, which would probably have met with much more resistance in its absence. First was an even greater flexibility in what individual team members were responsible for. They took on new responsibilities as the need arose, often responsibilities very different from their existing ones. Nearly every member of the team found that his or her role changed in relation to MAD1, often expanding several times. "If you'd told me a year ago that I would be producing a conference today," Williams told me, "I wouldn't have believed it."

Changing roles usually means that team members take on new and different responsibilities. They are often reluctant to do this, being unwilling to have to learn new things or worried that their performance might drop. Here, this resistance was overwhelmed by individual and collective desperation because the project was so clearly beyond the team's existing capabilities and structure and was irrevocable. There was barely even a discussion of whether roles should change—it was taken for granted that they would. Team members were repeatedly thrust against their will into situations that gave them opportunities for individual growth and learning.

Before and during the actual days of the symposium, the team encountered unanticipated situations that they had to respond to immediately. "When we're working on a new dish, we just all slide into how we normally do things," Nutter said, "but we couldn't do that for MAD because stuff just kept happening and we had to figure out how to deal." Because they were irrevocably committed, these unanticipated situations forced the team to break existing habits and patterns for working with each other. The project forced team members to take on new roles but also forced the team as a whole to figure out new ways to work together.

## ONE THING LEADS TO ANOTHER

Noma's upheavals didn't end after MAD1. They seemed to get progressively more dramatic. The next year, they organized MAD2 ("It was much easier the second time," Williams told me)—and completely redesigned the R&D facility, uprooting it from its long-time location on the houseboat and relocating it to a smaller space above the restaurant.[2] At the end of 2014, Noma closed for five months to do a two-month popup in Tokyo with a completely different menu. Because of Noma's commitment to using indigenous ingredients, the move to Japan meant learning how to use an entirely new set of ingredients and surveying traditional Japanese cooking methods and equipment. The R&D team began their work nearly a full year before Noma Japan opened its doors in January 2015. The year after that, Noma Australia opened for ten weeks in Sydney, with the R&D for that menu taking a similar amount of time. In Tokyo, Noma partnered with the Mandarin Oriental Hotel, renovating and moving into one of its recently vacated restaurant spaces. In Sydney, they partnered with a real estate developer and went into a vacant restaurant spot in a new development. Even with basic restaurant infrastructure in both places, both Noma Japan and Noma Australia pushed the team beyond its limits.[3]

The year after Australia, they took a major step up by relocating Noma for seven weeks in 2017. This time, the restaurant moved to Tulum in Mexico. The ingredient and process R&D for Noma Mexico took over six months and opened up new conceptual territory in terms of how the R&D team thought about Noma's distinctive style. For one thing, as Redzepi said, "It is the first time that Noma has ever been influenced by [spice]. Nordic food is essentially based on fat and sugars with hits of umami through our fermentations. Discovering spice is like uncovering a sixth flavor."[4]

Mexico was a major advance into unknown territory for other reasons, too. Though Noma partnered there with a hotel operator, there was almost no existing infrastructure this time. Noma Mexico's site was a jungle. In addition to the ingredient and process R&D for the Mexico menu, the Noma team had to find local architects, builders, and craftspeople with whom to plan and build a whole kitchen and dining area and to design and manufacture much of the furniture and service ware. The restaurant and kitchen would be largely open to the elements, and it would seat twice as many people as Noma's original space in Copenhagen. These fundamental and profound changes to the service model forced the kitchen and front of house teams into rethinking and adapting ways of working together that had been carefully refined over a decade.[5]

But even before Noma Mexico opened, an even bigger disruption was in the works. In 2015, Noma had announced that it would close, move out of its original location in Copenhagen, and build an entirely new restaurant nearby. This was a long-term project, which also pushed the team beyond its ability. The new location would be in a derelict former munitions store that would have to be comprehensively redesigned and refurbished. The goal was for Noma to be able to grow ingredients on premises and to enable a completely different approach to the logic of the menu, the way ingredients were sourced, and the mode of service. Noma 2.0 opened in early 2018.

These projects all had intended objectives—to move the restaurant to Japan or Mexico, to relocate the test kitchen, and so on—but these intentional objectives are not what this chapter focuses on. Though it was not their intention to do so, these projects created desperation that was productive in the sense that it pushed teams and their members into the discomfort zone that lay just beyond the limits of their ability. To understand desperation by design, it's essential to look more closely at how these teams designed the projects they committed to.

## DESIGNING FOR PRODUCTIVE DESPERATION

The various desperation projects I saw across the different R&D teams had several design principles in common. Before describing these principles, I should emphasize that (like open-ended roles and open-ended style) desperation by design probably only makes sense for teams that are tasked to innovate and do new and unfamiliar things. Motivating other types of teams using desperation by design is misguided. If a team's goals are clearly specified and understood in advance, and the actions that it must take to achieve those goals are also clearly specified and well-understood, the best way to motivate the team is to tie rewards to the output and train them in the actions that are known to be needed[6]—artificially injecting desperation into such a team is counterproductive. Well-understood projects are precisely the ones for which the leader's role is to minimize the amount of uncertainty and disruption the team faces through proper scoping and appropriate resource allocation. More importantly, because such desperation is clearly at odds with the stated goals of the team and the well-understood actions it has to take, it is perceptibly artificial. It may work once, or even several times, but more often it is immediately or quickly perceived as a ruse or a gimmick. This demotivates team members and weakens trust in the team's leaders.

### *Real Commitment with the Possibility of Failure*

Desperation is driven by emotion: "It's under control, sort of, but really it's panic you feel in your gut," a ThinkFoodTank chef told me as the days counted down to the simultaneous opening of the three ThinkFoodGroup restaurants in Las Vegas. If the situation doesn't feel viscerally real, it won't a team out of its rut. This visceral sense of fear drives individuals and teams to do things that they would otherwise be reluctant to do.

A desperation project must therefore represent a real commitment. This requires a level of maturity in team leaders which is hard to find. The project must really be beyond the team's ability, there must be a real risk that it might fail, and there must be an irrevocable commitment to it. True desperation only emerges when these three conditions exist.[7] The sharp focus that productive desperation creates comes from knowing that the stakes are real, the drive to action comes from knowing that inaction has real consequences, and the learning comes from having to do things that are not part of the team's current repertoire. As Redzepi put it: "There is no option to quit." In order for the the risk of failure to be real, the leader has to have made peace with the idea that failure is truly possible.

## *Listening for a Different Signal*

Desperation can benefit a team by pushing members and the team as a whole to learn new things, adopt new roles, and figure out new ways of working together. These increase the team's ability to innovate by coming up with new ideas and by taking on new kinds of challenges. But these benefits come at a price. Even if they don't fail, desperation projects require a massive investment of energy and can thus be psychologically exhausting. Teams and individuals can be stretched—often further than they think—but beyond a point, they snap instead of springing back.[8] Successful desperation projects manage to find that point where the project's demands push the teams beyond their current capacities but not so far that they snap.

Successful teams committed to projects that were difficult enough to break down routines and habits, forcing the team to grow in ways that built capacity—but not so difficult that they caused the team to collapse. This fine balance was not simply a matter of good judgment by their leaders.

Though successful projects were the ones which created desperation once they had been committed to, this did not mean that the teams were impulsive or haphazard about these commitments. On the contrary, the precommitment process was methodical and prolonged. While the ultimate decision about committing to any given desperation project was almost always made by the team leaders—in the case of MAD, Redzepi's enthusiasm eventually wore down opposition to the idea—the successful teams spent a lot of time together discussing and evaluating projects before committing to them. The process closely resembled a consultation on the project between the teams and their leaders. This fairly extended consultation process was an opportunity for the team to explore various facets of the project and establish a preliminary sense of how far beyond their current ability it was.

Team leaders weren't listening primarily to figure out whether the project was possible or not given current parameters. Instead, they seemed to use these consultations to figure out their teams' emotional states. The signal they were looking for was the team's degree of calm (or lack thereof) when thinking through the ramifications of the project. The leaders didn't take their teams at face value when they were told that projects were impossible. Instead, they looked for situations where the team seemed only moderately agitated despite the project being clearly beyond their ability. The best leaders were therefore sensitive to the subtext of what their teams said, in large part because they created opportunities for their teams to reflect this kind of information to them when making decisions about committing to projects beyond their capability.

### Rhythm, Rest, and Escalation

For Noma, each successive project gradually pushed the team further from where it had begun. The first disruptions were relatively minor, then they got more ambitious. With each project, the team became more confident going beyond its comfort zone.

Its members became more practiced at being in uncomfortable situations, so these situations felt less uncomfortable. The limits of the team's comfort zone also expanded, as each project stretched their collective idea of what they could achieve.

Reflecting on this, Redzepi told me that, "MAD was the first time I knew that I could push the guys this way." Each disruption drove the team to desperation but also pushed them to grow in ways that allowed them to absorb more disruption the next time. Each desperation project built resilience in the team and forced it to learn new things. "Each of these things we have done," Redzepi said, "we take with us to the next step. Noma 2.0 is like the crystallization of all the things we've done so far. Each time we forced ourselves to do something hard that seemed impossible, it was like pushing through a closed door. It seemed impossible but when you give yourself no choice, it has to work, there is no possibility to quit."

Some of the teams in this book seemed especially successful at repeatedly pushing the limits of their ability. They set a regular program for desperation: commit to a desperation project with a determinate end-time, push through to completion, rest and recover, then find and commit to another project. The regularity of this rhythm allowed them to muster their willpower for each push because they knew approximately when the end time would be.[9] It allowed the team and its members to plan for the bursts of effort that desperation projects required, which was necessary since such expenditure of effort cannot be sustained indefinitely. The rest period after each project also gave the teams time to decompress and recover to become ready for the next project. Finally, anticipating the next desperation project prevented them from falling back into a state of complacency, which would eventually make it harder to nerve themselves up for entering the discomfort zone again. The frame of mind that supports productive desperation cannot be sustained forever, but is easier to recall if it is not too far in the past.

Successive desperation projects train a team to respond to desperation better. Rhythmic engagement in progressively more ambitious desperation projects allowed the teams to take small, then larger steps towards working in the discomfort zone—it was a way to train them to grow increasingly comfortable with discomfort and for them to gradually grow their capacity.[10]

## DESPERATION BY DESIGN

One of the most intractable problems in managing innovation teams is overcoming the deeply ingrained aversion people have to doing unfamiliar, therefore uncertain and uncomfortable, things. The urge to comfortably exploit the known is insidious and instinctive. It often overrides the imperative or even the desire to explore and change—motivating innovation teams is thus notoriously difficult. Organizations that fail to push themselves out of the comfort zone enter a plateau that, while comfortable, eventually begins to pall. Their most valuable members, the ones who thrive on and seek learning and challenge, eventually grow bored and leave. Decline and death ensues (figure 12.1 illustrates).[11]

The teams I observed overcame this aversion to discomfort and were able to repeatedly put themselves into the discomfort zone in which innovation can happen. This resulted from a counterintuitive strategy. Like Odysseus tying himself to the mast, these teams committed themselves irrevocably to projects that were beyond their abilities and where there was a chance of real failure. Because these projects pushed them beyond their current abilities, they created a visceral sense of desperation among their members.[12] This desperation was productive for innovation in that it drove the teams and their members to seek out new information and perspectives, take on new roles, and develop new

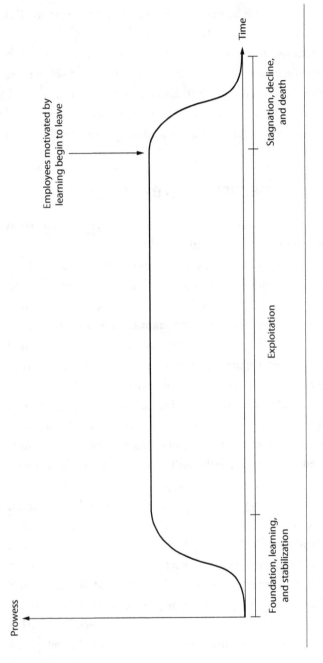

**FIGURE 12.1** Birth, life, and death of the typical organization.

ways of working with each other—all of which made them better able to come up with new problems to solve and new ways to solve them. They seemed to keep organizational death at bay and keep growing capacity through carefully progressive overload, taking on more and more ambitious desperation projects with relatively shorter rest periods and smaller initial performance declines (illustrated in figure 12.2).[13]

There were patterns of similarity across the teams in how they designed projects that successfully created a productive sense of desperation. Decisions to commit to projects were made only after extensive team consultation. Team leaders had to be sensitive enough to their teams to only commit to projects that struck the balance between being too difficult and not being difficult enough. This ended up being more an emotional judgment than one based on a formal-rational evaluation of facts—though these consultations allowed team leaders to gather facts about the projects, their real value was that they were opportunities for the teams to communicate to leaders their emotional responses to desperation projects.

Successful teams also evolved a rhythmic pattern of engaging in progressively more ambitious desperation projects followed each time by a recovery period (figure 12.2 illustrates). Much like building a muscle, this progressive approach allowed the teams to manage their resources and expend them at the right time, recover from the stresses and exertions of each project, and avoid the sense of complacency that would make the next desperation project psychologically too difficult to engage in.

These teams demonstrate the value of thinking unconventionally about motivation in the context of innovation work. Instead of searching for better carrots with which to motivate themselves, they used an unconventional but very effective stick—and they did so repeatedly in ways that gradually increased their

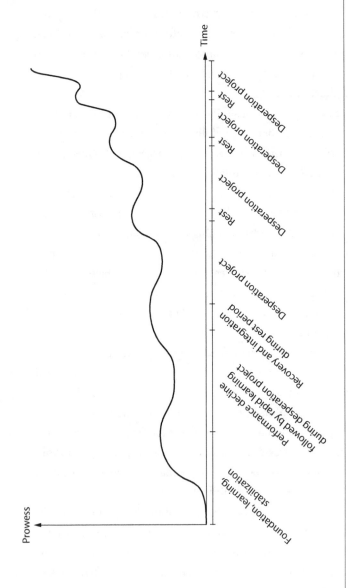

**FIGURE 12.2** A succession of desperation projects staves off organizational decline by progressively increasing a team's capacity and ability to deal with discomfort.

The labels along the Time axis, in order:

Foundation learning, stabilization

Performance decline followed by rapid learning during desperation project

Recovery and integration during rest period

Desperation project

Rest

Desperation project

Rest

Desperation project

Rest

Desperation project

individual and collective capacity to do new things and respond to change.

## Insight 6

*Carefully designed progressive overload pushes organizations to adapt and innovate.*

# PART VII

Insights from the Frontiers of Food

# 13

## ALL CHANGE

**E**VERYTHING in this book so far is history. The already rapid change I described in chapter 1 has accelerated. Today, the frontiers of food are changing more quickly and in more different ways than ever. Between when I began research for this book and when I finished writing it in 2019, each team moved on to projects that neither they nor I could have anticipated when I first visited them.

### THE COOKING LAB: *MODERNIST BREAD*

Between 2012 and 2018, The Cooking Lab released *Modernist Cuisine at Home* (2012), *The Photography of Modernist Cuisine* (2013), and *Modernist Bread* (2017).[1] It also announced that work was underway on its next book, *Modernist Pizza*, and Nathan Myhrvold, The Cooking Lab's founder, opened the Modernist Cuisine Gallery. These projects were the result of The Cooking Lab's increasingly sophisticated understanding of its unique configuration of competencies and novel business model—but also profoundly shifted the domains of knowledge The Cooking Lab had to cover and thus the roles its members had to perform in the team.

In making *Modernist Cuisine*, The Cooking Lab had created both a new category of culinary book as well as a new business model in publishing. Nearly every culinary research and development (R&D) lab that produces books or other forms of media works with traditional publishing houses or production companies who take on the responsibility of design, manufacture, and marketing. The Cooking Lab did not do this. "No publishing house wanted *Modernist Cuisine* for what we wanted to sell it for. They didn't think it would be able to make costs back," Myhrvold said. "So we ended up doing it ourselves." For *Modernist Cuisine*, they vertically integrated by taking nearly the entire publishing function in-house. The Cooking Lab did everything from research and writing to design, print management, pricing, and marketing, contracting out only the actual printing and final distribution of the books. This business model innovation meant that it did not have a publisher imposing constraints on how *Modernist Cuisine* developed.

The Cooking Lab's distinctive photographic style was one result of this unprecedented creative freedom. In the course of producing *Modernist Cuisine* and *Modernist Cuisine at Home*, Myhrvold and The Cooking Lab had developed an array of distinctive but also expensive, laborious, and technically demanding methods of photographing food, often building custom equipment to make the photography possible. For instance, while visiting the lab in 2018, I found two team members working on a jerry-rigged setup to photograph the moment two masses of liquid collide in midair. Through many failed shots, they had learned that simply launching liquids at each other resulted in messy-looking photos. The solution they eventually devised was to catapult two liquid-filled latex balloons at each other. A fraction of a second later, two linked droppers released droplets of limonene timed to reach the balloons just before they collided.

In less than 50 milliseconds, the limonene would weaken the latex enough to rupture the balloons, leaving two globes of liquid traveling intact toward each other. If the timings of the balloon catapults, the limonene delivery, the strobe light, and the camera shutter were perfectly calibrated, the entire setup would produce the effect of a casual collision of two liquid masses. This level of problem-solving was needed for many of the illustrations in The Cooking Lab's books. They were therefore not only effective illustrations but also spectacular and unique photography—which became a distinct line of business through the publication of *The Photography of Modernist Cuisine* (which collected a few hundred of the *Modernist Cuisine* photographs) and the Modernist Cuisine Gallery (which sells fine art prints of Myhrvold's own food photography).

The Cooking Lab's vertical integration made *Modernist Cuisine* a commercial success for two reasons. It offered creative freedom to develop the book's content and presentation in unconventional but effective ways. In turn, this allowed it to successfully price the book at what conventional publishers had erroneously believed to be an unfeasibly high price: both *Modernist Cuisine* and *Modernist Cuisine at Home* were more far expensive than a conventional publisher would have priced them but nonetheless swiftly sold out of their initial print runs and have continued to be strong sellers. The books also turned out to be extremely profitable because vertical integration allowed The Cooking Lab to retain most of the sales revenues, where a conventional publishing arrangement would have given the author only a relatively small royalty.

The flip side of The Cooking Lab's unusual business model as an R&D lab was that they had no closely matching exemplars to learn from. Since 2011, they have begun to develop a project rhythm appropriate for the extremely long-cycle research and development work they do. Given the efficacy of producing *Modernist Cuisine at Home* after *Modernist Cuisine*, they began to alternate between working on major, long-duration projects resulting in expensive landmark books and shorter-duration projects to develop more accessible books. Early on, Myhrvold had identified bread as another extensive domain of practical culinary activity in which knowledge was scattered and largely empirical in nature. Bread seemed ripe for the The Cooking Lab's unique approach of gathering and synthesizing an unprecedented amount of information, identifying underlying mechanisms, then using that information and understanding to make the synthesis appealing (through clear writing, effective information design, and beautiful photography) and practically useful (through rigorously tested recipes appropriate to the target audiences).

Francisco Migoya, The Cooking Lab's current head chef, said that, "When they started, as usual, they thought it would be a slightly simpler book [than *Modernist Cuisine*]." As development on the book ramped up, they realized how much more extensive the project actually was. While the book synthesized much of the relevant science behind bread, it eventually also asked and answered entirely new sets of questions about the bread-making process. One such question (which The Cooking Lab accidentally stumbled upon[2]) is, "What happens to bread when you cook it in a hermetically sealed container?" *Modernist Bread* contains the answer. Bread cooked this way, being sterilized by cooking, can then be stored at room temperature for months. When finally released in late 2017, the book spread over five volumes and more than 2,300 pages, and had taken more than four years of research and development. "We actually could have made it a seven-volume book," Myhrvold said via email. "We developed a lot of content that we ultimately decided to cut."

*Modernist Bread* organized the world of bread by clarifying the foundational science and the mechanisms by which bread is made: the biology and chemistry of various grains and grain-processing methods, the physics of different doughs and their mixing and baking processes. This mechanistic understanding made it possible for The Cooking Lab to identify crucial differences between different stylistic categories of bread—they ended up with twenty-six master breads in total—which then allowed them to introduce variations in each category that went beyond flavoring variations. "Breads everywhere are essentially the same because of the empirical nature of bread learning," Migoya said, "but once you learn why bread behaves the way it does, you have the tools to make many different kinds of bread."

As with *Modernist Cuisine*, *Modernist Bread* was written with careful consideration of its audience. The team recognized that writing it for professional bakers working in bakeries would limit the audience to an unfeasibly small number considering the project's scope and expense. To make the book economically viable, they decided to extend it to also serve home bakers and professionals baking bread not in bakeries but in hotels, restaurants, and other catering operations—this last audience was both especially large and underserved.

The book's inclusiveness made it a challenge to develop. Home bakers, professionals bakers working in bakeries, and professional bakers working in hotels, restaurants, and catering would likely use different types of baking equipment. To take just one example, a professional bakery deck oven, a home oven, a restaurant combi-oven, and a wood oven all perform differently. To be genuinely useful to each type of user, the recipes had to take differences in equipment into account. This meant that The Cooking Lab had to develop, test, and write each recipe to accommodate all the major types of equipment commonly available to the different audiences.

These recipes benefited from The Cooking Lab's mechanism-based approach. The empiricist nature of most breadmaking knowledge meant that most bread books presented recipes that implicitly assumed that users would get things right at each stage of the recipe process. *Modernist Bread*, in contrast, could be written more comprehensively and with an emphasis on preventing poor outcomes in part by illustrating how varying key parts of the process along the way would affect the final product. Ultimately, surmounting this challenge required an innovation in information design—of the bread recipe itself. The Cooking Lab ended up developing a new and more effective bread recipe format that integrated mechanistic understanding and presented it in a way that would allow different users to extract recipe and process instructions appropriate for their equipment.

Some of the technical information in *Modernist Bread* predated the project, and The Cooking Lab's task was to gather and synthesize it. However, the book's real value lay in its classification of master bread types, the novel recipe format, the rigorously tested recipes themselves, and the flexible variation they enabled. To produce these, the team ended up having to ask whole new ranges of questions about bread that had never been asked before. Researching and producing *Modernist Bread* represented a new set of tasks and a new body of practical knowledge for The Cooking Lab. This meant reorganizing a team built over the course of more than five years to develop *Modernist Cuisine* and *Modernist Cuisine at Home.* Seeing key gaps in expertise on the team, The Cooking Lab brought Migoya in as head chef for his expertise in bread and pastry pedagogy (he had taught for years at the Culinary Institute of America and written several cookbooks).

The Cooking Lab also hired a food scientist, a publisher, and a senior editor.

The team grew to accommodate the work on *Modernist Bread*, but The Cooking Lab did not hire an entirely new set of research chefs despite how different the bread project was compared to its previous projects. Instead, they each retrained to specialize in a subset of the twenty-six master bread styles so they could develop and test the bread recipes that are such a crucial component of the book: the existing team reconfigured itself, and individual team members learned new skillsets and took on new roles. As Migoya said, "When you have limited resources but your organization is not rigid, you can figure it out."

## AMAJA: FERMENTATION AND RADICAL REDESIGN

Amaja's test kitchen organization and focus have evolved significantly in the intervening years. These changes were, as usual, intertwined. The test kitchen had always explored different food processing methods to develop new dishes for Amaja. Fermentation had become a key pillar of the test kitchen's work early on; it had developed a suite of novel fermentation processes as a result. Some of these processes adapted existing fermentation methods so they could be used on new ingredients. One example was modifying the koji process—originally developed in Japan and primarily used in brewing sake to convert rice starches into sweet sugars that yeasts can digest into alcohol—to work on a wide range of unconventional grains and legumes. Other processes grew out of attempts to develop fermentation processes that would produce entirely new flavors and products. The goal overall had been to develop new ingredients that Amaja could use in dishes or which could be developed into saleable products.

As these specialized fermentation products became more widely used at Amaja, the test kitchen became responsible for more and more production to supply the service kitchen with fermentation products in the volumes needed for daily service. Extensive fermentation R&D and production requires specific equipment—especially temperature-controllable incubation chambers that take up lots of space—and people with specialized knowledge. Eventually, in 2014, the fermentation projects were spun off into a separate fermentation-focused R&D and production facility run by Norma Gamba (a biochemist on staff at the time) and César Pareto (who had left the Patagonia Food Lab and returned to Amaja as head of R&D) and located in a series of repurposed shipping containers behind the original Amaja location.

The shipping containers have since been reincarnated as the Amaja Fermentation Facility, an integrated research and production unit within the new Amaja building. In addition to manufacturing the fermentation products used in the restaurant, having dedicated R&D facilities and staff time allowed the team to produce a book documenting a wide range of existing and novel fermentation techniques for a general audience.

Like a growing number of restaurants and independent chefs, Amaja had also done a series of extended pop-ups in countries around the world. Each of these had changed how the test kitchen team thought and worked. "Being always at home is very comfortable," Tomás Irigoyen told me. "When we go away, we're forced to learn all these new things, we became more sensitive. Now we can see a carrot in a different way because we have been in different places." Each relocation forced the test kitchen team to uproot itself from its original context and closely examine a different culinary tradition with unfamiliar ingredients, cooking methods, and ways of eating.

These self-imposed learning opportunities began to fundamentally change the dishes the R&D team developed for Amaja. For instance, exposure to the use of spices in South America and the unusual bush spices of Australasia catalyzed what had previously been an inchoate approach to spicing in the food. Going to countries with long traditions of communal festive dishes shared among people at the same table and people at different tables also changed how the test kitchen team thought about how dishes should work at a table. Where previously the entire Amaja menu was plated for individual diners, future menus will begin to incorporate shared dishes. More broadly, these relocations showed the team the numerous benefits of having coherent menus each running for a determinate length of time compared to a menu evolving continually through the year. When Amaja reopened in 2017, the new menu divided the year into three menu seasons— seafood (winter to late spring), vegetables (summer to early fall), and game and forest (fall through winter)—separated by three to four weeks of rest for the Amaja team.

The disruptions also changed how Amaja worked more generally. Systematic innovation had always been the test kitchen's responsibility. Leaving Amaja's homebase periodically spurred the service kitchen, front of house, and management teams to also begin to systematically reexamine their respective domains. Each relocation pushed the management team to experiment with Amaja's service and business model. "When we came back [to open Amaja 2.0], we voted all of us for what kind of service model to have," Irigoyen said, "and everyone, no exceptions, voted for five days without lunch. Working in different countries with other setups made us realize that the restaurant can be more about you and how you want to live. Our last pop-up, it was too hot in the middle of the day to do lunch. So we did a big dinner service. It was the first time we did a full turn during service[3] and the dining room was twice the size of [the original] Amaja at least. It was a huge change for the front of house team but they made it work. And it worked very well because everyone got three to four extra hours in the morning when we dropped lunches. That makes a big, big difference."

I met with Irigoyen in October 2018, at Amaja 2.0. The first seafood season had just concluded and the restaurant was closed to guests but filled with staff and stagiaires preparing for the upcoming vegetable season. Irigoyen told me that, "[Amaja had been] changing ourselves as much as we can every year as we figured out better ways to do things. But we couldn't make all the changes we wanted in the old location. We were too tied to the space and how things had to work there. Moving here [to the new space] was our opportunity to break away from everything we wanted to change. It would have been impossible to do this all at once. We had to do it bit by bit to get used to it, and now here we are."

## THE FAT DUCK: NARRATIVE PERSONALIZATION

In 2015, the Fat Duck closed for its first major renovation since opening. The renovation was slow and expensive, as the restaurant is housed in a heritage-listed building nearly eight hundred years old—it took almost nine months. While the original building was being refurbished, the Fat Duck's kitchen team relocated to Australia for six months, temporarily reopening the restaurant there. The temporary closure was also an opportunity to also radically reconsider the Fat Duck's menu. It had become known for whimsical, technically precise food, on the cutting-edge because it was based on insights from the social and natural sciences incorporated for the first time into high-end cuisine. With the growing prevalence of technical cooking in high-end cuisine, it was time to move the Fat Duck's menu in a new direction.

The idea, which developed gradually, was to create a new menu in which the entirety of the guest's experience—each course and the transitions between them, the interactions with the servers—would hold together and be narratively coherent, analogous to a novel or film. Additionally, to the greatest extent practical, the menu and service model was to be designed so that parts of it could be customized to individual guests.

Narrative and personalization are not entirely new in high-end cuisine. Previous Fat Duck menus already contained kernels of this idea. Some dishes, like the Mad Hatter's Tea (a beef broth shaped into the form of a golden watch, and transformed at the table into a beef, mushroom, and vegetable soup) were references to stories in themselves. Restaurants elsewhere had also been experimenting with weaving narrative into food.[4] The Fat Duck's innovation was in the scope of its ambition. Previous attempts at narrative in food had been restricted to individual dishes or groups of dishes in a menu; no one had yet attempted to bring an entire meal—all its courses and the interactions before, during, and after the meal—into a coherent story for the guest. The Fat Duck's new menu was intended to leap from a narrative contained in a single dish to one that tied a guest's experience of the entire restaurant together.

Tailoring a meal to the individual diner is also not new in the world of high-end cuisine. Such personalization is common in the most rarefied forms of kaiseki and sushi in Japanese cuisine. A regular guest at a traditional kaiseki establishment might, for instance, receive a different starter from her dining companions, one cooked using ingredients indigenous to her hometown. This level of personalization requires deep knowledge of the guest, which is possible in the social and cultural context these restaurants operate in. There is a convention of long-term patronage that is enhanced by a practice (now far less common) known as *ichigen-san okotowari*: in essence, declining to serve guests not previously known to the establishment or who had not been introduced to the establishment by a known and trusted regular guest. This practice filters out first-time customers and allows restaurants to serve only guests who are repeat customers. Many repeated interactions over the course of many years allows the chef at an establishment like this to tailor the whole meal to what he or she has learned of an individual guest's preferences or personal history.

Beyond the guest's pleasure from having something custom-made precisely to her tastes, personalization—especially in food—can also provoke strong emotional and psychological responses. One of the best-known examples of this is in Proust's *In Search Of Lost Time*, when a madeleine with linden tea involuntarily calls forth in the narrator an intricately detailed memory of childhood time spent with his aunt during which she fed him pieces of a madeleine dipped in her cup of linden tea.[5] Analogously, restaurants saw that some dishes could evoke intense emotion in guests, though the effect was often serendipitous instead of intentional.

The difficulty with creating this effect by intent was partly that it was unclear what mechanisms caused these emotions and memories to surface. Some memories are personal yet common and pervasive; these seem easier to communicate. The French Laundry's dish of soup and a sandwich (heirloom tomato soup served with vintage sharp cheddar grilled on brioche) calls up one of these by analogy: the memory shared by hundreds of thousands of people of a grilled cheese sandwich made with Wonder bread and Kraft Singles dunked into a bowl of Heinz's cream of tomato soup. Other memories are intensely personal and distinctive and so much harder to communicate. An early fish dish by Alinea's head chef, Grant Achatz, was served on a bed of hyacinth flowers. Their scent would be released by the boiling water poured on them at service—a reference to a spring day in Achatz's youth when he ate on the riverbank among wildflowers while fishing with his father.[6] Diners and critics alike reported that some guests at Alinea involuntarily experienced intense emotion as they ate, as waves of memory washed over them.[7]

The new Fat Duck menu's ambition was to reach beyond such serendipitous evocations of emotion through memory. Its goal was to deliberately and systematically create similar effects by personalizing aspects of each guest's meal—anything from a flavor in a dish to a postcard from a recent holiday location. This was an ambitious leap in hospitality made even more challenging because the nature of the Fat Duck's business meant that the personalization often could not be predicated on a long association with the guest in question.

Weaving personalization and narrative into the Fat Duck required the Fat Duck Experimental Kitchen (FDEK) to fundamentally reconsider how they developed new dishes. To begin with, they had to think from first principles about the concept of narration in order to develop testable hypotheses about how various aspects of the dining experience could be made to serve different narrative functions. These control points would not only guide the guest's movement through particular narratives but also become potential candidates for personalization. This represents almost completely new ground in cooking. Not much is known at the moment about how to tell stories through the medium of food. The current culinary understanding of narrative is thus in an embryonic state—similar to the understanding of science in application to cuisine two decades ago. It took several decades for many people working individually and collectively to build the technical foundations for creativity we have today.

The team explored narrative and personalization for almost the entire nine-month period the original Fat Duck was closed. As they experimented with these ideas, they saw that the project's ramifications would reach much further than had originally been envisioned. Most dishes at high-end restaurants require too much preparation to accommodate the kinds of last-minute changes personalization requires, and few restaurants conceive of their front of house staff as actors helping to move the narrative of a meal along. The Fat Duck had to invent a new service model and menu logic in order to accommodate narrative personalization. This required enormous amounts of training before the reopening to create a kitchen team and floor staff that could handle personalized narrative menus. A separate workflow and dedicated team of people had to be created to get the information that would allow each guest's meal to be personalized. Needless to say, much ongoing planning and coordination was also needed to integrate this information into the service plan for each table and to coordinate between the kitchen and floor staff before and during the meal.

All this required an unprecedented level of interdependent work and collaboration at the Fat Duck. Redesigning the menu was a qualitatively different challenge compared to what had come before. While the many new dishes on the menu required the usual difficult and failure-prone R&D work, the real conceptual difficulty and thus the real innovation lay not at the level of the food itself but at the level of the guest's holistic experience of the entire restaurant. The Fat Duck was attempting to ask and answer extremely difficult questions through the medium of an entire restaurant experience. A prominent UK newspaper critic, reviewing the Fat Duck after the reopening, expressed the opinion that the new approach to the menu was so unprecedent-edly brave and groundbreaking that "it has left the food section altogether. This is what rocking, unmediated genius tastes like."[8]

## MAD: MISSION SEARCH

Since MAD1 in 2011, the team has grown and changed in structure. Noma and its staff are still closely connected to and supportive of MAD, but the MAD team is now a separately incorporated organization with a U.S.-based fundraising entity.

The MAD Symposium series has continued annually with only two interruptions. A series of smaller but more frequent and thematically focused public discussions called MAD Mondays now happen in both Sydney, Australia (organized by Sydney-based chef Kylie Kwong) and Copenhagen (organized by the MAD core team). In 2016, MAD partnered with Yale University to host a week-long summit for chefs designed to address questions of sustainable leadership. In 2017, it launched a program called VILD MAD ("wild food" in Danish) to introduce children and adults to the landscape and wildlife around them through foraging for wild food. In 2018, MAD launched a book series titled Dispatches, edited by *Lucky Peach* cofounder Chris Ying. Each Dispatch explores a single focused issue from many perspectives. The first MAD Dispatch examines immigration and the exchange of people and ideas through the lens of food.[9]

The logic underlying this diverse set of initiatives grows out of the founding impetus behind MAD. This was an inchoate, amorphous urge to create a setting that could materially change the food industry. MAD1 emerged from the belief that change—broadly conceived—would come when chefs were exposed to new and different ways of thinking and had opportunities to discuss them. MAD1 was thus structured as a two-day event at which participants heard from speakers about topics that were unusual in the context of a chefs' conference. This helped MAD swiftly become the food industry's preeminent conference of ideas. MAD1 also provided a meeting venue for innovation-oriented people in the food industry that had previously not existed and thus strengthened a network of relationships between innovation-oriented chefs and other people in and adjacent to the food industry. Subsequent MADs stimulated the same sense of excitement among both organizers and participants.

Nonetheless, there remained a niggling sense of dissatisfaction after each symposium. The symposia stimulated conversations among participants, but the desired changes in the industry were elusive. The team gradually came to realize that they wanted MAD to go beyond being a conference of ideas. They wanted it to not only spark change but also to facilitate that change. The educational initiatives (VILD MAD and the MAD-Yale partnership) were in part an attempt to move in that direction. A more fundamental problem was that the nature of the change desired was still amorphous. The MAD team continued to grasp for a clear understanding of what they were trying to do in the first place, a crisp statement of what they were trying to change and how they wanted those changes to be enacted.

Some of the thinking about MAD's overarching goals as an organization has been done in action, through experimenting with the programming of each successive MAD symposium. Each MAD symposium to date has had a different thematic focus. MAD1 was loosely about vegetation and planting the seeds of new ideas in chefs' minds. With each successive symposium, the themes became less focused on the relatively uncontroversial content of cooking and more focused on the increasingly problematic, challenging contexts in which cooking and the food industry exist. One important context was how restaurants and the food industry fit into the broader world around them. However, successive symposia also examined the internal context of the restaurant as a place where people work and the often conflicted landscape of the chef's psyche.

The symposia gradually broached increasingly difficult topics that were more ambiguous, that cut closer to the bone. Discussions of mental health problems, the challenges of maintaining family life and working in restaurants, personal emotional insecurity, sexual harassment and discrimination, and restaurant business model sustainability—to name just a few—became an increasingly large part of the programming, eventually coming to dominate MAD5 and MAD6.

These thematic changes were partly the result of repeated experimentation with the symposium's organizational approach and structure. This happened despite MAD1's success; success which made it psychologically difficult for the team to change how subsequent MADs would be run. Nonetheless the team experimented with the symposium. After programming the first two MADs, the team turned MAD3 over to David Chang (chef-owner of the Momofuku group of restaurants) and the editors of *Lucky Peach* (a progressive journal of food culture) and MAD4 to Alex Atala (chef-owner of DOM in Brazil). The first four MAD symposia were single-track in structure: fifteen to twenty speakers presenting individual talks to the entire audience of participants in the big tent over two days.

For MAD5, they went further by changing the symposium's structure. This was an attempt to include many more different perspectives and topics and further increase interaction among participants. MAD5 split the symposium into a mix of big-tent talks and an array of much smaller concurrent sessions run by nearly eighty of MAD5's participants. (The MAD team brought me in to help program MAD5 and develop the concurrent session structure.)

The proliferation of MAD initiatives and the team's experimentation with different formats for the MAD symposium are the visible consequences of an unwillingness to settle into a superficially successful and popular format of work. In turn, this reflects MAD's founding urge to always reach further than its grasp allows. The team recognized early that it had to do a lot of work and a lot of difficult internal questioning and problem-finding to understand its mission and how to achieve it. What problems are worth focusing on? What are the questions that need to be asked? Who should be involved in these conversations? What are the best platforms through which to pose these questions? At the last symposium—MAD6 in August 2018—these disparate threads came together when MAD announced its next step: transforming itself into MAD Academy, an educational program akin to a school of advanced studies for the food industry.[10]

## THINKFOODGROUP:
## POSTDISASTER FOOD RELIEF AT SCALE

ThinkFoodGroup is perhaps most revealing of how the uncertainty mindset can be relevant beyond the high-end culinary context. Between 2011 and 2019, ThinkFoodTank moved into a dedicated lab space in Washington DC and continued to play a key role in developing menus and running the openings for the many new restaurants that were added to the ThinkFood-Group portfolio. However, the uncertainty mindset that permeated how ThinkFoodGroup worked was also instrumental in creating a new way to run postdisaster emergency food relief operations at massive scale.

ThinkFoodGroup's portfolio includes humanitarian work driven by José Andrés. After the 2010 earthquake in Haiti, Andrés founded a nonprofit named World Central Kitchen

(WCK) to support economic development, education, and health, primarily in postdisaster situations. WCK runs independently from ThinkFoodGroup, but it uses Andrés's time and ThinkFoodGroup's resources—including its chefs, operational expertise, and organizational approach. WCK's driving idea was to focus on problem areas and draw on expertise directly connected to food and the cooking profession. It swiftly built a network of chefs around the world who could be activated to initiate projects requiring practical cooking expertise, such as developing school kitchens and meal programs to improve student attendance and developing culinary training programs intended to make trainees economically independent. In 2016, WCK also started providing food relief by preparing and supplying meals to people affected by Hurricanes Matthew and Harvey when they hit Haiti and Houston in 2016.[11]

In 2017, the need for WCK to provide food relief at massive scale suddenly became apparent. That September, Hurricane Maria hit the eastern Caribbean, catastrophically damaging infrastructure and killing hundreds of people on a swathe of islands and especially on Puerto Rico and Dominica. Immediately after Maria, nearly all of Puerto Rico was without power or running water, and many islanders were displaced from their homes.[12]

Andrés and documentary filmmaker Nate Mook (who would later become WCK's executive director), visited Puerto Rico a few days after Maria subsided. The enormous scale of the food relief that would be needed was immediately evident. The 3.4 million people living on the island when the hurricane hit would require many millions of meals per week. Many Puerto Ricans, especially in more remote parts of the island, had nowhere to cook and neither adequate power nor water to cook with. Restoring power and supply chains was initially estimated to take many weeks; in the end it took much longer as the extent of the destruction became clearer.

The coordinating government agency in Puerto Rico—the Federal Emergency Management Agency (FEMA)—operated under the standard operating procedure for postdisaster food relief, which is to ship in MREs (Meals, Ready to Eat) produced elsewhere. MREs are shelf-stable, fully cooked foods sealed in plastic pouches, essential when ingredients, supplies, and cooking facilities are not available. Intended as wartime food for soldiers in the field, MREs are more expensive than fresh meals and make for dispiriting eating. FEMA contracted for 30 million MREs to be produced in the mainland United States and shipped in several weeks.[13]

For the first few weeks, Andrés and Mook were the entire WCK team on the island. Seeing that no government or nongovernmental agency working on Puerto Rico had an immediate plan for feeding people until the MREs arrived from the mainland, the team began to mobilize whatever chefs, equipment, and food supplies they could find. The team saw that the situation in Puerto Rico in those first post-Maria weeks was uncertain and rapidly changing. Their organizational approach there was analogous to how ThinkFoodTank managed the chaos of a restaurant opening.

They did not spend a lot of time developing a detailed plan of action that would likely become immediately irrelevant while being hard to change. Instead, WCK rapidly assessed the situation and created solutions that used available resources. They found or built temporary kitchens and kitchen teams across the island to produce fresh meals from the stocks of ingredients that had been warehoused on Puerto Rico before Maria hit. They also activated their global network of volunteer chefs and began to line up infusions of money, food, supplies, and equipment from private donors on Puerto Rico and the U.S. mainland. Their goal, as Andrés put it, was simply to respond to the continually evolving situation so they could feed the absolute maximum number of people given the massive shortages of prepared food at the time.

WCK's Puerto Rico operation was opportunistic by design. While off-island chefs flew in to help, they were vastly outnumbered by local volunteer chefs and other helpers. To the greatest extent possible, WCK also used facilities, ingredients, and materials already on the island—including delivering prepared food with anything from private vehicles, to borrowed helicopters, to Homeland Security teams. This opportunistic operational model was inherently flexible enough to adapt to a situation that could not be fully understood in advance and which was constantly in flux.

This approach allowed WCK to handle unexpected problems and use unanticipated resources, such as a shortage of fuel (handled by bartering food for fuel), finding a warehouse full of useable ingredients, or being contacted by a pastor and his congregation wanting to set up a production kitchen in their neighborhood. It also meant that it was willing to call in external expertise when necessary. As soon as the team realized the scale of the food provision problem (hundreds of thousands of meals needed to be cooked each day), they saw that they lacked expertise in producing and distributing meals in large quantities. To fill this gap, they called in a team of chefs from Compass, a large foodservice company with chefs who knew how to cook for thousands of people at a time.

Immediately after Hurricane Matthew in 2016, WCK had provided about 15,000 meals in Haiti through mobile kitchens. The organization had also provided food at several other natural disaster sites.[14] The feeding operation in Puerto Rico a year later represented a food relief logistics effort that ultimately was at least two orders of magnitude larger than what it had done in Haiti. Eventually, it operated twenty-six kitchens across the island and prepared and distributed over 150,000 meals daily when operating at peak capacity. By the time World Central Kitchen scaled down their Puerto Rico operation, they had served over 3.5 million meals.

WCK's approach to food relief was—and remains—diametrically opposed to the conventional approach to disaster relief, which is driven by the risk mindset and relies on detailed advance planning and centralized control. The team brought the uncertainty mindset with it when it arrived on Puerto Rico, a mindset I've described in earlier chapters in the context of ThinkFoodTank. Sharing this mindset meant that WCK and ThinkFoodTank worked in analogous ways. Both teams were comfortable with dropping people into an uncertain situation and giving them the freedom to work out what to do in real time instead of forcing them to do a lot of advance planning. The uncertainty mindset made WCK willing to confront the complex, changing, and emergent reality on the ground and thus gave it the ability to create a food relief operation that was highly effective because it embraced instead of denied that uncertainty.[15]

# 14

## A MINDSET FOR AN UNCERTAIN WORLD

**H**IGHLY innovative organizations cannot stand still while remaining innovative. The teams in this book designed themselves to not only constantly kick themselves out of ruts but also to be good at being kicked out of ruts. Effective innovation management involves training people and designing teams to be willing and able to discard what they have become good at and become good at something else.

This is fortunate because high-end cuisine is changing faster than ever, and the teams that work in it have had to change to keep up. As the industry has matured, it has become more open-minded about what constitutes innovation. In the early days, it was mainly concerned with the food on the plate. Today, the frontiers of food are moving ever further outward. Innovation efforts now pervade the entire guest experience. Even further removed from that, high-end cuisine is increasingly aware of the serious problems of gender inequity, mental illness, poor staff welfare, and organizational unsustainability that plague the industry. These problems can only be addressed through new thinking and experimentation with new business models and ways of treating employees, and by engaging differently with the world outside the industry. From conferences to provoke conversations about serious industry problems, to building guest experiences around narrative, to new ways of thinking about entire classes of foods, to food-based emergency relief, the teams in this book have innovated in response to the changing industry they work in—and the changing world they live in.

## HARD TRUTHS

Innovation requires the paradoxical ability to be simultaneously creative and nondelusional about the world; to see what's actually there but also to actively imagine how that shapes the range of meaningful, not-yet-existent, possible outcomes. This requires both making sense of things as they are and also being able to break that framework of sensemaking and interpretation to allow room for the new.[1]

Innovation is inherently truly uncertain. With innovation work, you don't know what you're looking for until you find it or create it. Uncertainty is an inescapable part of trying to do something that has not been done or even imagined before.[2] It follows that innovation cannot be solely a process of rational analysis and problem-solving—if that were true, machines would be able to do it for us. What makes innovation work hard is that uncertainty makes it both a rational problem-solving process and an interpretive, open-ended process of finding problems by bringing different perspectives together and negotiating how they interact.[3]

The lived reality of innovation work is that it is therefore messy and chaotic, filled with ambiguity and friction. Innovation arises out of creative dissonance between different worldviews, different domains of work, and different ideas of value.[4] Innovation and creativity depend on the organization achieving a continually moving state of balance between having enough structure to coordinate its members and the looseness and freedom needed to ensure that they can find new things and bring them into the organization.[5]

Innovation work, being messy, uncertain, and interpretive, is emotionally difficult. Though the cognitive and technical challenges of innovation are always highlighted, the emotional and affective challenges are seldom identified, let alone discussed. Yet, as these teams show, the emotional hurdles of doing innovation work are considerable.

Making something genuinely new and useful requires combining rational problem-solving with messy interpretation. Creative dissonance and realistic imagination help. Innovation work is ambiguous, subjective work that is neither certain nor predictable—when done well, it helps organizations adapt to the changing demands imposed on them by the environment. The hard truths of innovation are thus aspects of the same insight: organizations that want to be innovative cannot also be neat, predictable, stable, and unchanging. They have to be able to change inside as the demands on the outside change, and they are likely to experience ambiguity and dissonance and be untidy as they change.

These hard truths have been identified by innovation and management researchers before, yet researchers and managers continue to grasp at the seductive idea that innovative organizations can be built to plans that are neat, knowable in advance, stable, and unchangingly understandable.

## MINDSETS, DECISIONS, ACTIONS, RESULTS

The teams in this book look messy and unpredictable, but they were able to keep innovating and adapting because they used the unconventional organizational practices I've described. These, in turn, result from having a mindset that acknowledges and embraces uncertainty.

The cutting-edge, high-end culinary community emerged due to a concatenation of events that made it unignorably evident that the cutting-edge culinary industry was uncertain instead of risky. The culinary innovation teams I spent time with could not ignore the uncertainty they faced nor pretend it was risk. They had an uncertainty mindset that influenced how they approached key questions about how to design and organize themselves. This uncertainty mindset led them to make unusual and counterintuitive decisions about how to think about membership and hiring, what types of goals to pursue, and how to motivate themselves.

Roles for members of these R&D teams were modular and provisional, the teams pursued goals that were open-ended and abstract, and they intentionally committed themselves to projects far beyond their current abilities. In these teams, member roles were unstable and changeable, team goals were uncertain and impossible to articulate, and the teams were periodically consumed by desperation. Yet these teams could consistently come up with new ideas that worked. They could innovate so effectively not in spite of but *because of* these counterintuitive organizational decisions.

Crucially, these were not implemented in isolation. They worked because they were deployed together with each other and were supported by specific ways of working. Without robust role negotiation processes, provisional and open-ended roles would not have created adaptable and responsive teams. Without iterative processes for teaching and learning style during routine work, open-ended goals would not have generated consistently familiar innovation. And without calibration processes, the ability to work with open-ended goals in place, and adaptability from open-ended roles, desperation projects would not have been productive in creating teams that could systematically reconfigure themselves to do things they were previously incapable of.

The teams featured in this book were effective innovators not only because they saw and could accept that their industry was changing. They were also good at changing themselves to adapt to or drive those changes. This was not because they possessed some special, ineffable, unreplicable property. In this book, I've argued the opposite, that this ability springs from a simple but unconventional approach to thinking about organization which is rooted in an uncertainty mindset. The uncertainty mindset is a foundation for teams that are more able to innovate and adapt to change.

## SELF-ADMINISTERED UNCERTAINTY

Cutting-edge culinary R&D shows us a fundamentally different approach to organizing innovation because it is a world that until recently was almost entirely uncontaminated by conventional management wisdom. As a result, the teams in this book worked in ways that violated this conventional wisdom.

I've argued that these ways of working led the teams in this book to continually find, lose, and regain the ability to perform well in their changing environment. These teams were constantly pushing themselves off-balance and into situations of uncertainty,[6] and that seems to have allowed them to continually adapt to their unpredictably changing environment.

Becoming and staying innovative as an organization may be less about finding a highly adapted, stable state of optimal innovation performance and more about investing energy and time in ongoing processes of seeking, finding, losing, and then regaining balance and equilibrium. These exhausting processes of staying in dynamic equilibrium are intimately bound up with innovation and adaptation because organizations, like their members, must be changeable and unpredictable in order to innovate.[7]

Organizations seem to succeed when they deliberately inject unpredictability into themselves, as these teams did by making roles open-ended and provisional, pursuing open-ended style, and committing to desperation projects. They were innovative and adaptable to an uncertain external environment not in spite of but because they made their internal environment uncertain. While uncertainty is hard for organizations to deal with, the benefit of uncertainty is that it creates space for something that doesn't yet exist—and the motivation to fill that space.

How can we build continually innovative and adaptable organizations? One facet of the answer is that it can be as simple as starting with a mindset that explicitly acknowledges that the future is uncertain instead of risky. This uncertainty mindset led to counterintuitive ways of working, these unconventional ways of working generated internal uncertainty, and this internal uncertainty stimulated the teams to search for new ideas and change to implement them.

## BEYOND THE FRONTIERS OF FOOD

I've argued that cutting-edge cuisine is a model system in which the nature of the uncertainty mindset is clearly visible. From where I stand, the insights about how to design organizations that emerge from understanding the uncertainty mindset are relevant beyond cuisine. Having worked with small businesses and with consulting companies whose clients are large corporations, there is clear evidence from the frontlines that the pace of change businesses face is growing ever greater, that the complexity and uncertainty they face is increasing—and that old ways of designing organizations are not adequate to these new challenges.

An advisor to the senior leadership of one of the world's largest infrastructure investment banks told me that, "Across nearly every industry we touch, we're seeing that the business environment is changing more quickly and more unpredictably than ever. The conventional ways of thinking about organizing big companies are not up to this new challenge—they produce organizations that are extremely good at doing predictable things, but terrible at responding well to change." In a similar vein, an advisor to one of the largest consumer internet companies in the world said, "For them, it's starting to look like every week, sometimes every day, brings a new crisis from way out of left field. How they're structured makes it nearly impossible for them to innovate their way out of the mess they're in. They need a new way to thinking just to keep up, let alone get ahead."

Broadly, adopting the uncertainty mindset makes sense for organizations and businesses facing uncertainty in the future or their business environments. However, it seems most relevant to three particular categories of businesses.

1. **Startups in (or trying to create) emerging industries:** Here, the ground rules of the industry are still forming. Who customers are, how the underlying technologies work, the nature of regulation, and the use-cases that are relevant are in the process of being worked out. Quantum computing, personalized pharmaceuticals, legally produced cannabis; these are just a few of the profusion of industries emerging at the moment. Adopting the uncertainty mindset from the beginning could help businesses in these types of industries set strategy and grow in ways that allow them to survive and succeed despite fundamental changes in how their industries operate.

2. **Startups disrupting established industries:** Startups often take organization design principles from big businesses—even though they face far greater uncertainty due to their size and position as new entrants trying to find gaps in markets dominated by much larger, entrenched incumbents. As a general partner at a major venture capital fund told me, "Every early-stage startup I have seen essentially faces a deeply uncertain future. The business model is untested, the market is basically unknown, the technology is still in development. They should be doing their best to

233

stay nimble while they learn what their business is, yet many of them raise capital and spend huge amounts of effort to build infrastructure for large scale." Adopting the uncertainty mindset instead could lead these startups to the gradually scaling, adaptable organization design that is more appropriate for the uncertainty they face.

3. **Leading incumbents in rapidly and unpredictably changing industries:** In these industries, leading incumbents are likely to have their business models disrupted by smaller and more agile upstarts, rapidly changing customer behavior, or new technology. We see this in industries like news media, advertising, advanced manufacturing, and consumer healthcare provision. These disruptions to business-as-usual produce uncertainty, which incumbents must absorb and manage effectively—or eventually be destroyed by. Unfortunately, the leading incumbents in any industry are likely to be hamstrung by investors (or stock market wariness) who generally insist on short-term performance even at the expense of long-term performance and survival. Combined with their size, this makes it seem unlikely that they will be able to systemically adopt the uncertainty mindset and overhaul their entire organizations. For leading incumbents, the answer may lie in building internal teams with the uncertainty mindset to drive organizational adaptation to uncertain change. R&D divisions, new product development teams, and business development units (to name only a few examples), are more likely to detect and respond appropriately to unexpected changes in the business environment if they are organized around the uncertainty mindset.

## SIX INNOVATION INSIGHTS FROM THE FRONTIERS OF FOOD

In previous chapters, I described how the uncertainty mindset manifested in the concrete tactics—the organizational design and work practices—of some of the best culinary R&D teams in the world. The uncertainty mindset will probably manifest quite differently in other industries. The correct approach to applying insights from cutting-edge cuisine to other industries is not to try and transfer the tactics used in high-end cuisine directly. Instead, as I have tried to do, it is to try and understand their underlying principles. How did the uncertainty mindset produce those concrete practices? How did those concrete practices make individuals and teams responsive, adaptable, and innovative? Understanding these principles is the key to developing concrete tactics appropriate for contexts outside cuisine.

1. **Modular, provisional roles lead to adaptable organization members.** Conventionally, roles are presented (and perceived) as being static and monolithic; it should come as no surprise that they lead to dissatisfied and ossified employees. Modularity allows roles to evolve and adapt, component by component. Setting expectations that roles are provisional leads members to actively explore and modify their roles to adapt to changing demands on the organization (explained in detail in chapter 8).

2. **Continually adjusting member roles leads to responsive, adaptable, high-performing organizations.** The continual evolution of each member's role forces other members to pay close attention to how their own roles are affected. Organizations whose members' roles are continually evolving and adjusting are more likely to have members that have detailed and accurate understandings of what their colleagues are good at doing and how to work well interdependently. Such a detailed understanding allows these organizations to work well with minimal supervision and under considerable uncertainty (chapter 9).

3. **Choosing to pursue open-ended goals permits and encourages familiar innovation.** Conventional wisdom suggests that goals must be clearly defined to be effective—by definition, such goals exclude the possibility of innovation and are inappropriate for innovation teams. In contrast, open-ended goals are partly undefined or ambiguously defined. They offer room for organizations to innovate within the parameters of what the team has historically produced (chapter 10).

4. **Organization members learn how to pursue open-ended goals by doing actual and consequential work.** Conventional approaches to learning and development rely heavily on putting employees through targeted training programs that may simulate actual work but are nearly always separated from it. The learning

these programs enables is thus disconnected from how people actually work. In contrast, routine work can be designed to offer multiple, effective opportunities for teaching, learning, and feedback. This unconventional approach provides less certainty about precisely what organization members learn and when they learn it—however, it enables learning which is both faster and more effective because it occurs constantly and in context (chapter 11).

5. **Innovation work is best motivated not with carrots but with well-chosen sticks.** Innovation work is uncertain and fraught with failure—it is cognitively desirable but emotionally challenging. Visceral aversion to uncertainty and failure is an obstacle to innovation work that incentives alone cannot surmount. Carefully overloading an organization with an irrevocable and consequential project can create a sense of productive desperation that is a better motivator for doing innovation work than incentives alone (chapter 12).

6. **Carefully designed progressive overload pushes organizations to adapt and innovate.** Overloading organizations with desperation projects creates intense stress which can be productive by breaking down old routines and stimulating learning—but it can also be destructive by stifling internal communication and narrowing focus unnecessarily. The key to making overload productive is to overload progressively so that the organization's individual and collective capacity grows gradually and with a rhythm that incorporates time between desperation projects for rest and integration of new knowledge and ways of working (chapter 13).

## A MINDSET FOR AN UNCERTAIN WORLD

On the frontiers of food, it is difficult to be self-delusional about whether the future is risky or truly uncertain. In contrast, risk and uncertainty are often conflated in the world outside cutting-edge, high-end cuisine, and often this conflation has dire consequences.[8] Regardless of whether or not we recognize it, the world is becoming more uncertain as it becomes more complex and interconnected.[9]

Against this backdrop of increasing uncertainty in work and life, the teams in this book have something important to teach us that goes beyond their ability to create new ideas in food. Their uncertainty mindset gave them the ability to sense changes in their environment and respond to these changes. They demonstrate that an innovative organization can be functionally identical to one that can detect and adapt to unpredictable change.

The vast majority of organizations are founded, figure themselves out, plateau, stagnate, then die. The teams in this book managed to defer this fate by kicking themselves out of the plateau—the combination of open-ended roles, open-ended goals, and desperation projects allowed them to move on upwards, repeatedly.

I've argued that the uncertainty mindset is fundamentally different from the risk mindset, and it pushes organizations in the direction of counterintuitive but effective approaches to organizing for innovation and adaptability. As World Central Kitchen's operations in Puerto Rico suggest, the uncertainty mindset works beyond high-end cuisine. Other kinds of teams working on other kinds of projects in uncertain and rapidly changing environments could benefit from the innovation capacity that comes from seeing uncertainty clearly and embracing it, instead of desperately pretending it doesn't exist or wishing it away. The uncertainty mindset makes organizations messy, dissonant, unpredictable. The hidden benefit is that it gives them the continuing ability to innovate and adapt. In an increasingly unpredictable world, organizations need the uncertainty mindset.

# NOTES

## PREFACE

1. In the last decade, scientists and engineers have become increasingly interested in understanding innovation in high-end cuisine (see, for instance, Humphries (2012) and Kummer (2014)). The R&D teams in this book are among the handful worldwide that have featured most prominently in science, technology, and innovation coverage of cutting-edge cuisine.

## 1. FROM THE MARGINS TO THE CENTER

1. Garum is a liquid condiment originating in the Roman Era, produced by the slow decomposition of salted fish; *yuba* is a fragile, edible skin produced by cooking soy milk until the top surface dehydrates enough to remove an intact layer of soy protein; lacto-fermentations preserve foods by acidification through lactic acid produced by *Lactobacillus* bacteria; a fumet is a light-bodied broth made from fish.
2. See Sandler (1988).
3. See Fernandez-Armesto (2002).
4. See Hermé (2015).
5. On sealing meat, see McGee (2004, 161); on salting dry beans, see Lopez-Alt (2015, 256).
6. Author's fieldnotes, June 2011.

## 2. THE UNDERCURRENTS OF THE NEW

1. Food at any level is a cultural product and so must be understood in the context of the culture that produces it. Writing about the embeddedness of cuisine in the context of France, Priscilla Clark notes that, "The strictly culinary or alimentary product concerns the cook, the kitchen, the dining room and the diner. The *discours alimentaires* join chef and diner as well as cook and diner, and implants the culinary product in an ambient culture. For consumers may be readers as well as diners (if only by reading the menu). Chefs have an immediate public in the restaurant, but a long range one through cookbooks, guidebooks, even novels. The fate of French or any other cuisine involves the whole culinary system, for cuisine, like other cultural products, needs to be examined with reference to the society of which it is part and which it in turn expresses" (Clark 1975b, 198). Embeddedness remains important even when the internationalized nature of modern high-end cuisine—diners, workers, and even restaurants routinely move to and fro across the world—makes understanding the nature of the culture in which it is embedded harder than when cuisines were more closely associated with the cultures of particular regions.

2. See Scattergood (2015).

3. James Leff, personal conversation, 10 January 2013.

4. *Food Snob*: https://foodsnobblog.wordpress.com; *Gastroville*: blog deleted; *Docsconz*: http://docsconz.com; *Chuck Eats*: http://www.chuckeats.com/; *A Life Worth Eating*: http://www. alifewortheating.com; *The Ulterior Epicure*: https://ulteriorepicure.com.

5. A former Michelin Guide employee has written about the structure of the reviewer teams; for more on this, see Remy (2004).

6. Information about the 50 Best jury, formally known as the World's 50 Best Restaurants Academy, was provided by the World's 50 Best Restaurants (see https://www.theworlds50best.com/voting/the-academy, accessed 26 December 2019). For more on how the 50 Best restaurants are chosen, see L. Collins (2015). And for a detailed consideration of how influencers are affecting high-end cuisine, see Abend (2017).

7. See Cassi (2011).

8. René Redzepi, personal conversation at MAD1, 27 August 2011.

9. Fieldnotes from observations during planning for MAD1 (June 2011), during MAD1 (26 and 27 August 2011), during MAD3 (25 and 26 August 2013), during planning for MAD5 (January to August 2016), and during MAD5 (28 and 29 August 2016) and MAD6 (26 and 27 August 2018).
10. See McGee (1984) and McGee (2004).
11. See Fay Jai (2004).
12. Aki Kamozawa and Alex Talbot: https://blog.ideasinfood.com; Shola Olunloyo: https://www.studiokitchen.com; Michael Laiskonis: https://mlaiskonis.wordpress.com; Mikael Jonsson: blog removed; Dave Arnold and Nils Noren: http://www.cookingissues.com; Martin Lersch: https://blog.khymos.org.
13. See Myrhvold, Young, and Bilet (2011).
14. Wayt Gibbs, personal conversation, 5 March 2012.
15. See Varenne (1651).
16. Quoted in McClusky (2011).
17. See Myrhvold, Young, and Bilet (2011, vol. 6, 305).
18. For more on platforms and their dynamics in the technology industry, see Gawer and Cusumano (2002) and Gawer (2009). On the relationship between modularity of resources and platform dynamics, see Baldwin and Clark (2000).
19. High-end cuisine is a field in which legitimacy is crucial and identity is intimately connected with legitimation. When cutting-edge cuisine was first emerging, it faced a legitimation problem analogous to the one nouvelle cuisine faced when it emerged in 1960s France in the context of classic haute cuisine. Nouvelle cuisine chefs emphasized the extent of their creative control, thus defining themselves against the rigid constraints on classic cuisine chefs imposed by Escoffier's codification of cooking—but at the same time emphasized that nouvelle cuisine was still haute cuisine. In high-end cuisine, what is new and different must somehow both distinguish itself from *and* identify itself with what it is different from. For more on institutional patterns in French gastronomy, see Clark (1975a), Clark (1975b), Ferguson (1998), and Rao, Monin, and Durand (2003). For more on how organizational practices become legitimized, see Meyer and Rowan (1977).

20. The early cutting-edge restaurants played an important role in creating an environment in which today's cutting-edge culinary community could form. For instance, El Bulli was one of the first restaurants to invest time and effort in internal systems for coming up with new ideas in food. It also invested considerable resources in documenting and disseminating these ideas through books, workshops for chefs at other restaurants, and by hosting *stagiaires* (unpaid interns) who learned about those new ideas in their time at El Bulli. These institutionally entrepreneurial actions helped promote El Bulli's new ideas in food in the world of high-end cuisine, and they also legitimized its way of organizing culinary innovation. For more on El Bulli's strategy for managing culinary innovation externally and legitimizing it as an activity, see Svejenova, Mazza, and Planellas (2007), and Opazo (2016).

21. See Adrià, Adrià, and Soler (2008), Blumenthal (2008), and Aduriz (2012).

22. See Abend (2011).

23. See Andrews (2010).

24. The growing numbers of acclaimed cutting-edge restaurants offered social proof that focusing on innovation was a legitimate strategy in high-end cuisine, thus creating room for change in its institutional structure. For more on social proof, see Rao, Greve, and Davis (2001). On previous instances of institutional change in cuisine (from traditional haute cuisine to nouvelle cuisine in France), see Rao, Monin, and Durand (2003) and Rao, Monin, and Durand (2005). And on imitation and mimetic practices within industries, see Haveman (1993).

25. For more on how individual chefs think about their creative work and choose what dishes they put on their menus, see Leschziner (2015).

26. See Hermé (2012).

27. For more on the dynamics of knowledge-sharing in high-end cuisine, see Stefano, King, and Verona (2014).

28. The dynamics underlying the emergence of cutting-edge cuisine as a coherent segment of high-end cuisine are consistent with the idea that innovation and invention happen when knowledge and practices flow across overlapping networks from where they are well-known to where they are novel. For more on how innovation emerges out of interactions between networks, see Padgett and Powell (2012).

29. The development of the cutting-edge culinary community is also consistent with the conceptualization of innovation within industries as intrafirm innovation activity in the context of interfirm competition and collaboration in creating and using innovations. For more on this, see Baumol (2002). The now-global, cutting-edge culinary community exists in part because of how people within the community move and circulate interregionally and interorganizationally, bringing ideas and ways of working with them. It is thus a virtual analogue of geographic regions that become innovative in part by evolving decentralized systems of interrelated organizations. For more on the structure and mechanisms of regional advantage, see Saxenian (1996) and Saxenian (2007).

## 3. WELL-KNOWN, BARELY UNDERSTOOD

1. For more on the production and use of miso, see Shurtleff and Aoyagi (1976).
2. The pea did not originate in Patagonia but has been grown there for long enough that it is now commonly thought of as a native crop. It is believed to have been originally domesticated in the Middle East. For more on early pea domestication, see Mikić et al. (2014).
3. For more on the winner effect in humans and mood-repair through success, see Zilioli and Watson (2014) and Rieger et al. (2014). For more on fear of failure, learned helplessness, and defensive pessimism, see Abramson, Seligman, and Teasdale (1978), Norem and Cantor (1986), and Martin, Marsh, and Debus (2001).
4. For a Britain-focused historical analysis of the emergence and dynamics of the Industrial Revolution, see Hobsbawm (1999). For a critical analysis of the modernist movement in painting, see Greenberg (1965).
5. A useful way to think of each of the communities that gave rise to cutting-edge cuisine (for instance, the community of high-end cuisine) is as a network containing the necessary components (people, ideas, ways of working, and so forth) necessary for the network to reproduce itself—what John Padgett and Woody Powell have labeled an autocatalytic network. When multiple autocatalytic networks are connected together, the transposition and feedback of components recombine in ways that are new to the entire connected set of networks. When cutting-edge cuisine emerged, this invention affected each of the interacting communities but

had the greatest effect on one of them: high-end cuisine. For more on autocatalysis, organizational genesis, and novelty, see Padgett and Powell (2012).

6. For more background on how innovations are conceptualized in terms of their potential for creating discontinuities in a given context, see Leifer et al. (2000), Garcia and Calantone (2002), and Alexander and Van Knippenberg (2014).

7. For a synthesis of the nutritional implications of cereal fermentation, see Poutanen, Flander, and Katina (2009).

8. Claiborne (1981).

## 4. FOUR TYPES OF NEW IDEAS IN FOOD

1. For more on the distinction between new dishes as final outcomes, and inventions or conceptual innovations that permit many new dishes to be created, see Opazo (2016).

2. Incremental innovation, knowledge translation, and combinatorial innovation have been examined by innovation researchers in other contexts. For more on incremental innovation, see Ettlie, Bridges, and O'Keefe (1984) and Baumol (2005). On knowledge translation, see Cremades, Balbastre-Benavent, and Sanandrés Domínguez (2015). On combinatorial innovation, see Yoo et al. (2012).

3. Though innovation is often constrained by known parameters (such as budget or staffing), innovation work itself is not rational in the conventional sense because of the uncertainty it entails—uncertainty that arises from the need to imagine possibilities, from the necessarily incomplete knowledge that characterizes exploration, and from the need to interpret what exploration discovers. For more on innovation as imagination grounded in pragmatism, see Pendleton-Jullian and Brown (2018b, ch. 19). On the interpretive and reflexive aspects of innovation work, see Stark et al. (2009) and Lester and Piore (2004). On how conventional rationality breaks down in the context of innovation, see Elster (1990).

4. For more on affordances as a way of understanding the relationship among individuals, their actions, and the conditions in the environment that constrain them, see Gibson (1977), Greeno (1994), Hutchby (2001), and Leonardi (2011).

5. See Grigson (1974, xiv).

6. Yellowtail (*Seriola quinqueradiata*) are known in their stages of increasing maturity as *wakashi* (fry and juveniles), *inada*, *warasa*, and finally *buri* (when fully mature).

7. Lars Williams, personal conversation, 13 June 2011.

8. See Adrià, Soler, and Adrià (2006) for more information about the evolution of spherification by El Bulli.

9. See A. Talbot (2009).

10. See Arnold (2009b) and Arnold (2009a).

11. See Hesser (2005).

12. For more on early distributed efforts to understand sous vide cooking, see chapter 2, note 11.

13. See Page and Dornenburg (2008).

14. See Pinel (2015).

15. See Ahn et al. (2011) and De Klepper (2011).

16. For accounts of life in restaurant service kitchens, see Ruhlman (1997), Fine (1999), and Buford (2006).

## 5. A NONDELUSIONAL WORLDVIEW

1. The conceptualization of mindsets as affecting perception and action is rooted in a phenomenological view of how individuals interact with the world (Husserl [1913] 1982). For a more recent survey of research on mindsets and their implications, see Dweck (2012).

2. For more on the formal distinction between risk and uncertainty, see Knight (1921) and Ellsberg (2001).

3. One of the foundational theories of organization explains organizational action as attempts to reduce exposure to the unknown and the unpredictable. For more on this, see Thompson (1967) and Kamps and Pólos (1999).

4. Rumsfeld was responding to a question about U.S. military operations in Iraq in the context of the apparent absence of evidence of weapons of mass destruction in Iraq. For the full transcript, see Rumsfeld and Myers (2002).

5. For more perspectives on how complexity and interdependence can cause systems to collapse, see Perrow (1984) and Vaughan (1996).

6. For a vigorous account of this, see Taleb (2007).

7. See Lewis (2011) and Nelson and Katzenstein (2014).

8. One way to think about historical change is to imagine it as punctuated equilibrium: short periods of abrupt upheaval separated by long stable periods. For more on the concept of punctuated equilibrium in evolutionary biology (where it was introduced) see the review in Gould (2007). Punctuated equilibrium in our time is giving way to routine uncertainty: "We are in an era of profound change, in which acceleration, instability, and disturbance may become the norm. This is a white water world—a world of dynamic flows in which so much of what we do and know is radically contingent on the context at the moment one is looking at it, or operating in it" (Pendleton-Jullian and Brown 2018a, 28). This uncertainty arises because the world is becoming both more complex and more interconnected. This is the other side of connecting autocatalytic networks (Padgett and Powell 2012): incumbents may perceive the organizational novelty that arises as desirable and serendipitous change or undesirable unpredictability. For more on complexity and uncertainty, see Christensen (1997) and Wheatley (2006).

9. Jobs's talk also predicted an array of products that seemed outlandish at the time—that Apple went on to develop—including ultraportable computers and the ability to purchase software through the internet. For more, see Jobs (1983). On innovation and pragmatic imagination, see Pendleton-Jullian and Brown (2018b).

## 6. THE UNCERTAINTY MINDSET

1. This perspective on understanding how teams work is ultimately phenomenological in the sense that, as entities, teams act based on what they believe about the world, and those beliefs depend on how they perceive the world. This perception, in turn, is shaped by the type of intentionality the entity has about the world. For more on this extensive and diverse approach, begin with Husserl ([1913] 1982).

2. Interdependent coordination involves a "delicate choreography that maintains actors' shared orientation toward the future while accommodating motion, ambiguities, and missteps" (Tavory and Eliasoph 2013, 909).

3. For a biological perspective on swarm organization, see Janson, Middendorf, and Beekman (2005), Seeley, Camazine, and Sneyd (1991), and Garnier, Gautrais, and Theraulaz (2007).

4. The conventional view of hiring assumes stable roles (Ilgen and Hollenbeck 1991; Ilgen 1994) which organizations fill through a selection and matching process (Granovetter 1995; Judge and Cable 1997; Jovanovic 1979; Stewart and Carson 1997; Mortensen and Pissarides 1999; Singh 2008).

5. For more on goals, see Hackman (1987), Locke and Latham (1990), and Hackman (2002a).

6. For more on the inarticulatability of tacit knowledge, see H. M. Collins (2010).

7. Clear and stable roles and goals are the default recommendation for building and managing effective teams (for instance, see Hackman 1990, 2002b). Desperation is also conventionally thought to damage team efficacy by overloading the teams (Weick 1993).

## 7. INNOVATION IMPLIES CHANGE

1. For more on cocoa butter crystallization and tempering, see Manning and Dimick (1985) and G. Talbot (2009).

2. For more on the inherent unrationality of innovation, see Elster (1990).

3. This approach contrasts sharply with the conventional view of hiring as a process of analyzing work within the organization to develop accurate descriptions of job roles (Singh 2008), recruiting candidates for those descriptions, then selecting the people who are the best match for those descriptions (Jovanovic 1979; Mortensen and Pissarides 1999; Ployhart and Schneider 2002). In this conventional view, roles in organizations are implicitly assumed to be stable and defined in advance of hiring.

4. A change like this increases overall welfare without making anyone worse off. For more on this idea of a system-level Pareto improvement, see chapter 6 on economic equilibrium in Pareto ([1906] 2014).

5. For more on the benefits of clear and stable jobs, see Hackman and Oldham (1980), Ilgen and Hollenbeck (1991), Ilgen (1994), and Hackman (2002b).

6. Eliminating the unpleasant sensation of the unknown seems to be a basic human motivation (Kagan 1972). This basic motivation finds expression in a wide range of human behaviors. In the organizational context, this includes groupthink (Janis 1983), group-centrism (Kruglanski et al. 2006), and a preference for jobs with clearly defined responsibilities. Management theory and practice recognize that jobs can never be

fully and formally defined. Formal job descriptions are known to be incomplete, which is why work-to-rule is effective as a method of worker protest. Yet, despite widespread awareness that job roles change and consist of both formal and informal components, in practice leaders in organizations often insist on having stable, clear job descriptions. This aggravates the underlying problem—which is that individuals instinctively seek stability in their roles.

7. See Barabba (2011).

8. For more on this view of the eventual failure of Digital Equipment Corporation, see Christensen (1997) and Schein et al. (2004).

9. Team structure—member roles and interpersonal ways of working—is believed to be relatively rigid. This structure needs to be unfrozen before change can occur (Lewin 1947).

10. While the conventional view of jobs is that they are monolithic, stable, and created ahead of being filled by a specific person, research increasingly shows a different picture of what jobs could be. Jobs can be idiosyncratic when they are created specifically for particular new members or when incumbents' jobs evolve over their tenure in an organization (Miner and Estler 1985; Miner 1987; Miner and Akinsanmi 2016). Jobs can be assembled over time out of multiple tasks instead of being predefined and integral (Cohen 2012; Tan 2015). And jobs can be plastic enough for respondents to increase their work satisfaction by adjusting the boundaries of their job roles (Wrzesniewski and Dutton 2001).

## 8. BUILDING INNOVATION DREAM TEAMS

1. The first edition of Glasse's *The Art of Cookery Made Plain and Easy* (1747) records recipes for Irish, Scotch, and Welsh rarebits. The FDEK called the dish a Welsh rarebit, though the original spelling of the dish is rabbits (Grigson 1974).

2. For more on the social implications of honest signaling, see Pentland (2008). For the original biological conceptualization, see Zahavi (1975).

3. For more on internal conflicts of this type, see Wilson (2000) and Milgrom and Roberts (1988).

4. Highly effective interdependent team or ensemble work has been observed and analyzed in chamber music (Lehman and Hackman 2002), improvisational jazz performance (Barrett 1998; Faulkner and

Becker 2009), and sports teams (Hackman 2002a). For more on such self-managing work groups, see Hackman (1976). For more on teaming as an active process by which interdependent work can be done in organizations, see Edmondson (2012).

5. For more on negotiated joining, see Tan (2015).
6. For more on the flow state, see Csikszentmihalyi ([1990] 2002).

## 9. THE POWER OF FAMILIAR NOVELTY

1. Wine is an example of an experience good that can only be evaluated through consumption and direct experience—in contrast with inspection goods, the quality of which can be evaluated by observation, without needing direct experience (Stigler 1962; Nelson 1970; Hirshleifer 1973).
2. For more on tacit knowledge, see Polanyi (1958), and H. M. Collins (2010).
3. This consistency is, of course, an oversimplification. The same wine may vary from bottle to bottle and will almost certainly change over time with cellaring.
4. See, for instance, Coates (2008) on Burgundy.
5. See chapters 2 and 3.
6. The conceptualization of open-ended style in this book builds on the traditional art historical concept of style as (implicitly detectable) forms, elements, qualities, or expressions that are constant in the artistic output of an individual or a group (Schapiro 1953). More recently, there is a growing awareness that the style infused into an object by its producer isn't necessarily the same as the style that the consumer interprets it as having: what the creator puts into the work isn't necessarily what the consumer sees in it (Winter 1998). In cutting-edge cuisine, stylistic infusion and interpretation are often mutually responsive to the narratives that form around the cuisine. Critics and consumers provide consumption narratives, but chefs also provide production narratives (through cookbooks, blogposts, speeches at chef conferences, social media posts, and such) that attempt to frame and explain the food they produce.
7. For more on contesting systems of value and how how creativity and innovation can emerge out of the friction and dissonance between those systems when they interact, see Boltanski and Thévenot (2006) and Stark et al. (2009).

## 10. LEARNING HOUSE STYLE

1. For more on tacit knowledge in use, see H. M. Collins (2010), and Ribeiro and Collins (2007).
2. There are two fundamentally divergent views on learning tacit knowledge in organizations. The organizational knowledge creation perspective holds that tacit and explicit knowledge are interconvertible with each other (Nonaka 1991; Nonaka and Krogh 2009). From this perspective, tacit knowledge can be converted to explicit knowledge and then learned through conventional, intentional training (Szulanski, Ringov, and Jensen 2016). These intentional training methods are ineffective for style knowledge because intentional training definitionally can only take up a small proportion of organizational life, and each member must learn an enormous amount of style knowledge to become an effective team member. In contrast, this book takes the social-practice perspective that not all tacit knowledge can be converted to explicit knowledge (Cook and Brown 1999; Brown and Duguid 2001; Tsoukas 2003; Ribeiro and Collins 2007). Inherently tacit knowledge (such as knowledge of open-ended style) requires a fundamentally different approach to teaching and learning.
3. Iterative prototyping is one name for a broad class of related processes for product development. Other names include experimentation (Thomke 1998) and rehearsal (Harrison and Rouse 2015). These processes usually involve workers repeatedly building and testing successive prototypes to explore hypotheses about the final product's design, functionality, or production method. Each prototype informs the next, the repeated cycles stopping when a satisfactory prototype is created or when the project is abandoned. Iterative prototyping is most often viewed as a method for accelerating innovation, reducing its cost, or improving its quality (Iansiti 2000; Thomke 2003); it is now common practice in R&D—say in software development or consumer product development—as a way to get to the final product more quickly. Cutting-edge culinary R&D teams used iterative prototyping to develop new products in a way that allowed them to use failure as an intelligent way to learn and innovate more effectively (Cannon and Edmondson 2005).
4. The value of learning by using knowledge is recognized in practical training settings. Apprenticeship models of teaching and learning (including the "see one, do one, teach one" model of medical training) are often good

250

examples of this. For accounts of tacit knowledge learning in a range of settings, see Jordan (1989) and Singleton (1998).

5. This exchange was also reported in Tan (2015).

6. Social norms and expectations within these cutting-edge culinary R&D teams—for instance, the expectation that every team member should comment on prototypes regardless of their seniority—seemed to create a sense of psychological safety (Edmondson 1999) that permitted more honest and direct feedback on prototypes both in formal and informal feedback sessions.

7. Complex systems often exhibit equifinality, wherein "the same final state may be reached from different initial conditions and in different ways" (Bertalanffy 1962, 40). For example, a person navigating through a city can reach the same destination via many different routes and modes of transport and beginning from many different starting points. A nervous driver who loves to cycle and doesn't mind a longer journey would take a different route and method of transport to the office than her colleague who loves to drive (and is a nervous cyclist)—even if they both live in the same apartment building. Equifinality increases potential freedom in how individuals can act within the system. In this example, equifinality allows the nervous driver to cycle instead of drive, giving her a more optimal way to get to work.

8. For more on the association between diversity and innovation performance, see Kogut and Zander (1992), Brown and Eisenhardt (1995), Grant (1996), Reagans and Zuckerman (2001), and Page (2007).

9. This approach to giving direction for action has similarities to the ground forces command approach known originally as *Aufragstaktik* when it was introduced in late nineteenth-century German ground war doctrine and variously translated in English as mission-type tactics, mission-oriented tactics, mission command, or commander's intent. Mission command calls for communication of the desired mission outcome and motivation as concisely and precisely as possible, with care taken to define acceptable and unacceptable tradeoffs to achieve that outcome. Crucially, wherever possible, operational details are intentionally left to the discretion of the commander's subordinates who are expected to respond appropriately and with discretion to the concrete resources and constraints they face in executing the mission. For more on the history of mission-oriented command, see Shamir (2011).

10. See Anderson (2012).

11. As Gehry put it, "You're bringing an informed aesthetic point of view to a visual problem. You have freedom, so you have to make choices—and at the point when I make a choice, the building starts to look like a Frank Gehry building. It's a signature" (2011).

12. The distinctiveness of Serra's work results from his particular approach to art-making. As he described it: "I was very involved with the physical activity of making . . . It struck me that instead of thinking about what a sculpture is going to be and how you're going to do it compositionally, what if you just enacted those verbs in relation to a material, and didn't worry about the result?" (quoted in Tomkins (2010, 81)).

13. For more on the intentional transfer of knowledge within organizations, see Nonaka (1994), Almeida and Kogut (1999), Gupta and Govindarajan (2000), and Szulanski, Ringov, and Jensen (2016).

14. What I describe here—learning how to innovate within an open-ended style through and in the course of routine work—is consonant with the social-practice view of knowledge in organizations. This perspective distinguishes between knowledge and knowing (knowledge in action) and pays special attention to both knowledge and knowing in collectivities. For more on this perspective, see Cook and Brown (1999) and Brown and Duguid (2001). For a foundational conceptualization of the interrelationships between work, learning, and innovation, see Brown and Duguid (1991).

## 11. THE MOTIVATION PARADOX

1. The physical design and equipping of a kitchen affects what can be cooked, how it is cooked, how the people cooking work individually and with each other. Redesigning a kitchen is one of the most disruptive things an established high-end restaurant functioning at a high level can do to itself.

2. For more accounts of how a kitchen can rapidly unravel during the course of service, see Ruhlman (1997), Fine (1999), and Buford (2006).

3. When everyone working in a service kitchen pushes, it can enter into a state of collective flow. For more on flow states, see Csikszentmihalyi ([1990] 2002).

4. There is a tradeoff when using the tension of service to motivate a kitchen team. The constant push needed in a service kitchen aspiring to a high

standard of execution imposes immense stress on people working in it. Many chefs report mental health problems and cope with the stress with drugs or alcohol. For more on mental health in the culinary industry, see http://chefswithissues.com.

5. For more on mood-repair, fear of failure, learned helplessness, and defensive pessimism, see chapter 3, note 3.

6. Management research has long recognized the tension and need for balance between exploring the unknown and exploiting the known (Smith and Tushman 2005; Raisch et al. 2009). Doing something unknown is hard partly because performance in doing an action becomes easier to measure as the action becomes better understood—and this feeds the organizational inclination to allocate resources to measurable and controllable actions (Foucault 1977; Scott 1999; and Drucker 1993).

7. Organizational researchers know that individuals vary in their need for personal growth through learning, and that this is an important consideration in designing work (Hackman and Oldham 1975; and Oldham and Hackman 1980).

8. René Redzepi, personal conversation at MAD1, 27 August 2011.

## 12. DESPERATION BY DESIGN

1. Desperation is a reaction to the prospect of catastrophe—and can be productive when channeled toward avoiding catastrophe: "A major catastrophe that frustrates a central goal of life will either destroy the self, forcing a person to use all his psychic energy to erect a barrier around remaining goals, defending them against further onslaughts of fate; or it will provide a new, more clear, and more urgent goal: to overcome the challenges created by the defeat" (Csikszentmihalyi [1990] 2002, 198).

2. Just as redesigning a service kitchen forces a restaurant to change what it cooks, redesigning the test kitchen forced the Noma R&D team to change how it developed dishes for Noma.

3. For more details about Noma Japan and Noma Australia, see Swinnerton (2016) and Gordinier (2016).

4. Quoted in Pérez (2017).

5. For more details about Noma Mexico, see Gold (2017).

6. See Hackman (1987) and Wageman and Baker (1997).

7. For a related perspective on the importance of having a real stake in an activity, see Taleb (2018).

8. For more on the collapse of teams in crisis conditions, see Weick (1988) and Weick (1993).

9. On a much shorter timescale, service kitchens also respond to immediate deadlines (for instance, as reported in Fine 1999). More generally, individuals and teams seem to pace or entrain themselves in the course of work (Ancona and Waller 2015; Ancona and Chong 1999; and Gersick 1988).

10. For more on rhythm in social life, see Zerubavel (1981).

11. Organizations are believed to change and adapt generally in the direction of stability, inertia, and exploitation of known opportunities (Hannan and Freeman 1984; Levinthal 1991). For more on the tendency for organizational adaptation to favor exploitation and thus have ultimately destructive consequences, see March (1991).

12. For more on the possibilities of using emotion to support organizational change, see Hodgkinson and Healey (2011).

13. Crises threaten an organization's survival (Weick 1988; Nystrom and Starbuck 2004) and can create conditions that unfreeze the organization, allowing it to change and adapt in response (Lewin 1958; Hedberg 1981; Mitroff et al. 1989; Christianson et al. 2009; Hodgkinson and Healey 2011). In particular, crises deliberately instigated by leaders (autogenic crises) are believed to allow organizational preadaptation to future changes in the environment (Barnett and Pratt 2000). Desperation projects thus lie between stretch goals and crises that ultimately destroy an organization. They pose a threat but a manageable one that induces change and growth instead of paralysis, denial, and death. For more on stretch goals, see Sitkin et al. (2011).

## 13. ALL CHANGE

1. See Myrhvold and Bilet (2012), Myrhvold (2013), and Myrhvold and Migoya (2017).

2. See Ray (2017).

3. *Turns* refer to the number of times the seats in a restaurant are used during any service. In a forty-seat restaurant, a maximum of forty guests can be accommodated without turning any tables (no turns). If the restaurant manages a half-turn, it will seat sixty guests (turning half the seats in the restaurant); if it manages to seat eighty guests, it will have done a full turn.

4. Two of the best-known examples were at Osteria Francescana in Modena, Italy and Eleven Madison Park in New York City. Osteria Francescana's dishes were meant to capture stories. For instance, a dish like An Eel Swimming Up the Po River (*saba*-glazed eel, apple jelly, and polenta) was designed around components that referred to "the flight of the Estense dukes to Modena in 1598, after Clement VIII seized their capital at Ferrara and claimed its eel marshes and fisheries for the Church" (Kramer 2013). And when Eleven Madison Park relaunched in 2012, it attempted to capture the history of New York City in a four-hour menu that drew on familiar imagery and local products. A *New York Times* review noted that "the cheese course, for instance, is supposed to evoke an old-fashioned outing in Central Park; it will incorporate a handmade picnic basket by Jonathan Kline of Black Ash Baskets; a bottle of Picnic Ale, specially brewed for the restaurant by Ithaca Beer Company; a wedge of cheese whose rind has been basted in the ale by the affinage team at Murray's Cheese Shop; and a pretzel and mustard infused with the ale. Even the label on the bottle has been created by Milton Glaser, the designer of the 'I♡NY' logo in the 1970s" (Gordinier 2012).

5. See Proust (2002).

6. About this dish—wild turbot, a shellfish mousse, water chestnuts, and hyacinth vapor—Achatz wrote: "My father would frequently take me on the boat out into the St. Clair River to drift fish for walleye . . . . The extremely humid and sultry climate that the Midwest summer is known for producing a very distinctive fish/sea smell as the air met the water. And inevitably the banks of all the bodies of water were lined with many types of plants in bloom. So for me the two smells—seafood and the perfume of flowers—were permanently fused in my mind . . . once [the dish] was all together, I instantly remembered a day when I was 12 years old, fishing for walleye with my dad in the late spring. We would tuck in along the shore and eat lunch among the wildflowers. Fish and flowers made sense to me not for any culinary reason, but for sentimental ones" (2009).

7. See Lam (2008).

8. See Gill (2016).

9. See Ying (2018).

10. See MAD Foundation (2019).

11. See Burton (2017).

12. See Glanz and Robles (2018).

13. The contractor awarded the main $156 million FEMA contract for producing MREs for Puerto Rico after Hurricane Maria ended up delivering only a small fraction of the meals needed, and even those were not to the specifications of the contract. This FEMA contract was eventually canceled. For more on FEMA's MRE contract for Puerto Rico, see Mazzei and Armendariz (2018).

14. See McCarthy (2018).

15. For Andrés's account of the World Central Kitchen operation in Puerto Rico, see Andrés and Wolffe (2018).

## 14. A MINDSET FOR AN UNCERTAIN WORLD

1. For more on pragmatic imagination and its role in enabling action in an increasingly interconnected and unpredictable world, see Pendleton-Jullian and Brown (2018b, especially ch. 19). This is part of a broader argument about how increasing connectedness and complexity make it necessary to design not for absolute states but for emergent ones. This way of conceptualizing design treats it as a practice applicable not only to physical objects but also to human interactions, systems, and organizations.

2. For more on how innovation goes beyond the limits of rationality, see Elster (1990). For more on the emergent nature of innovation outcomes, see Stark et al. (2009), especially chapters 1 and 3.

3. For more on the importance of interpretive work in the innovation process, see Lester and Piore (2004).

4. For more on creative dissonance and the idea of coordination through misunderstanding, see Stark et al. (2009).

5. A continual process of renegotiating the tension and balance between under- and overorganization is what enables creative chaos (Chen 2009).

6. For more on beneficial ambiguity in the context of individual roles in organizations, see Tan (2015).

7. Focusing on achieving a currently adapted state may compromise longer-term adaptability. As David Stark and Monique Girard point out, "Under conditions of radical uncertainty, organizations that simply improve their *adaptive fit* to the current environment risk sacrificing *adaptability* in subsequent dislocations" (Stark et al. 2009, 83). Adaptability emphasizes dynamic processes and the potential for change rather than the stable

adapted states implied by adaptation; on this, also see Alexander (1979), especially chapters 2, 3, and 8.

8. For more on this, see chapter 6.

9. This appears to be true anecdotally, as illustrated by examples like the 2008 global financial crisis and the abrupt shift to the right in Western Hemisphere polities beginning in 2016. Increasingly, subsystems (such as individual banks or individual states) and the larger systems they belong to behave in unexpected ways because the subsystems are themselves growing in complexity, increasing in number, and connected in complex ways. Consequently, subsystem-level effects that would have been trivial and mostly contained within unconnected subsystems now ripple through their containing systems with unanticipated effects. To illustrate with just one example, this seems to have been the case with how social media interacted with geopolitics and changing demography in influencing the swing to the right in the developed world polities. The uncertainty and unpredictability of highly interconnected complex subsystems is a central tenet of complexity theory (Bertalanffy 1962; Pendleton-Jullian and Brown 2018a; Wheatley 2006).

# REFERENCES

Abend, Lisa. 2011. *The Sorceror's Apprentices*. New York: Free Press.
———. 2017. "Welcome to the Food Circus." *Fool*, no. 7: 38–49.
Abramson, Lyn Y., Martin E. P. Seligman, and John D. Teasdale. 1978.
"Learned Helplessness in Humans: Critique and Reformulation." *Journal of Abnormal Psychology* 87 (1): 49–74.
Achatz, Grant. 2009. "Fish, Flowers, and the Taste of Youth." *The Atlantic Online*, September 23, 2009. https://www.theatlantic.com/health/archive/2009/09/fish-flowers-and-the-taste-of-youth/27013/.
Adrià, Ferran, Albert Adrià, and Juli Soler. 2008. *A Day at El Bulli*. London: Phaidon.
Adrià, Ferran, Juli Soler, and Albert Adrià. 2006. *El Bulli 2003–2004*. New York: Ecco.
Aduriz, Andoni Luis. 2012. *Mugaritz: A Natural Science of Cooking*. London: Phaidon.
Ahn, Yong-Yeol, Sebastian E. Ahnert, James P. Bagrow, and Albert-László Barabási. 2011. "Flavor Network and the Principles of Food Pairing." *Nature Scientific Reports* 1 (196).
Alexander, Christopher. 1979. *The Timeless Way of Building*. New York: Oxford University Press.
Alexander, Lameez, and Daan Van Knippenberg. 2014. "Teams In Pursuit of Radical Innovation: A Goal Orientation Perspective." *Academy of Management Review* 39 (4): 423–438.

# References

Almeida, Paul, and Bruce Kogut. 1999. "Localization of Knowledge and the Mobility of Engineers in Regional Networks." *Management Science* 45 (7): 905–917.

Ancona, Deborah, and Chee-Leong Chong. 1999. "Cycles and Synchrony: The Temporal Role of Context in Team Behavior." *Research on Managing Groups and Teams* 2: 33–48.

Ancona, Deborah, and Mary J. Waller. 2015. "The Dance of Entrainment: Temporally Navigating across Multiple Pacers." *Research in the Sociology of Work* 17: 147–177.

Anderson, Wes. 2012. "Wes Anderson: Creating A Singular 'Kingdom.'" Interview by Terry Gross. NPR *Fresh Air*, May 29.

Andrés, José, and Richard Wolffe. 2018. *We Fed An Island: The True Story of Rebuilding Puerto Rico, One Meal at a Time.* New York: Ecco.

Andrews, Colman. 2010. *Ferran: The Inside Story of el Bulli and the Man Who Reinvented Food.* New York: Gotham.

Arnold, Dave. 2009a. "Agar Clarification Made Stupid-Simple: Best Technique Yet." *Cooking Issues* (blog), July 14, 2009. http://www.cookingissues.com/index.html%3Fp=1439.html.

———. 2009b. "Major Clarification Breakthrough from Ideas in Food." *Cooking Issues* (blog), July 14, 2009. http://www.cookingissues.com/index.html%3Fp=1426.html.

Baldwin, Carliss, and Kim Clark. 2000. *Design Rules: The Power of Modularity.* Cambridge, MA: MIT Press.

Barabba, Vincent P. 2011. *The Decision Loom: A Design for Interactive Decision-Making in Organizations.* Charmouth, UK: Triarchy.

Barnett, Carole K., and Michael G. Pratt. 2000. "From Threat-Rigidity to Flexibility: Toward a Learning Model of Autogenic Crisis in Organizations." *Journal of Organizational Change Management* 13 (1): 74–88.

Barrett, Frank J. 1998. "Creativity and Improvisation in Jazz and Organizations: Implications for Organizational Learning." *Organization Science* 9 (5): 605–622.

Baumol, William J. 2002. *The Free-Market Innovation Machine: Analyzing the Growth Miracle of Capitalism.* Princeton, NJ: Princeton University Press.

———. 2005. "Education for Innovation: Entrepreneurial Breakthroughs versus Corporate Incremental Improvements." *Innovation Policy and the Economy* 5: 33–56.

Bertalanffy, Ludwig von. 1962. "General System Theory: A Critical Review." *General Systems* 7: 1–20.

Blumenthal, Heston. 2008. *The Big Fat Duck Cookbook*. London: Bloomsbury.

Boltanski, Luc, and Laurent Thévenot. 2006. *On Justification: Economies of Worth*. Princeton, NJ: Princeton University Press.

Brown, John Seely, and Paul Duguid. 1991. "Organizational Learning and Communities-Of-Practice: Toward a Unified View of Working, Learning, and Innovation." *Organization Science* 2 (1): 40–57.

———. 2001. "Knowledge and Organization: A Social-Practice Perspective." *Organization Science* 12 (2): 198–213.

Brown, Shona L., and Kathleen M. Eisenhardt. 1995. "Product Development: Past Research, Present Findings, and Future Directions." *Academy of Management Review* 20 (2): 343–378.

Buford, Bill. 2006. *Heat: An Amateur Cook in a Professional Kitchen*. London: Vintage.

Burton, Monica. 2017. "The Story of World Central Kitchen, the Nonprofit Serving Millions of Meals to Puerto Rico." *Eater*, November 10, 2017. https://www.eater.com/2017/11/10/16623204/world-central-kitchen-jose-andres-bahamas-puerto-rico-haiti-houston.

Cannon, Mark D., and Amy C. Edmondson. 2005. "Failing to Learn and Learning to Fail (Intelligently): How Great Organizations Put Failure to Work to Innovate and Improve." *Long Range Planning* 38 (3): 299–319.

Cassi, Davide. 2011. "Science and Cooking: The Era of Molecular Cuisine." *European Molecular Biology Organisation Reports* 12 (3): 191–196.

Chen, Katherine K. 2009. *Enabling Creative Chaos: The Organization behind the Burning Man Event*. Chicago: University of Chicago Press.

Christensen, Clayton. 1997. *The Innovator's Dilemma*. Boston: Harvard Business Review Press.

Christianson, Marlys K., Maria T. Farkas, Kathleen M. Sutcliffe, and Karl E. Weick. 2009. "Learning through Rare Events: Significant Interruptions at the Baltimore & Ohio Railroad Museum." *Organization Science* 20 (5): 846–860.

Claiborne, Craig. 1981. "Logic Loses Out, but Taste Triumphs." *New York Times* (March 25): C1 (national edition).

Clark, Priscilla. 1975a. "Thoughts for Food I: French Cuisine and French Culture." *French Review* 49 (1): 32–41.

———. 1975b. "Thoughts for Food II: Culinary Culture in Contemporary France." *French Review* 49 (2): 198–205.

Coates, Clive. 2008. *The Wines of Burgundy*. Berkeley: University of California Press.

Cohen, Lisa E. 2012. "Assembling Jobs: A Model of How Tasks Are Bundled into and across Jobs." *Organization Science* 24 (2): 432–454.

Collins, Harry M. 2010. *Tacit and Explicit Knowledge*. Chicago: University of Chicago Press.

Collins, Lauren. 2015. "Who's to Judge?: How the World's 50 Best Restaurants Are Chosen." *New Yorker* (November 2).

Cook, Scott D. N., and John Seely Brown. 1999. "Bridging Epistemologies: The Generative Dance between Organizational Knowledge and Organizational Knowing." *Organization Science* 10 (4): 381–400.

Cremades, Enrique, Francisco Balbastre-Benavent, and Elena Sanandrés Domínguez. 2015. "Managerial Practices Driving Knowledge Creation, Learning and Transfer in Translational Research: An Exploratory Case Study." *R&D Management* 45 (4): 361–385.

Csikszentmihalyi, Mihaly. (1990) 2002. *Flow: The Classic Work on How to Achieve Happiness*. London: Rider.

De Klepper, Maurits. 2011. "Food Pairing Theory: A European Fad." *Gastronomica* 11 (4): 55–58.

Drucker, Peter F. 1993. *Management: Tasks, Responsibilities, Practices*. New York: HarperBusiness.

Dweck, Carol. 2012. *Mindset: Changing the Way You Think to Fulfil Your Potential*. London: Hachette UK.

Edmondson, Amy C. 1999. "Psychological Safety and Learning Behavior in Work Teams." *Administrative Science Quarterly* 44 (2): 350–383.

———. 2012. *Teaming: How Organizations Learn, Innovate, and Compete in the Knowledge Economy*. Hoboken, NJ: Wiley.

Ellsberg, Daniel. 2001. *Risk, Ambiguity, and Decision*. New York: Garland.

Elster, Jon. 1990. "When Rationality Fails." In *The Limits of Rationality*, ed. Karen Cook and Margaret Levi, 19–50. Chicago: University of Chicago Press.

Ettlie, John E., William P. Bridges, and Robert D. O'Keefe. 1984. "Organization Strategy and Structural Differences for Radical versus Incremental Innovation." *Management Science* 30 (6): 682–695.

Faulkner, Robert R., and Howard S. Becker. 2009. *Do You Know—? The Jazz Repertoire in Action.* Chicago: University of Chicago Press.

Fay Jai. 2004. "Sous Vide: Recipes, Techniques & Equipment (Part 1)." eGullet Forums, February 23, 2004. https://forums.egullet.org/topic/144243-sous-vide-recipes-techniques-equipment-part-1.

Ferguson, Priscilla Parkhurst. 1998. "A Cultural Field in the Making: Gastronomy in 19th-Century France." *American Journal of Sociology* 104 (3): 597–641.

Fernandez-Armesto, Felipe. 2002. *Near a Thousand Tables: A History of Food.* New York: Free Press.

Fine, Gary Alan. 1999. *Kitchens: The Culture of Restaurant Work.* Berkeley: University of California Press.

Foucault, Michel. 1977. *Discipline and Punish.* New York: Pantheon.

Garcia, Rosanna, and Roger Calantone. 2002. "A Critical Look at Technological Innovation Typology and Innovativeness Terminology: A Literature Review." *Journal of Product Innovation Management* 19 (2): 110–132.

Garnier, Simon, Jacques Gautrais, and Guy Theraulaz. 2007. "The Biological Principles of Swarm Intelligence." *Swarm Intelligence* 1 (1): 3–31.

Gawer, Annabelle. 2009. "Platform Dynamics and Strategies: From Products to Services." In *Platforms, Markets, and Innovation,* ed. Annabelle Gawer, 45–76. Cheltenham, UK: Edward Elgar.

Gawer, Annabelle, and Michael A. Cusumano. 2002. *Platform Leadership: How Intel, Microsoft, and Cisco Drive Industry Innovation.* Boston: Harvard Business School Press.

Gehry, Frank. 2011. "Project: Design the Building For the New World Symphony in Miami." *Atlantic Monthly* (May).

Gersick, Connie. 1988. "Time and Transition in Work Teams: Toward a New Model of Group Development." *Academy of Management Journal* 31 (1): 9–41.

Gibson, James Jerome. 1977. "The Theory of Affordances." In *Perceiving, Acting, and Knowing: Toward an Ecological Psychology,* ed. Robert Shaw and John D Bransford, 67–82. Hillsdale, NJ: Lawrence Erlbaum.

Gill, Adrian Anthony. 2016. "Table Talk: AA Gill reviews The Fat Duck, Bray, Berkshire." *Sunday Times* (April 24).

Glanz, James, and Frances Robles. 2018. "How Storms, Missteps and an Ailing Grid Left Puerto Rico in the Dark." *New York Times* interactive online feature, May 6, 2018. https://www.nytimes.com/interactive/2018/05/06/us/puerto-rico-power-grid-hurricanes.html.

Glasse, Hannah. 1747. *The Art of Cookery Made Plain and Easy.* London.

Gold, Jonathan. 2017. "The World's Best Restaurant Opens a Pop-Up in Mexico." *Los Angeles Times* (May 5).

Gordinier, Jeff. 2012. "A Restaurant of Many Stars Raises the Ante." *New York Times* (July 27).

———. 2016. "In Australia, Noma Forages for Ingredients and Inspiration." *New York Times* (March 1).

Gould, Stephen Jay. 2007. *Punctuated Equilibrium.* Cambridge, MA: Harvard University Press.

Granovetter, Mark. 1995. *Getting a Job: A Study of Contacts and Careers.* Chicago: University of Chicago Press.

Grant, Robert M. 1996. "Toward a Knowledge-Based Theory of the Firm." *Strategic Management Journal* 17 (Winter Special Issue): 109–122.

Greenberg, Clement. 1965. "Modernist Painting." *Art & Literature* 4 (Spring): 193–201.

Greeno, James G. 1994. "Gibson's Affordances." *Psychological Review* 101 (2): 336–342.

Grigson, Jane. 1974. *English Food.* London: Macmillan.

Gupta, Anil K., and Vijay Govindarajan. 2000. "Knowledge Flows Within Multinational Corporations." *Strategic Management Journal* 21 (4): 473–496.

Hackman, J. Richard. 1976. *The Design of Self-Managing Work Groups.* Technical report. Yale University School of Organization and Management, December.

———. 1987. "The Design of Work Teams." In *Handbook of Organizational Behavior,* ed. Jay Lorsch, 315–342. Englewood Cliffs, NJ: Prentice-Hall.

———. 1990. *Groups That Work (And Those That Don't).* San Francisco: Jossey-Bass.

———. 2002a. *Leading Teams: Setting the Stage for Great Performances.* Boston: Harvard Business Review Press.

———. 2002b. "New Rules for Team Building." *Optimize* July: 50–62.

# References

Hackman, J. Richard, and Greg R. Oldham. 1975. "Development of the Job Diagnostic Survey." *Journal of Applied Psychology* 60 (2): 159–170.

———. 1980. *Work Redesign.* Reading, MA: Addison-Wesley.

Hannan, Michael T., and John Freeman. 1984. "Structural Inertia and Organizational Change." *American Sociological Review* 49 (2): 149–164.

Harrison, Spencer H., and Elizabeth D. Rouse. 2015. "An Inductive Study of Feedback Interactions Over the Course of Creative Projects." *Academy of Management Journal* 58 (2): 375–404.

Haveman, Heather A. 1993. "Follow the Leader: Mimetic Isomorphism and Entry Into New Markets." *Administrative Science Quarterly* 38 (4): 593–627.

Hedberg, Bo. 1981. "How Organizations Learn and Unlearn." In *Handbook of Organizational Design: Adapting Organisations to Their Environment,* ed. Paul Nystrom and William Starbuck, 3–27. Oxford: Oxford University Press.

Hermé, Pierre. 2012. *The Architecture of Taste.* Lecture at the Harvard Graduate School of Design, November 27, 2012.

———. 2015. *Macaron.* New York: Harry N. Abrams.

Hesser, Amander. 2005. "Under Pressure." *New York Times* (August 14).

Hirshleifer, Jack. 1973. "Where Are We in the Theory of Information?" *American Economic Review* 63: 31–39.

Hobsbawm, Eric. 1999. *Industry and Empire.* New York: New Press.

Hodgkinson, Gerard, and Mark Healey. 2011. "Psychological Foundations of Dynamic Capabilities: Reflexion and Reflection in Strategic Management." *Strategic Management Journal* 32 (13): 1500–1516.

Humphries, Courtney. 2012. "Cooking: Delicious Science." *Nature* (June 21): S10–S11.

Husserl, Edmund. (1913) 1982. *Ideas Pertaining to a Pure Phenomenology and to a Phenomenological Philosophy—First Book: General Introduction to a Pure Phenomenology.* Trans. Fred Kersten. Dordrecht, Netherlands: Springer.

Hutchby, Ian. 2001. "Technologies, Texts and Affordances." *Sociology* 35 (2): 441–456.

Iansiti, Marco. 2000. *Technology Integration: Making Critical Choices in a Dynamic World.* Boston: Harvard Business School Press.

Ilgen, Daniel R. 1994. "Jobs and Roles: Accepting and Coping with the Changing Structure of Organizations." In *Personnel Selection and*

*Classification,* ed. Michael G. Rumsey, Clinton B. Walker, and James Harris, 13–32. New York: Psychology Press.

Ilgen, Daniel R., and John R. Hollenbeck. 1991. "The Structure of Work: Job Design and Roles." In *Handbook of Industrial and Organizational Psychology,* 2nd ed., ed. Marvin D. Dunnette and Leaetta M. Hough, 2: 165–207. Palo Alto, CA: Consulting Psychologists Press.

Janis, Irving L. 1983. *Groupthink: A Psychological Study of Policy Decisions and Fiascoes.* Boston: Houghton Mifflin.

Janson, Stefan, Martin Middendorf, and Madeleine Beekman. 2005. "Honeybee Swarms: How Do Scouts Guide a Swarm of Uninformed Bees?" *Animal Behaviour* 70 (2): 349–358.

Jobs, Steven. 1983. *Untitled speech.* Delivered at the International Design Conference (Aspen, CO), June 15, 1983. Original cassette recording, digitized and available at https://soundcloud.com/mbtech_1434547055436/talk-by-steven-jobs-idca-1983.

Jordan, Brigitte. 1989. "Cosmopolitical Obstetrics: Some Insights from the Training of Traditional Midwives." *Social Science & Medicine* 28 (9): 925–937.

Jovanovic, Boyan. 1979. "Job Matching and the Theory of Turnover." *Journal of Political Economy* 87 (5): 972–990.

Judge, Timothy A., and Daniel M. Cable. 1997. "Applicant Personality, Organizational Culture, and Organization Attraction." *Personnel Psychology* 50 (2): 359–394.

Kagan, Jerome. 1972. "Motives and Development." *Journal of Personality and Social Psychology* 22 (1): 51–66.

Kamps, Jaap, and László Pólos. 1999. "Reducing Uncertainty: A Formal Theory of Organizations in Action." *American Journal of Sociology* 104 (6): 1776–1812.

Knight, Frank H. 1921. *Risk, Uncertainty, and Profit.* Boston: Houghton Mifflin.

Kogut, Bruce, and Udo Zander. 1992. "Knowledge of the Firm, Combinative Capabilities, and the Replication of Technology." *Organization Science* 3 (3): 383–397.

Kramer, Jane. 2013. "Post-Modena." *New Yorker* (November 4).

Kruglanski, Arie W., Antonio Pierro, Lucia Mannetti, and Eraldo de Grada. 2006. "Groups as Epistemic Providers: Need for Closure and the Unfolding of Group-Centrism." *Psychological Review* 113 (1): 84–100.

Kummer, Corby. 2014. "Fun With Food." *Technology Review* (October 3).

Lam, Francis. 2008. "A Restaurant That's Really This Good." *Gourmet* (October).

Lehman, Erin V., and J. Richard Hackman. 2002. *Nobody on the Podium: Lessons for Leaders from the Orpheus Chamber Orchestra (Case No. 1644.9)*. Harvard University Kennedy School of Government Case Services.

Leifer, Richard, Christopher M. McDermott, Gina Colarelli O'Connor, Lois S. Peters, Mark P. Rice, Robert W. Veryzer Jr., et al. 2000. *Radical Innovation: How Mature Companies Can Outsmart Upstarts*. Boston: Harvard Business School Press.

Leonardi, Paul M. 2011. "When Flexible Routines Meet Flexible Technologies: Affordance, Constraint, and the Imbrication of Human and Material Agencies." *MIS Quarterly* 35 (1): 147–167.

Leschziner, Vanina. 2015. *At the Chef's Table: Culinary Creativity in Elite Restaurants*. Stanford, CA: Stanford University Press.

Lester, Richard Keith, and Michael J. Piore. 2004. *Innovation: The Missing Dimension*. Cambridge, MA: Harvard University Press.

Levinthal, Daniel A. 1991. "Organizational Adaptation and Environmental Selection—Interrelated Processes of Change." *Organization Science* 2 (1): 140–145.

Lewin, Kurt. 1947. "Frontiers in Group Dynamics: Concept, Method and Reality in Social Science; Social Equilibria and Social Change." *Human Relations* 1: 5–41.

———. 1958. "Group Decision and Social Change." In *Readings in Social Psychology*, ed. Eleanor Maccoby, Theodore Newcomb, and Eugene Hartley, 197–211. New York: Holt, Rinehart & Winston.

Lewis, Michael. 2011. *The Big Short: Inside the Doomsday Machine*. London: Penguin.

Locke, Edwin A., and Gary P. Latham. 1990. *A Theory of Goal Setting and Task Performance*. Englewood Cliffs, NJ: Prentice-Hall.

Lopez-Alt, J. Kenji. 2015. *The Food Lab: Better Home Cooking Through Science*. New York: Norton.

MAD Foundation. 2019. *Danish Government and MAD Announce the Creation of an Academy*. Press release from the MAD Foundation, March 12, 2019. https://www.madfeed.co/2019/danish-government-and-mad-announce-the-creation-of-an-academy/.

Manning, Douglas M., and Paul S. Dimick. 1985. "Crystal Morphology of Cocoa Butter." *Food Microstructure* 4 (2): 249–265.

March, James G. 1991. "Exploration and Exploitation in Organizational Learning." *Organization Science* 2 (1): 71–87.

Martin, Andrew J., Herbert W. Marsh, and Raymond L. Debus. 2001. "Self-Handicapping and Defensive Pessimism: Exploring a Model of Predictors and Outcomes from a Self-Protection Perspective." *Journal of Educational Psychology* 93 (1): 87–102.

Mazzei, Patricia, and Agustin Armendariz. 2018. "FEMA Contract Called for 30 Million Meals for Puerto Ricans. 50,000 Were Delivered." *New York Times* (February 6).

McCarthy, Amy. 2018. "José Andrés, the Accidental Humanitarian." *Eater*, February 7, 2018. https://www.eater.com/2018/2/7/16982476/jose-andres-interview-puerto-rico-relief-efforts.

McClusky, Mark. 2011. "Microsoft's Former CTO Takes on Modernist Cuisine." *Wired* (February 28).

McGee, Harold. 1984. *On Food and Cooking: The Science And Lore Of The Kitchen.* New York: Scribner.

———. 2004. *McGee on Food and Cooking: An Encyclopedia of Kitchen Science, History and Culture.* London: Hodder & Stoughton.

Meyer, John W., and Brian Rowan. 1977. "Institutionalized Organizations: Formal Structure as Myth and Ceremony." *American Journal of Sociology* 83 (2): 340–363.

Mikić, Aleksandar, Aleksandar Medović, Živko Jovanović, and Nemanja Stanisavljević. 2014. "Integrating Archaeobotany, Paleogenetics and Historical Linguistics May Cast More Light onto Crop Domestication: The Case of Pea (*Pisum sativum*)." *Genetic Resources and Crop Evolution* 61 (5): 887–892.

Milgrom, Paul, and John Roberts. 1988. "An Economic Approach to Influence Activities in Organizations." *American Journal of Sociology* 94 (1): 154–179.

Miner, Anne S. 1987. "Idiosyncratic Jobs in Formalized Organizations." *Administrative Science Quarterly* 32 (3): 327–351.

Miner, Anne S., and Olubukunola Akinsanmi. 2016. "Idiosyncratic Jobs, Organizational Transformation, and Career Mobility." In *The Structuring of Work In Organizations: Research in the Sociology of Organizations* 47: 61–101. Bingley, UK: Emerald.

Miner, Anne S., and Suzanne E. Estler. 1985. "Accrual Mobility: Job Mobility In Higher Education Through Responsibility Accrual." *Journal of Higher Education* 56 (2): 121–143.

Mitroff, Ian I., Thierry Pauchant, Michael Finney, and Chris Pearson. 1989. "Do (Some) Organizations Cause Their Own Crises? The Cultural Profiles of Crisis-Prone vs. Crisis-Prepared Organizations." *Industrial Crisis Quarterly* 3 (4): 269–283.

Mortensen, Dale, and Christopher Pissarides. 1999. "New Developments in Models of Search in the Labor Market." In *Handbook of Labor Economics*, ed. Orley Ashenfelter and David Card, 3: 2567–2627. Amsterdam: Elsevier.

Myrhvold, Nathan. 2013. *The Photography of Modernist Cuisine.* Bellevue, WA: The Cooking Lab.

Myrhvold, Nathan, and Maxime Bilet. 2012. *Modernist Cuisine at Home.* Bellevue, WA: The Cooking Lab.

Myrhvold, Nathan, and Francisco Migoya. 2017. *Modernist Bread.* Bellevue, WA: The Cooking Lab.

Myrhvold, Nathan, Chris Young, and Maxime Bilet. 2011. *Modernist Cuisine: The Art and Science of Cooking.* Bellevue, WA: The Cooking Lab.

Nelson, Phillip. 1970. "Information and Consumer Behavior." *Journal of Political Economy* 78 (2): 311–329.

Nelson, Stephen C., and Peter J. Katzenstein. 2014. "Uncertainty, Risk, and the Financial Crisis of 2008." *International Organization* 68 (2): 361–392.

Nonaka, Ikujiro. 1991. "The Knowledge-Creating Company." *Harvard Business Review* (November): 96–104.

——. 1994. "A Dynamic Theory of Organizational Knowledge Creation." *Organization Science* 5 (1): 14–37.

Nonaka, Ikujiro, and Georg von Krogh. 2009. "Tacit Knowledge and Knowledge Conversion: Controversy and Advancement in Organizational Knowledge Creation Theory." *Organization Science* 20 (3): 635–652.

Norem, Julie K., and Nancy Cantor. 1986. "Defensive Pessimism: Harnessing Anxiety as Motivation." *Journal of Personality and Social Psychology* 51 (6): 1208–1217.

Nystrom, Paul C., and William H. Starbuck. 2004. "To Avoid Organizational Crises, Unlearn." In *How Organizations Learn*, 2nd ed., ed. Ken Starkey, Sue Tempest, and Alan McKinlay, 100–111. London: Thomson Learning.

Oldham, Greg R., and J. Richard Hackman. 1980. "Work Design in the Organizational Context." *Research in Organizational Behavior* 2: 247–278.

Opazo, Maria Pilar. 2016. *Appetite for Innovation: Creativity and Change at el Bulli.* New York: Columbia University Press.

Padgett, John Frederick, and Walter W. Powell. 2012. *The Emergence of Organizations and Markets.* Princeton, NJ: Princeton University Press.

Page, Karen, and Andrew Dornenburg. 2008. *The Flavor Bible: The Essential Guide to Culinary Creativity, Based on the Wisdom of America's Most Imaginative Chefs.* Boston: Little, Brown & Company.

Page, Scott. 2007. *The Difference: How the Power of Diversity Creates Better Groups, Firms, Schools, and Societies.* Princeton, NJ: Princeton University Press.

Pareto, Vilfredo. (1906) 2014. *Manual of Political Economy: A Critical and Variorum Edition (1906).* Ed. Aldo Montesano, Alberto Zanni, Luigino Bruni, John S. Chipman, and Michael McLure. Oxford: Oxford University Press.

Pendleton-Jullian, Ann, and John Seely Brown. 2018a. *Design Unbound: Designing for Emergence.* Cambridge, MA: MIT Press.

———. 2018b. *Design Unbound: Ecologies of Change.* Cambridge, MA: MIT Press.

Pentland, Alex. 2008. *Honest Signals: How They Shape Our World.* Cambridge, MA: MIT Press.

Pérez, Christina. 2017. "Noma's René Redzepi on What to Expect at His Much-Anticipated Tulum Pop-Up." *Vogue* (April 10).

Perrow, Charles. 1984. *Normal Accidents: Living With High-Risk Technologies.* New York: Basic Books.

Pinel, Florian. 2015. "What's Cooking with Chef Watson? An Interview with Lav Varshney and James Briscione." *IEEE Pervasive Computing* 14 (4) (October): 58–62.

Ployhart, Robert E., and Benjamin Schneider. 2002. "A Multi-Level Perspective on Personnel Selection Research and Practice: Implications for Selection System Design, Assessment, and Construct Validation." *Research In Multi-Level Issues* 1: 95–140.

# References

Polanyi, Michael. 1958. *Personal Knowledge*. Chicago: University of Chicago Press.

Poutanen, Kaisa, Laura Flander, and Kati Katina. 2009. "Sourdough and Cereal Fermentation in a Nutritional Perspective." *Food Microbiology* 26 (7): 693–699.

Proust, Marcel. 2002. *The Way by Swann's*. Translated by Lydia Davis. London: Allen Lane.

Raisch, Sebastian, Julian Birkinshaw, Gilbert Probst, and Michael L. Tushman. 2009. "Organizational Ambidexterity: Balancing Exploitation and Exploration for Sustained Performance." *Organization Science* 20 (4): 685–695.

Rao, Hayagreeva, Henrich R. Greve, and Gerald F. Davis. 2001. "Fool's Gold: Social Proof in the Initiation and Abandonment of Coverage by Wall Street Analysts." *Administrative Science Quarterly* 46 (3): 502–526.

Rao, Hayagreeva, Philippe Monin, and Rodolphe Durand. 2003. "Institutional Change in Toque Ville: Nouvelle Cuisine as an Identity Movement in French Gastronomy." *American Journal of Sociology* 108: 795–843.

——. 2005. "Border Crossing: Bricolage and the Erosion of Categorical Boundaries in French Gastronomy." *American Sociological Review* 70 (6): 968–991.

Ray, Joe. 2017. "*Modernist Bread* Slices Into the Science of the Loaf." *Wired* (November 7).

Reagans, Ray, and Ezra W. Zuckerman. 2001. "Networks, Diversity, and Productivity: The Social Capital of Corporate R&D Teams." *Organization Science* 12 (4): 502–517.

Remy, Pascal. 2004. *L'Inspecteur Se Met à Table*. Paris: Équateurs.

Ribeiro, Rodrigo, and Harry Collins. 2007. "The Bread-Making Machine: Tacit Knowledge and Two Types of Action." *Organization Studies* 28 (9): 1417–1433.

Rieger, Diana, Tim Wulf, Julia Kneer, Lena Frischlich, and Gary Bente. 2014. "The Winner Takes It All: The Effect of In-Game Success and Need Satisfaction on Mood Repair and Enjoyment." *Computers in Human Behavior* 39: 281–286.

Ruhlman, Michael. 1997. *The Making of a Chef: Mastering Heat at the Culinary Institute of America*. New York: Henry Holt.

Rumsfeld, Donald, and Richard Myers. 2002. *Untitled U.S. Department of Defense news briefing*. Delivered February 12, 2002. Transcript prepared by Federal News Service Inc., available at https://archive.defense.gov/Transcripts/Transcript.aspx?TranscriptID=2636.

Sandler, Irving. 1988. *American Art of the 1960s*. New York: Harper & Row.

Saxenian, AnnaLee. 1996. *Regional Advantage: Culture and Competition in Silicon Valley and Route 128*. Cambridge, MA: Harvard University Press.

———. 2007. *The New Argonauts: Regional Advantage in a Global Economy*. Cambridge, MA: Harvard University Press.

Scattergood, Amy. 2015. "What Happened to Chowhound?" *Los Angeles Times* (October 9).

Schapiro, Meyer. 1953. "Style." *Anthropology Today*, ed. Arthur L. Kroeber. Chicago: University of Chicago Press.

Schein, Edgar H., Paul J. Kampas, Peter S. Delisi, and Michael M. Sonduck. 2004. *DEC Is Dead, Long Live DEC: The Lasting Legacy of Digital Equipment Corporation*. San Francisco: Berrett-Koehler.

Scott, James C. 1999. *Seeing Like a State: How Certain Schemes to Improve the Human Condition Have Failed*. New Haven, CT: Yale University Press.

Seeley, Thomas D., Scott Camazine, and James Sneyd. 1991. "Collective Decision-Making in Honey Bees: How Colonies Choose among Nectar Sources." *Behavioral Ecology and Sociobiology* 28 (4): 277–290.

Shamir, Eitan. 2011. *Transforming Command: The Pursuit of Mission Command in the U.S., British, and Israeli Armies*. Stanford, CA: Stanford University Press.

Shurtleff, William, and Akiko Aoyagi. 1976. *The Book of Miso*. Soquel, CA: Autumn.

Singh, Parbudyal. 2008. "Job Analysis for a Changing Workplace." *Human Resource Management Review* 18: 87–99.

Singleton, John Calhoun, ed. 1998. *Learning in Likely Places: Varieties of Apprenticeship in Japan*. New York: Cambridge University Press.

Sitkin, Sim B., Kelly E. See, C. Chet Miller, Michael W. Lawless, and Andrew M. Carton. 2011. "The Paradox of Stretch Goals: Organizations in Pursuit of the Seemingly Impossible." *Academy of Management Review* 36 (3): 544–566.

Smith, Wendy K., and Michael L. Tushman. 2005. "Managing Strategic Contradictions: A Top Management Model for Managing Innovation Streams." *Organization Science* 16 (5): 522–536.

Stark, David, Daniel Beunza, Monique Girard, and János Lukács. 2009. *The Sense of Dissonance: Accounts of Worth in Economic Life.* Princeton, NJ: Princeton University Press.

Stefano, Giada di, Andrew King, and Gianmarco Verona. 2014. "Kitchen Confidential? Norms for the Use of Transferred Knowledge in Gourmet Cuisine." *Strategic Management Journal* 35 (11): 1645–1670.

Stewart, Greg L., and Kenneth P. Carson. 1997. "Moving beyond the Mechanistic Model: An Alternative Approach to Staffing for Contemporary Organizations." *Human Resource Management Review* 7 (2): 157–184.

Stigler, George J. 1962. "Information in the Labor Market." *Journal of Political Economy* 70 (5): 94–105.

Svejenova, Silviya, Carmelo Mazza, and Marcel Planellas. 2007. "Cooking up Change in Haute Cuisine: Ferran Adrià as an Institutional Entrepreneur." *Journal of Organizational Behavior* 28: 539–561.

Swinnerton, Robbie. 2016. "When Rene Redzepi Brought Noma to Japan." *Japan Times* (December 13).

Szulanski, Gabriel, Dimo Ringov, and Robert J. Jensen. 2016. "Overcoming Stickiness: How the Timing of Knowledge Transfer Methods Affects Transfer Difficulty." *Organization Science* 27 (2): 304–322.

Talbot, Alex. 2009. "Compression Clarification." *Ideas in Food* (blog), July 12, 2009. https://blog.ideasinfood.com/ideas_in_food/2009/07/compression-clarification.html, July 12.

Talbot, Geoff. 2009. "Chocolate Temper." In *Industrial Chocolate Manufacture and Use,* 4th ed., ed. Stephen T. Beckett. Oxford: Blackwell.

Taleb, Nassim Nicholas. 2007. *The Black Swan.* New York: Random House.

———. 2018. *Skin in the Game: Hidden Asymmetries in Daily Life.* New York: Random House.

Tan, Vaughn. 2015. "Using Negotiated Joining to Construct and Fill Open-Ended Roles in Elite Culinary Groups." *Administrative Science Quarterly* 60 (1): 103–132.

Tavory, Iddo, and Nina Eliasoph. 2013. "Coordinating Futures: Toward a Theory of Anticipation." *American Journal of Sociology* 118 (4): 908–942.

Thomke, Stefan H. 1998. "Managing Experimentation in the Design of New Products." *Management Science* 44 (6): 743–762.

———. 2003. *Experimentation Matters.* Boston: Harvard Business School Press.

# References

Thompson, James D. 1967. *Organizations in Action: Social Science Bases of Administrative Theory.* New York: McGraw-Hill.

Tomkins, Calvin. 2010. *Lives of the Artists: Portraits of Ten Artists Whose Work and Lifestyles Embody the Future of Contemporary Art.* New York: Henry Holt.

Tsoukas, Haridimos. 2003. "Do We Really Understand Tacit Knowledge?" In *The Blackwell Handbook of Organizational Learning and Knowledge Management,* ed. Mark Easterby-Smith and Marjorie A. Lyles, 410–427. Oxford: Blackwell.

Varenne, Pierre François la. 1651. *Le Cuisinier François.* Paris: Chez Jacques Canier.

Vaughan, Diane. 1996. *The Challenger Launch Decision: Risky Technology, Culture and Deviance at NASA.* Chicago: University of Chicago Press.

Wageman, Ruth, and George Baker. 1997. "Incentives and Cooperation: The Joint Effects of Task and Reward Interdependence on Group Performance." *Journal of Organizational Behavior* 18 (2): 139–158.

Weick, Karl E. 1988. "Enacted Sensemaking in Crisis Situations." *Journal of Management Studies* 25 (4): 305–317.

———. 1993. "The Collapse of Sensemaking in Organizations: The Mann Gulch Disaster." *Administrative Science Quarterly* 38 (4): 628–652.

Wheatley, Margaret J. 2006. *Leadership and the New Science.* San Francisco: Berrett-Koehler.

Wilson, James Q. 2000. *Bureaucracy: What Government Agencies Do and Why They Do It.* New York: Basic Books.

Winter, Irene J. 1998. "The Affective Properties of Styles: An Inquiry into Analytical Process and the Inscription of Meaning in Art History." In *Picturing Science, Producing Art,* ed. Caroline A. Jones and Peter Galison, 55–77. London: Routledge.

Wrzesniewski, Amy, and Jane E. Dutton. 2001. "Crafting a Job: Revisioning Employees as Active Crafters of Their Work." *Academy of Management Review* 26 (2): 179–201.

Ying, Chris, ed. 2018. *You and I Eat the Same: On the Countless Ways Food and Cooking Connect Us to One Another.* New York: Artisan.

Yoo, Youngjin, Richard J. Boland Jr., Kalle Lyytinen, and Ann Majchrzak. 2012. "Organizing for Innovation in the Digitized World." *Organization Science* 23 (5): 1398–1408.

# References

Zahavi, Amotz. 1975. "Mate Selection: A Selection for a Handicap."
*Journal of Theoretical Biology* 53 (1): 205–214.

Zerubavel, Eviatar. 1981. *Hidden Rhythms: Schedules and Calendars in Social Life*. Chicago: University of Chicago Press.

Zilioli, Samuele, and Neil V. Watson. 2014. "Testosterone Across Successive Competitions: Evidence for a 'Winner Effect' in Humans?" *Psychoneuroendocrinology* 47: 1–9.

# INDEX

# Index

McGee, Harold, 24, 25, 28, 29, 182
media, about culinary industry, 69
mental health problems in culinary
    industry, 221, 253
Michelin Guide, 18–20, 34
Microsoft, 26
microteaching and microlearning,
    92, 154–156
    (*See also* open-ended style:
    teaching and learning)
microtesting, 88, 117–118, 120,
    121, 127–129
    (*See also* negotiated joining)
Migoya, Francisco, 208, 210, 211
mindsets, 77, 83
    (*See also* uncertainty mindset)
miso, 41–43
mission search, 220
*mlaiskonis* (blog), 25
*Modernist Cuisine* series of books.
    *See* Cooking Lab
Molecular and Physical Gastronomy
    (conference), 21
Momofuku, 31, 221
mood-repair, 43
Mook, Nate, 223, 224
motivation
    for discomfort, 93, 188
    for innovation work, 177–179,
        188, 230
    from exhilaration, 176
    from learning and personal
        growth, 177–178
MREs (Meals, Ready to Eat),
    224
Mugaritz, 30
Myhrvold, Nathan, 26, 205

narratives in food. *See* approaches to
    culinary innovation
negotiated joining, 86–88, 110, 230,
    235
neophiles, 16–18
networks. *See* chef networks
Noëls de Montbenault (a profound
    wine), 134
Nolan, Eugene, 112–117, 119, 120
Noma, x, 20–22, 31, 57, 179–185,
    188–192, 195–196,
    219, 253
Noma 2.0, 192
nondelusional worldview, 75–77,
    83–86, 222–226, 228–229
Nordic Food Lab, 184
Noren, Nils, 25
Nutter, Sam, 185
Nørretranders, Tor, 182

Odysseus, 197
Okumura, Robert, 16
Olafur Eliasson Studio, 91
Olsen, Justin, 153
Olunloyo, Shola, 25
*On Food and Cooking*, 24, 28
    (*See also* books about culinary
    industry)
online forums, 16–18, 24–25, 34
open-ended style, 90–92, 134,
    139–141, 164–165, 230, 235
    defined, 137–139
    information about, 155
    making arguments about, 155
    management challenges of,
        141–142, 164
    tacit knowledge of, 149